RUNNING MAN

RUNNING MAN

**How Running Saved Me From Addiction
and Transformed My Life**

CHARLIE ENGLE

SIMON &
SCHUSTER

London · New York · Sydney · Toronto · New Delhi

A CBS COMPANY

First published in Great Britain by Simon & Schuster UK Ltd, 2016
A CBS COMPANY

1 3 5 7 9 10 8 6 4 2

Simon & Schuster UK Ltd
1st Floor
222 Gray's Inn Road
London WC1X 8HB

www.simonandschuster.co.uk

Simon & Schuster Australia, Sydney
Simon & Schuster India, New Delhi

The author and publishers have made all reasonable efforts to
contact copyright-holders for permission, and apologise for any omissions or errors
in the form of credits given. Corrections may be made to future printings.

A CIP catalogue record for this book is available
from the British Library.

ISBN: 978-1-4711-3952-9
Trade paperback ISBN: 978-1-4711-3953-6
Ebook ISBN: 978-1-4711-3955-0

Interior design by Erich Hobbing
Printed and bound by CPI Group (UK) Ltd, Croydon, CR0 4YY

Simon & Schuster UK Ltd are committed to sourcing paper that
is made from wood grown in sustainable forests and support the Forest Stewardship
Council, the leading international forest certification organisation. Our books
displaying the FSC logo are printed on FSC certified paper.

For Momma

Bid me run, and I will strive with things impossible.
—WILLIAM SHAKESPEARE,
Julius Caesar

RUNNING MAN

PROLOGUE

I always heard the keys—those awful jangling keys—coming toward me, then fading as the guard moved down the corridor. I learned to block out the big bald guy who banged on his locker half the night and the scrawny dude in the corner always yelling something about Jesus. But no matter how exhausted I was or how hard I had crammed the foam earplugs into my ears, I heard those damn keys. It wasn't the sound itself that got me; it was that the keys were attached to a guard—and where there was a guard, there might be trouble.

The keys meant it was 5:00 a.m.—head count. I peeked out from under the corner of the blindfold I had made with a strip of gray cloth ripped from a pair of old sweatpants. Lots of inmates left their lights on all night; some were reading or writing, some prowling around, doing things I was not interested in knowing about. The blindfold helped me escape all that. I saw the guard moving away from my cellblock. Good. Not my turn to be harassed.

I lifted the cloth off my eyes, dug out my earplugs, and lay motionless on my top bunk, listening to the two hundred other men in my unit stirring. My cellmate, Cody, an affable kid who had been slammed with a ten-year sentence for buying weed, was still snoring in the bunk beneath me. Through the high, dirt-flecked double-paned window in my cell, I could see a square of black sky.

- - - -

Just before I reported to Beckley Federal Correctional Institute, I had been a guest speaker at a big AA meeting in Charlotte, North Caro-

1

lina. At the refreshment table, a burly, tattooed guy came up to me and told me to make sure I got a nickname in prison.

"Why's that?" I had asked as I helped myself to an Oreo from a paper plate.

"You get yourself a nickname so that when you get out of the joint and you're walking down the street and somebody yells out your prison name, you ignore that son of a bitch and keep on walking."

In the three months I had been locked up, I had encountered a Squirrel, a Shorty, a Pick-n-Roll, a Swag, a Gut, a Tongue, a Beaver, and a Glue Stick. They called me Running Man. I was the middle-aged white guy who ran laps alone on the quarter-mile dirt track in the prison's recreation yard, past the smirking smokers and the guys playing hoops. When we were in lockdown, I was the fool pounding out miles on the hard floor next to my bunk.

"You don't belong in prison," an inmate I knew as Butterbean said after watching me run in place for more than an hour. "You belong in a fucking insane asylum."

Running Man. They couldn't know how well it fit me. I had been running all my life; trying to find something, trying to lose something. Running helped me kick a ten-year addiction to cocaine and had kept me sober for going on twenty years. Running saved my life—and then it gave me a life. On the outside, people in the ultrarunning world knew who I was. I'd run across the Sahara Desert, setting records along the way. I had been on Jay Leno. I had paid sponsorship deals, now long gone. I was getting hired to give inspirational speeches to auditoriums full of pharmaceutical salesmen, war heroes, corporate bigwigs, and weekend warriors. In prison, running—thinking about running, reading about running, writing about running—was the only thing I had left.

One morning, just before 10:00 a.m. head count, I was on my bunk reading a *Runner's World* magazine article about Badwater, the 135-mile ultramarathon that takes place in Death Valley, California, every July. Lots of people think it's the toughest race in the world, and I wouldn't argue with them. The course starts below sea level and ends at Whitney Portal, a lung-busting 8,300 feet up Mount Whitney. The blacktop in the desert is so hot—often more than two hundred degrees—it can melt the soles off your shoes and blister the skin off the bottoms of your feet. I'd run Badwater five times and placed in the top five all but once. I loved that race and the people who ran it. I thought of myself as part of the big, crazy Badwater family.

I was still thinking about Badwater when I went out to run that afternoon. I had two hours before I had to be back in my cell for 4:00 p.m. count. From the grassy place where I always did my warm-up stretches, I could see the rooftops of a few houses on a distant ridge. Sometimes I even heard music drifting up from the wooded valley below. The track was the only place I could almost convince myself that I wasn't in prison.

I started to run, easy at first, then faster. I felt the sun on my face. I let myself think about Badwater, about the wavering heat and the beckoning horizon. I pictured the hazy mountains looming over Furnace Creek and the furrowed dunes of Stovepipe Wells and that long, desolate climb up to Townes Pass. I remembered the desert light: russet at dawn, lavender at dusk. I thought about winding my way up Mount Whitney, knowing that with every S-curve, the torturous climb was closer to being done. And I remembered the pain. I ached for that exquisite, illuminating pain now, the kind that exposes who you really are—and asks you who you want to be.

About five miles into my run, I picked up the pace. And I started to hear something in my head I had heard before—a sound like the whir and clatter of a spinning roulette wheel, with the metal ball rolling in the opposite direction of the wheel, waiting to drop into play. You think you know where the ball is going to land, but then it bounces around and settles in a place you never saw coming. In my mind, I saw the ball ricochet and hop and, finally, land. I stopped running. Breathing hard, I clasped my hands behind my head and looked up at the sky. I would run Badwater this year after all. Yeah. *Hell*, yeah.

I would run the race on this shitty dirt track. I calculated the distance in my head. It would mean doing 540 laps, probably about twenty-four total hours of running over two days. I'd have to call in some favors and I'd have to fit it all in between head counts, but with some luck, I thought I could do it. I started to run again and felt a familiar happiness wash over me. It was the buzz I always got when I committed to a big race. This time it came with an oddly exhilarating—and undeniably ironic—sense of freedom: there were no entry fees, no application, no crowds, no airport security lines, no Twitter feed, no fund-raising, no finisher's medal, no pressure. All I had to do was run 135 miles. On the morning of July 13, 2011, the first day of the Badwater race, I would be standing on a starting line of my own.

CHAPTER 1

You loved me before seeing me;
You love me in all my mistakes;
You will love me for what I am.
—LUFFINA LOURDURAJ

I was born in 1962 in a small, backwoods town in the hills outside Charlotte, North Carolina. From the moment I could walk, I was a free-range kid. My mother and father were nineteen-year-old freshmen who met on a cigarette break during a summer-school literature class at the University of North Carolina at Chapel Hill. Richard Engle, my father—lanky, six feet three inches, clean-cut, in pressed khakis and button-down shirts—played freshman basketball at UNC for legendary coach Dean Smith. Rebecca Ranson, my mother—five feet two inches, unruly short brown hair, dark eyes, a budding playwright—was the daughter of an all-American runner who became a revered track and cross-country coach at UNC. But my mother's high school years had not been spent on a playing field or a cinder oval; at sixteen, she'd gotten pregnant and been sent to a home for unwed mothers, where she stayed until she delivered a baby girl, whom she gave up for adoption. I didn't find out I had a half sister until decades later.

My parents divorced when I was three years old. My father joined the Army in 1966 and shipped off to Germany. I didn't see him again for more than four years. I found out later that he and my mother had agreed to not say bad things about each other in front of me—

which explains why, from the day he left, my mother rarely mentioned him. He just disappeared. My mother threw herself into her schoolwork and her plays—and into protesting every injustice that rankled her. And North Carolina, in the mid-1960s, had a hell of a lot to get worked up about.

Momma remarried. Her new husband, Coke Ariail, was a director, producer, actor, photographer, painter, and sculptor whose favorite motif was my mother in the nude. A gentle man from a traditional Southern family, he had the impossible task of trying to replace my father. I ignored his rules and laughed off his punishments. We moved five times before I turned ten: Coke and my mother always found a new theater group to organize, a new degree to pursue, another wrong to right. September after September, I felt like a freak: the new kid with the scraggly, shoulder-length hair and the hippie parents, who spent his Saturdays not at Little League practices and games, but attending avant-garde plays and marching in antiwar protests. When court-ordered desegregation started, I rode the bus with the black students and befriended a soft-spoken boy named Earl, which, in the eyes of my conservative classmates, made me even more of a weirdo.

Just before I started fourth grade, we moved to the countryside outside Durham into a one-story house with peeling paint and a sagging front porch. My mother loved the place—she said it had "character" and "good bones"—so I said I loved it, too. Every month, I got to take the $100 rent check over to our landlord's place across the cow pasture that separated our houses. I felt like James Bond running across that field, hurdling electric fences, leaping over manure piles, and swinging wide around the bulls. I arrived at the Wimberleys' panting, my hair matted with sweat, tattered shorts drooping off my skinny hips, my legs splattered with mud and bits of grass. Sometimes they invited me in for cold cow-tongue sandwiches and cucumbers from their garden.

Coke and my mother were directing plays at the local theater—artsy and edgy stuff they had written themselves. They threw a lot of cast parties. On those nights, I'd sit in a beanbag chair in my bedroom and watch Johnny Carson, turning the volume up to drown out the noise. I kept the door shut, too, because the house smelled weird: pot and incense mixed with the chemicals from Coke's little darkroom. I never missed *The Tonight Show*, even on school nights. I liked Johnny, but I watched it mostly for Ed McMahon. I remember thinking he'd be a great dad with that big carnival-barker voice, that jolly rolling laughter. I imagined him coming in the front door at family gatherings.

"Where's Charlie?" he'd boom, first thing. "Where's my boy?"

When Johnny and Ed signed off for the night, I often padded out of my room, hungry and thirsty. By then, the party had usually spilled onto our front yard with the speakers facing an open window. I'd peer past the big moths banging on the screen door and spot my mother twirling in a long skirt while Coke danced with everyone and no one.

I remember one night making my way through the living room, stepping over empty bottles, guitar cases, and sandals on the way to the kitchen. I stopped in front of the sofa. A girl was lying there, one arm flopped awkwardly toward the floor. She was snoring. On the low table in front of her were two open bottles of beer, both still more than half-full. After a few seconds of watching her breathe, I went to the kitchen and opened the refrigerator. All we had was powdered milk mixed up in a jug—I hated that stuff—and Coke's homemade orange wine.

The record started to skip. I walked back into the living room, lifted the arm on the turntable, and put the needle down. The girl on the sofa was still out. I picked up one of the open bottles, sniffed it, brought it to my lips, and took a gulp. It tasted bitter, but I took another swig. I finished the first bottle and picked up the second. The beer made me feel warm and floaty and calm, as if someone had laid a magic hand on me and said, "See there, Charlie, nothing to worry about now."

On that humid late-summer night, with Janis Joplin wailing on the stereo, alcohol planted a little flag in my brain and claimed that territory as its own.

- - - -

About a half mile into the dense woods behind my house sat a cool, deep pond surrounded by pines, scrub oak, and azaleas. I spent hours at that pond, watching water bugs pulse between lily pads as big as Frisbees, swatting mosquitoes, skipping rocks, and fishing with a cane pole. When I got hot, I peeled off my clothes and swam, then lay on a warm rock and dried off in a patch of sunlight. Those woods were a place to dream—of places I'd rather be, of people I'd rather be. I was Marshal Matt Dillon, Detective Joe Mannix, Kwai Chang Caine practicing my kung fu moves. And I was Jonny Quest—oh, how I loved Jonny Quest—jetting off from Palm Key with my brilliant father, Dr. Benton Quest, on some supersecret world-saving mission to Tibet, Calcutta, the Sargasso Sea.

One afternoon at the pond, I heard a low roll of thunder. Greenish storm clouds were boiling above the treetops. Leaves began to rattle in the wind. I felt one raindrop and another and then a wall of them. I started for home, darting between trees, peeling off my T-shirt as I ran. When I emerged from the woods, I saw a jagged finger of lightning reach down to the field in front of me. The thunder, which had been distant, now boomed above my head. The storm seemed to be on top of me, matching my pace as I ran. I hopped a fence, leaped across a ditch filling with frothy fast-moving water, and cut through the long grass in our yard. I saw my mother standing in the porch doorway waiting for me. Waving my shirt over my head, I hollered and she waved back.

"I'm staying out here!"

"What?" she shouted, and cupped her hands to her ears.

I ran to the foot of the stairs, stripped off my shorts, balled up my drenched T-shirt, and tossed them up to her. She caught them and laughed.

"I'm staying out here!" I yelled again.

I dashed back out wearing only my cotton underpants. Yelping above the thunder and rain, whooping with every lightning flash, I sprinted around the yard. I brushed my hand against an overgrown honeysuckle vine and released its sweetness into the rain. I was soaked to the skin, but I felt free and smooth and happy. I wasn't scared of the storm. I was making my momma laugh and cheer. I will remember this always, I thought—the way it feels to run until you can't run anymore, the way it feels to not be afraid.

- - - -

The summer of 1973, my mother decided to move us to Attica, New York. She had been outraged by the Attica prison riot two years earlier, which left forty-three people dead—most of them inmates gunned down by prison guards from thirty-foot towers. Momma had been doing theater workshops with inmates in North Carolina prisons, crafting their lives and struggles into serious plays. She applied for and received a one-year grant to do the same at maximum-security Attica. The riot had started on her birthday—a sign, she said, that she was meant to go there.

Momma and I piled into our yellow VW Squareback, stuffed to the roof with our belongings, waved good-bye to Coke, who was reluctantly staying behind, and drove north to Attica. Coke told me later he thought it was a huge mistake, my mother taking me up there, but he was working all day and trying to do theater at night and had no way to take care of me alone.

We lived over a bakery in a tiny apartment that smelled of cinnamon and fresh-baked bread. My mother slept on a mattress on the floor of the only bedroom; I slept on a ratty sofa in the living room. A railroad track ran behind our place, and every morning at 6:30 a.m., a train rattled by, blowing its whistle. That train was my alarm clock, especially on those days when Momma got snowed in at the prison and couldn't get home. Some mornings, I would skip school and hang out down by the tracks with kids playing hooky or those who'd already dropped out. Most of their parents worked at the prison as guards. We killed time by stacking pennies on the rails and waiting for trains to flatten them. Sometimes, one of the older boys passed around a joint or a bottle of brown liquor. I didn't like pot—it made me slow and sleepy—but I liked booze. A few times I drank so much with the kids at the tracks I puked, but that didn't stop me. When I drank, relief washed through me; from what, I didn't know.

One day, my buddies and I spotted a man running alongside the last car of a slow-moving freight train. We watched him jump up, grab a handle near the door of a boxcar, and swing his body up and through the opening. Our mouths hung open as we watched that train disappear down the tracks.

I decided at that moment I was going to hop a train. I didn't tell any of my delinquent friends because I knew that if I failed or chickened out, I'd get teased about it. A week or so later, I worked up the courage to run beside the train and discovered it was much harder than it looked. The rocks in the rail bed were uneven and the railroad ties awkwardly spaced. I tripped and fell and landed about six inches from the train's moving wheels. I should have quit right there. Instead, I worked on my timing and figured out that if I stepped on every other tie as I ran, I could keep up with the train.

One Saturday morning, Momma was at work and I decided this was the day. I threw on my father's old, way-too-big-for-me Army jacket—one of the few things he'd ever given me—and ran down to the tracks. As a train approached, I hid in some bushes and watched the first few cars pass. When I saw the open doors of a boxcar, I ran, quickly pulling even with it. I leaped at the open doorway and threw my body forward, landing hard on my stomach. For one agonizing second, I teetered, half-in, half-out, and then found a finger hold in a space between the floorboards and pulled myself in. I rolled over onto my back, breathing hard, buzzing with the rush of what I had done.

My excitement lasted about five minutes. Empty boxcars were boring and smelled like piss. Ten minutes, twenty minutes, thirty minutes, and still the train sped on. I had to get off this thing. Peering out the open door, I thought about jumping. I pictured myself hitting the ground and rolling, like the guys I'd seen on TV. I looked ahead, hoping to see a soft place to land, but I saw only rocks and hard-baked dirt and scrubby bushes—all of them flashing by quickly. The only thing to do was dangle from the handle near the door and try to ease myself to the ground.

I grabbed the cold steel with a sweaty palm and swung out of the railcar. Now I was hanging over the moving ground, with the speed of the train pressing me against the boxcar. I realized that if I let go, I'd probably end up under the wheels of the train. But I couldn't swing my leg up to the open doorway and climb back up. My grip was slipping. I let one sneaker scrape along the ground, trying to get a sense of the speed of the train until I couldn't hold on any longer. I let go and landed on my feet at a run, taking lunging step after lunging step as I fought to keep my balance. Somehow I stayed upright while the train sped away from me.

"Yeah!" I shouted as I slowed to a trot. I raised my arms. I was invincible, a superhero. I was also, I realized, a hell of a long way from home.

Vibrating with adrenaline, I took off down the center of the track back toward Attica. I ran and ran, thinking I'd spot my ugly apartment building around each next bend. Every so often, I stopped and walked, then I'd force myself to run again. I ran for almost two hours until, at last, I saw our place. Not long after I let myself in and flopped onto our couch, my mother walked in.

"I got two cinnamon buns from downstairs. Day old, but just as good." She held up a small paper bag. "How was your day?"

"Okay."

"What have you been up to?"

"Nothing."

It's not that I thought I'd be in trouble if I told her what I'd done; I never got in trouble with Momma. But this adventure was something I wanted to keep to myself: the train ride and the rush of the jump and the miles and miles I had run to get home.

- - - -

Before eighth grade started, my mother asked me if I wanted to go live with my father, my stepmother, Molly, and my stepsister, Dina, in California. I don't know whose idea it was. I'd been to see my dad a few times and we'd had fun together: he'd taken me to Disneyland and the beach. He was not affectionate like Momma, but I

11

liked it out there. More than anything, I was excited that moving to California meant I would get to play organized sports. My mother and Coke were never in tune with what that entailed: uniforms and practices and games and schedules. I told Momma I wanted to go, then felt awful for saying it. She cried when I left, but somehow, I also sensed her relief. She would have more time for her projects if I wasn't underfoot. I knew how much her work meant to her. I got on the plane sick with guilt over leaving her—and bewildered that she could just let me go.

I signed up for Pop Warner football as soon as I got to California, even though the only football I had ever seen was on television. I was almost six feet tall and skinny as a rake handle, and I barely made the weight limit—125 pounds. I saw little playing time, but I liked how it felt to be a part of a team, and I enjoyed the practices—especially the running. One day after practice I was out doing some extra laps around the field while I waited for my stepmom to pick me up. I noticed the school cross-country coach watching me.

"Hey!" he shouted to me when I got close. "You look more like a runner than a football player. Why don't you come out for my team?"

I went to my first cross-country practice the next day. I wore my football cleats because I didn't have any running shoes. One of the other boys mumbled, "Nice shoes," as we took off on a three-mile trail run. I didn't care. I was just happy to be running. By the time that first workout was over, I knew I had found where I belonged.

- - - -

I remember my first race, the chaos of elbows and knees when the starter pistol fired, the jostling for position as dozens of boys tried to squeeze onto the narrow trail. Several hundred yards into the race, I tripped and fell. I tried to scramble to my feet, but it was like being caught in big surf. I kept getting knocked down. A shoe landed on my hand and spikes punctured my skin. I looked up to see who the hell had just stepped on me and spotted a kid in bright green shorts speeding away. When I finally got up and ran again, I was powered

12

by something new and potent—the rocket fuel of adrenaline and anger.

I surged forward, catching and passing runner after runner. I was flying—until I came to a stream. Since I had never run a cross-country race before and had never gotten my feet wet on a run, I didn't know what to do. I stopped abruptly, which caused the boy behind me to barrel into me and knock me over.

"Move, asshole," someone said as I tried once again to get to my feet. I watched the other runners splash through the water without missing a step. One of my teammates passed me.

"Come on, Charlie," he yelled.

C'mon, Charlie, I said to myself. *C'mon, Charlie.* I got up and ran again—picking my way through the stream on my toes, then lengthening my stride when I hit the trail. Now I had room to move. The field had spread out, and for a few minutes I was alone in the woods. I heard my feet hitting the dirt, and my rhythmic breathing. I felt myself moving with a kind of animal grace. When I emerged from the trees into an open area, I spotted the lead pack of six or seven boys. And in the middle of that group, I saw the kid in the green shorts. I was going to catch him.

Just as I closed in, he glanced back and saw me running in full attack mode. He took off, shooting right to the front of the group. I tried to push harder, but my legs were suddenly leaden, as if I were trying to run through thigh-deep mud. Green Shorts crossed the finish in first place. Having my blood on his spikes hadn't slowed him down.

I lurched across the finish line in fifth place and doubled over with hands on my knees, trying to get my breath. When I straightened up, I saw Green Shorts walking right toward me. *Oh, shit. What's this?*

"Good race," he said, giving me a slight lift of his chin, before walking on.

Good race. Good race. Those two little words changed my life. I had gotten recognition for my effort, for refusing to give up. I never lost another race that season, and I went on to win the sectional qualifier for the Junior Olympics. At the state meet, I came in thirteenth. Not bad for a rookie year, but I wanted more. I wanted to be the fastest.

I played basketball on the school team during the winter, but it was mostly so I would be in good shape for track and field in the spring. In my first-ever track meet, I won the half mile, the mile, and the triple jump. My teammates smacked me on the back, and my coach told me that I was a naturally gifted runner and that I could be really fast if I worked hard. When I showed my three blue ribbons to Dad, he seemed more surprised than impressed. I hoped he would come to see one of my meets, but he never did. I went undefeated that season.

At the end of the school year, my father announced we were moving back to North Carolina so he could start a new job working with his brother. I was upset because I wanted to run Junior Olympics in California so I could race against some of the guys who'd beaten me in cross-country. But Dad's decision was final. I felt better when my coach told me I could run in the North Carolina JOs if I could get there in time for the sectional meet. I didn't mind moving as long as I could run. At the sectionals, I won the half mile and the mile. When I found my father in the crowd, he said, "Good job . . . but if you had just pushed the pace a little harder on lap three, you could have gone faster by a second or two."

I threw myself into high school and into doing anything that I thought might make my father proud. I made the varsity football, basketball, baseball, and track teams. I produced, wrote, and performed a morning news show on the school's closed-circuit TV network. I was class president my sophomore and junior years and student-body president my senior year. I was top ten in my class of four hundred and voted Best All Around in the senior class. I was recruited by several colleges to play football, and I got an early acceptance to my dream school and family alma mater—the University of North Carolina.

On paper, I was a perfect kid, Mr. Wonderful. Except Mr. Wonderful was not what I felt like. Each new accomplishment and accolade brought only momentary relief, followed by the certainty that I was not doing enough. When I lived with Mom, I was never anything but myself, but with Dad, being myself felt inadequate. My father did little to refute that notion. He could, especially when he'd been drinking, flay me with a few choice words about a blown layup or bad pass, an A-minus instead of an A. I thought he focused on the negative; he saw it as just being honest. His dad had been that way, too. The grand Engle tradition: praise was for sissies; disparagement, ridicule—now *that* would make you a man.

Toward the end of football season senior year, I got caught with a beer in my hand at the State Fair in Raleigh and the coach suspended me for one game. My father was furious and we had a huge argument. I decided to run away, and I urged my girlfriend to come with me. We had only been dating for a few months, but things had gotten serious quickly. She was a senior with a lot to lose, but all that mattered in the moment was getting away. We loaded up her old Ford Pinto and drove south to Daytona Beach. In Daytona, nobody checked IDs, so even though we were only seventeen, we stocked up on rum and pineapple juice and got drunk in our motel room. I got a job as a busboy, but after two weeks of pretending to be grown-ups, we realized we had to go home. We hadn't even called our parents to let them know we were safe, and that cruelty weighed on both of us.

- - - -

My father ignored me for several days after my return—until one afternoon when I pulled into our driveway after football practice. He was outside, getting something from the trunk of his car. I took my time gathering up my books and my backpack, hoping he would just go back into the house and leave me alone. But when I looked up, he was glaring at me with his arms crossed. His face was red. Reluctantly, I got out of my car.

"What the *hell* were you thinking?" he said slowly.

"Don't worry about it. It's not your problem."

"It is my problem!" he shouted. "You just blew any chance you had for a scholarship. You blew your shot at playing college ball."

"All right! I know!" I yelled. "I don't give a shit!"

He took several steps toward me and drew one leg back to kick me. I dodged his foot, and the momentum of his missed swipe upended him. I saw the slick soles of his penny loafers as his legs went into the air and heard the sickening thud when he hit the asphalt. I didn't know what to do so I ran to my van and backed into the street. Before I drove away, I looked back and saw my father scrambling to his feet.

I knew he was right. This was a monumental screwup. By missing a few key games, I'd ruined my chances of playing college football. I had also been a candidate for the prestigious UNC Morehead Scholarship, which would have given me a free ride to UNC. I'd blown that, too. I had made a huge mess of things. But I knew I could redeem myself in college. All I had to do was study hard, make good grades, and stay out of trouble.

CHAPTER 2

Moderation means small, non-habit-forming amounts.
That's not you.

—CHAD HARBACH, *The Art of Fielding*

I arrived at the University of North Carolina at Chapel Hill as a seventeen-year-old freshman, half expecting a WELCOME CHARLIE ENGLE! banner to greet me. In only a few weeks at UNC I learned one troubling truth: I was average—at best. Four thousand shiny overachievers had descended on the campus, and way too many of them were smarter than me, better looking than me, and, it pained me to admit, more athletic than me.

I did get an invitation to try out as a walk-on for the football team, but soon after school started, I sprained my ankle in a pickup basketball game and football was out. I had missed my chance, unlikely as it may have been. What I should have done was go out for the cross-country team. I could have carried on the family tradition and kept myself in good shape. I thought I could make the team, but I doubted I could ever live up to my grandfather's legacy. I would have been training on a course that was named after him. I thought it would be easier to not even try than to risk failing.

- - - -

Several weeks into my first semester, I learned how to play backgammon. I also turned eighteen. For me, both these things translated into opportunities to drink. When I wasn't pounding shots in

17

the downtown bars, I was in the halls of my dorm, hunched over a backgammon board. Backgammon, as we played it, was a drinking game—BEER-gammon—with a complex set of rules and wagers that all led to the players getting shitfaced. Roll Acey-Deucy, drink. Roll Boxcars, drink. Roll Double Ducks, drink. Loser drinks, winner drinks, drinker drinks. I don't know if I was any good at the game, but I was a champion, varsity, first-string, starting-lineup, all-conference drinker. I had found my place to shine.

Despite my drinking, I went out for JV basketball, coached by Roy Williams, and made the team. It was an incredible time for UNC hoops: Michael Jordan, James Worthy, and Sam Perkins were all on varsity, playing for Coach Dean Smith. I knew I wasn't ever going to compete with those guys, but I wanted to be part of the team. I decided to be a team manager instead of a player. I hoped to move up to varsity eventually. I had a family legacy there. My uncle had been a varsity manager in the 1960s. Yes, I was sitting behind the bench and handing out towels and water bottles, but I was giving them to some of the greatest basketball players of all time. I was a tiny part of the team, but I felt overjoyed when they won the 1982 NCAA Championship.

I loved it—but I loved drinking more. I was occasionally so out of it at practice that I made mistakes on the stat sheets. Four JV managers were vying for one open varsity slot. I didn't get it. I didn't deserve it.

At the start of my sophomore year, my roommate Mike and I checked out the fraternity scene. We bounced from house to house, party to party, happy to provide entertainment for the brothers whose mission it was to get the new guys trashed. I decided to pledge Sigma Phi Epsilon; they were jocks who got decent grades and always seemed to have pretty girls hanging around. I liked that most of them wore jeans and T-shirts, not preppy penny loafers and button-downs.

I was happy to be a part of this group of guys who would watch my back—even if it was because I was bent over puking on my shoes. The drinking age was about to go up to twenty-one, and since bars would no longer be available to me, I was pleased to have snagged a guaranteed place to drink in the moldy basement of the frat house.

Road trips were big with the Sig Ep boys. My first one was to Boone in the mountains of North Carolina for a day of skiing and partying with the Appalachian State brothers. We loaded a keg onto our chartered bus, cranked up the Stones, and settled in for the two-hour trip.

About halfway to Boone, Steve, the kid next to me, fished something out of his pocket. "Want a bump?" He held up a small plastic contraption that looked like some kind of secret decoder ring.

"What?"

"Blow."

"Oh. Yeah. Sure," I said, not wanting to expose my cluelessness.

Steve lifted the bullet-shaped device to the light like a jeweler holding a gem. The sun revealed a small amber-colored round chamber at the bottom, about half-full of powder. A tiny handle on the side looked like the key on a windup toy. Steve twisted the handle, showing me the white powder in the top of the chamber waiting to be . . . what? What was I supposed to do now?

Steve saw my confusion and held up a hand in the way that said, *Pay attention, you're about to learn something*. He put the bullet up to his left nostril, tilted his head back, inhaled, and closed his eyes. "Ahhhhhhh."

He reloaded the bullet and handed it over. Self-consciously, I put it up to my right nostril, blocked my left, and breathed in. Steve gave me an expectant look, so I nodded with what I hoped was convincing enthusiasm, showing him I had indeed gotten the "bump."

He took back the device, fiddled with it, and handed it over again. "Other side."

I inhaled the powder, then remembered to close my eyes and tilt my head back the way he had. "Thanks, man." I returned the bullet to him.

I sat back and waited for the drug to take hold. Twenty minutes and two beers later, I was still waiting. Maybe it was all the alcohol I had consumed, or maybe it was bad coke, but I felt no different. If this was all cocaine did, who needed it? Not me. I had drinking. I understood drinking. Alcohol did exactly what it was supposed to do; it numbed everything. Drinking was reliable and I was excellent at it. I could outdrink most anyone, and I learned early on that the best way to recover from a hangover was to start drinking again. I remember being relieved that the coke hadn't affected me. I didn't want it—or anything else—to distract me from drinking.

Two weeks later, in the back of a bar on Henderson Street in downtown Chapel Hill, one of my buddies offered me coke again. To be sociable, I snorted two quick lines through a rolled-up dollar bill. After a minute or two of my feeling nothing, a klieg light switched on in my brain. I remember the electric tang of the lime I bit into before I downed the liquid fire of a tequila shot. And the way "Roxanne" seemed to come *out* of my ears instead of from the jukebox speakers. And that pitcher of cold beer with its drops of condensation on the side shining like rhinestones in the blue light of the bar's neon PABST BLUE RIBBON sign. I'd never seen anything so beautiful.

Suddenly, I had plans—big, big plans. I remember the looks on my friends' faces—Tom and Lenny and Carl. Really, did anyone have cooler friends than me? I reeled off my recipe for greatness. I would study hard, make straight A's, get back into prime running shape, volunteer at the local homeless shelter, get a part-time job, pay my father back, save the whales, find a cure for every god-awful thing that made nice people sick.

Cocaine rammed my alcohol-soaked brain into a hot forge and then hammered its edge ax-sharp. My thoughts were no longer the sentimental, looping ramblings of a drunken dreamer; they were a speeding train with a full cargo of clarity and purpose and unshakable resolve. *This*, at last, was who I really was, who I was born to be. I was made new, glowing with possibility. I could be the man I wanted to be—and, yes, even the man my father wanted me to be. All I needed was to score a few more lines.

I couldn't have known then that I would spend the next ten years looking for the magical combination of coke and alcohol and friends and vibe that would re-create that life-altering first high.

- - - -

Like many people my age in the early 1980s, I looked at coke as a risk-free, albeit expensive, way to ratchet up the fun. My friends and I would split a $100 gram and dance and drink the night away. I liked that coke seemed to give me drinking superpowers: I could down a case of beer and whatever else was put in front me—shots of tequila, kamikazes, you name it—and still be on my feet.

My friends loved to drink and do coke, too, but I soon realized we had one fundamental difference. At some point during the evening, they would remember that they had papers due and exams and classes. They would call it quits and head off to bed, leaving me alone and baffled by their departure; 2:00 a.m., 3:00 a.m., 4:00 a.m.—I was just getting rolling.

Soon, a shared gram wasn't nearly enough for me. My habit was getting more expensive; to keep myself supplied, I started to sell it. At first I dealt only to my fraternity brothers and close friends. Then I got bolder, selling to friends of friends and then to just about anyone who approached me. I told myself I wasn't some greedy lowlife, dealing so I could buy a fancy car or designer clothes. Selling cocaine allowed me to get more cocaine. *More* was what I wanted. It was simple.

Of course, the more drugs I got my hands on, the more I used. I lived in a single room in my frat house, and no one knew if I was in there or not. I'd keep to myself, drinking and doing drugs during the day, then appear at night, when it was officially time to go out and party. My grades plummeted and I quit going to class.

My multi-day binges ended only when I ran out of drugs and money. Crashing hard and sick with remorse, I'd promise myself I would never do it again. I swore I would get my shit together, eat healthy, study—right this sinking ship. Step one in my total transformation was almost always my lacing up my shoes and going out for a run.

Still intoxicated and operating on no sleep, I'd pull a ball cap low over my eyes and slip out the side door of the frat house. I cut between campus buildings and crossed a graveyard to reach the athletic fields and the light blue track. Then I ran as if in a trance, knees pumping, arms swinging, eyes straight ahead. The UNC bell tower chimed every fifteen minutes, then tolled the hour. Joggers came and went, and still I ran. Thirty, forty, fifty laps—I pushed the pace until my lungs and legs burned. The more I had partied, the worse the running hurt. The more it hurt, the harder I pushed. When I finally stopped, I drank from the water fountain until my stomach was bloated and then vomited into the bushes until my throat was raw. I knew that I deserved this pain. I hated myself for failing at school, for failing as a person. Running was my penance.

CHAPTER 3

I drank because I wanted to drown my sorrows, but now
the damned things have learned to swim.

— FRIDA KAHLO

My nosedive had not escaped my fraternity brothers' attention.
Engle, they agreed, was in deep shit. I owed money that I didn't
have to my drug supplier, and I had heard the cops had started asking around about me. Behind my back, my friend Jimmy called my
dad and told him he needed to come get me or something bad was
going to happen.

I had just returned from one of my purging runs when my father
walked into my room without knocking. He looked at me and shook
his head. I knew what he saw. I was ragged, unshaven, sweaty, dirty,
and red eyed. I turned away and started cramming my things into a
bag. In silence, my father and I loaded the rental car and drove to the
airport. College was over for me.

- - - -

When my father, my stepmother, Molly, and my stepsister, Dina,
moved to Carmel, California, I trailed along. It was just what I
needed, we all said; a fresh start. Molly and my dad bought two
Baskin-Robbins ice cream shops in Monterey and gamely hired me
to run one of them. I went off to franchise training in Burbank—
sundae school, I called it—and two weeks later returned with a document that proclaimed me a certified cake decorator.

I was grateful to Dad for giving me the opportunity. It was a leap of faith and I didn't want to let him down. Things went well for a while, but for reasons I couldn't comprehend, I could feel the pressure building again, the nagging need. After weeks of white-knuckling it, I started partying again. To feed my habit, I'd take $300 out of the Baskin-Robbins register, buy coke, sell enough to recoup the money I'd swiped, snort the rest, stay up all night, and get back the next morning in time to open the store and return the money to the cash drawer. Then I started to skip the part where I replaced the $300. I knew my behavior was despicable, but I did it anyway.

One morning, Dad walked into the store. I was in the back room counting cash and doing paperwork, getting ready to open.

"Morning," I said when he stepped into the office.

"I know what you have been doing."

I looked up.

His mouth was set in a hard straight line. "I hoped you would get your shit together but that's obviously not happening."

"What? I'm here, aren't I? Right on time."

"It's just more of the same. You can't do anything right, can you?" Dad glared at me.

"No." I looked at my hands. "No, I guess I can't. I'm sorry."

I walked past him, put my keys and franchisee name tag on the glass ice cream counter, and went out the front door.

- - - -

I fled to Chapel Hill to see some old buddies, who had somehow managed to stay in school, albeit on the six-year plan. Late one night, at a frat party, I met Pam Smith. I had just come back from a beer run; no matter how fucked-up I was, I almost always managed to get to the Happy Store for a twelve-pack just before it closed. Pam walked up to me shyly, smiling as if she already knew a secret about me. She asked for a beer and I was happy to share my stash with her. She was slender, with shoulder-length brown hair and bright, clear eyes—even at 2:00 a.m. Her shorts revealed tan, athletic legs. I popped the top off a cold can and handed it over. When she reached for the beer, I caught a whiff of some flowery fragrance that was nice but not too much.

She said she was about to finish her degree in biology at Carolina after taking a year off to earn money to pay for school. I told her I lived in California and was "between jobs." She was born in the Bay Area, but her folks had moved to North Carolina when she was a baby and she grew up certain she'd go to UNC. We spent the next few days hanging out together. I loved that she was as passionate as I was about the Tar Heels—and she laughed at my jokes. Pam's grandmother lived in the San Francisco Bay Area, and Pam said she visited her occasionally. I told her to look me up if she ever came West.

About a week after I returned to California, she called. She had just bought a plane ticket and was coming to see me. I was surprised, but excited.

Pam stayed with me in my tiny studio apartment in Carmel. One night, I took her to Jack London's, a downtown pub where I was a regular and the bartender was a good enough friend to not let on that I spent many more hours parked on those barstools than I should have. We sat at the bar and ate fish and chips and drank chardonnay from Monterey County. Though I wanted more wine, I kept my drinking in check. After dinner we walked barefoot, hand in hand, on the cold sand of Carmel Beach. We marveled at the big, beautiful houses overlooking the rocks and the water and talked about what it would be like to wake up every morning to that view. It all seemed so normal, so solid—things I had little experience with. My life always felt tenuous, as if it were dangling from a fragile thread. Having a normal person interested in me made me feel good.

Somehow during that week, Pam made me believe I was lovable, despite all the evidence to the contrary. I loved her—I guess mostly for loving me, which in retrospect was a shaky foundation for a relationship. I didn't see that then. I just wanted to be with someone who wanted me.

After spending a total of ten days together, we decided to move to Atlanta. My mother invited us to live with her until we could afford a place of our own. By then, she and Coke had separated and she was living with her partner, Julie. I wasn't shocked when Mom told me she was a lesbian; I had sensed that one or two of the women who had hung around our house over the years were more than friends. And Mom had been writing plays about the gay community for as long as I could remember. *Warren*, about her close friend Warren Johnston, who died of AIDS in 1984, was one of the first plays produced in the world to address the disease.

Pam got a job at the Emory University genetics research laboratory and I got one selling memberships at Bally's fitness. My mother and Julie liked booze almost as much as I did, so we spent many nights sitting around the kitchen table drinking and talking about theater and art and the scourge of AIDS. I loved seeing my mom happy and in love, and she was thrilled to have me living under the same roof again for a little while. I turned out to be good at selling memberships, and Pam and I were able to get our own place. But, for me, having money was not a good thing.

I started bingeing again, disappearing for days, then showing up wrecked and remorseful and pleading with Pam for forgiveness. That was the last time, I would tell her. Never again. Done, I'd said. I absolutely meant it. And then I'd feel it again, that hole that required filling.

One night after Pam went to bed, I slipped out of the house and headed to a bar down the street. I knew the bartender there had coke to sell. My plan was to have a beer or two, do a couple of lines, and head home. Instead, I spent the next two days bouncing from dive to dive, drinking and snorting coke. When I was out of money, I staggered back to our apartment reeking, trembling, famished, and distraught. I was relieved that Pam wasn't home when I arrived.

I went into the kitchen and riffled through our cupboards. I ripped open of package of Chips Ahoy! cookies and ate the entire thing. I gulped milk out of a gallon jug, then tore into a box of Froot Loops, cramming handfuls into my mouth and littering the countertop and floor with cereal. Then I heard the apartment door open, and Pam and my mother walked in.

I ran to the bathroom in a panic. I could not let my mother see me like this. She had no idea I was this awful person, this out-of-control low-life freak. I turned on the shower, stripped down, and stepped in, desperate for the hot water to make my skin stop crawling, to calm my pounding heart, to wash this nightmare away.

"Charlie!" Pam yelled through the closed door.

I heard my mother yell, "Are you okay?"

I was not okay. I hated myself. I hated what I was doing to the people I cared about. I hated that I would once again have to try to make up with Pam. I could not see even a sliver of light in my life.

I pulled my hand back and punched at the shower door. It shattered, sending glass shards everywhere. Blood streamed from my knuckles and down my arm. I slid down the wall of the shower, sobbing. My body blocked the drain, and water, tinted red, pooled on the tile floor. Then Pam and Mom were there, looking down at me. Pam was crying and my mother's hand was over her mouth, her eyes wide with fear.

Somehow, they got me out of the shower and into bed. Hours later, when I woke up, I had bandages on both arms and legs, and one above my right eye. I heard Pam and Mom speaking in quiet voices in the next room. I only caught a few words: "addicted" and "needs help" and "dangerous." I didn't want to hear it, so I let myself drift off again.

I kept things together for a week or two and then went off the rails again. When I slunk home after another three-day binge, I found Pam packing her things.

"What are you doing?"

"I can't live like this, Charlie."

"I'm sorry! I swear. That was the last time. I'm done. I swear."

"I'm leaving."

"No, you can't leave. I want to be better. But I can't do it alone. Please stay."

Pam looked at me and sighed. "Nothing will change."

"Yes, it will. I'll change. I want you with me."

"Why? So I can watch you kill yourself?"

"Stay. Marry me," I blurted out. "Please. Let's get married."

– – – –

Mom and Julie threw us a wedding shower. The invitation said it was a "bar stocking" shower: guests were expected to give us a bottle of top-shelf booze. Perfect. Just what I needed to launch my life of moderation. The wedding was small and simple, held in Pam's hometown of Weaverville, North Carolina. It was the first and only time I could remember having Mom and Coke and Dad and Molly in the same place. I loved seeing them together even if we'd never be one big happy family in a traditional sense. I had a few beers to calm my nerves, but I knew I had to limit myself and focus on demonstrating to my family and Pam that I was ready to get married.

Not long after we got back from our honeymoon, I drove to a bar, had a couple of beers, a few shots of tequila, and then . . . what? I don't know where I went or who I was with or how I drove home. When I reappeared a couple of days later, looking like hell, Pam and my mother were waiting for me at the kitchen table.

"We're worried about you," my mother said. She had a bourbon on the rocks in one hand and a cigarette in the other. She said that she had a friend who had joined AA and it had worked like a charm.

"We think you should try it," Pam said.

I wasn't sure what AA was, but I figured it could help me learn how to be a social drinker and get everyone off my back. Plus, I reasoned, reducing my intake of alcohol would leave me better able to manage my cocaine use.

The meeting was in a hospital cafeteria. I took a seat and Pam stood in the back of the room with her arms folded. My mother and Julie stayed outside to smoke while I got cured. Person after person stepped to the front of the room to speak. I was embarrassed for them—the way they sobbed as they told their stories about their drunken exploits. One had run over the family dog; one had made a scene at a PTA meeting. There were lost jobs, lost loves, deceptions, disasters. And something else about their tales I found very, very worrisome. These folks were referring to their drug and alcohol use as if it were *behind* them—a thing of the past. This, clearly, was not for me.

28

All I needed was a fresh start. I convinced Pam to move back to the Monterey Peninsula, where I got a full-commission job selling Toyotas. I went three weeks without selling a single car and came close to quitting. Peter, my Italian manager, yelled at me with his hands and his voice. Every day he pulled me aside to get me to tweak my sales pitch. Stop suggesting they look at less expensive vehicles, he said. Don't let them leave the showroom so quickly. Lighten up a little.

Eventually, I sold a car—and then another and another. I learned how to loosen up the buyers with some laughs, get them to like and trust me, and then steer them toward a shiny new car. Within a few months, I was one of the dealership's top salesmen. I even won Toyota's biggest prize—the National Walk-Around Contest, which recognized me as the top sales presenter in the United States. As the winner, I could choose between a new truck or the cash value of the vehicle. I took the cash.

Pam was smart to grab that check from me. We both knew the trouble I could get in with ten grand. We put the winnings toward buying our first house. I was twenty-six years old, and becoming a homeowner seemed like a box I needed to check; surely drug addicts didn't buy houses. Our broker, who was my boss's cousin, showed us a lot of great places—none of which we could afford. Then one day he called and said he had a perfect property for us: a nine-hundred-square-foot bungalow. It happened to be under high-tension power lines, but Jeff assured us that after a while we probably wouldn't even notice the buzzing.

We didn't love it, but since the Monterey housing market was so strong—"bulletproof," everyone said—and we didn't see ourselves living there for long, we decided it would be a good investment. The seller accepted our offer. Now all we had to do was get the bank to loan us money. We filled out the application forms and dropped them off the next day. The mortgage broker warned us that with our modest income, short time at our respective jobs, and our measly down payment, things didn't look great. But when he shook my hand, he leaned in and said the words I would hear from mortgage brokers many times in the next twenty years:

"Hey, don't worry about it. I'll get everything on the application squared away. We'll make this happen."

- - - -

After several weeks of supplying documents and information to the bank, our loan was approved and I was officially a homeowner and deeply in debt. The pressure was on to put up big numbers at Toyota and I did, selling more than thirty cars a month for several months in a row. For every qualifying sale I made, I got a cash bonus or "spiff." I squirreled that money away, thinking someday I'd surprise Pam with it. But that stash called and called to me until finally I decided to dip into it. I had been working so hard. Hadn't I earned the right to blow off a little steam?

I fell into a pattern of going to a bar for "a couple of beers" most days after work. Two beers turned into six or ten—and once I was buzzed, that voice in my head saying I deserved something *more*— the *more* being cocaine—became impossible to ignore. I'd score, stay out all night, then show up late to work, still half in the bag. I was just barely staying in the good graces of my boss and Pam. Whenever they confronted me, I gave them my solemn word that it was absolutely the last time. And the thing was, I meant it. I meant it even as I lifted the shot glass of tequila to my lips the next night and felt that deep relief, that unburdening flowing into me.

Weekends were always busy at the car dealership. One Saturday, I showed up at work an hour late. I had missed the weekly sales meeting.

My boss called me into his office. "Engle, what the fuck is wrong with you? You look like something a bird left on a rock. And you smell like shit, too. Did you drink all the booze in town last night?"

I took the berating silently. I believed that he wouldn't fire one of his best salesmen and that if I just took my punishment, I would be all right.

"I should send your ass home, but that would be too easy for you. Instead, you will stay here all day—outside on the lot. You will not take lunch. You will not speak to any customers. You're a good salesman and I want you here, but this is your last chance. Now get the fuck out of my office."

- - - -

Somehow, even with my escalating drinking and cocaine use, I was still running several times a week with a local running club. I had enough of an ego that I wanted to at least *look* good, and running was the most efficient way for me to keep my body lean and muscled. My chiropractor, Jay, was part of the group I ran with. He'd done several marathons and urged me to try one. He knew I was an addict. He thought a goal such as that might be just the motivation I needed to get clean.

A week before the Big Sur Marathon, I decided to enter. I'd run farther than ten miles only a few times in my life, but I figured it couldn't be that difficult. I'd just keep my feet moving. Pam was incredulous but seemed pleased that as part of my "training" I'd stop drinking that week. Jay had told me not to run the day before the marathon. I heeded that advice, but that left me with nothing to do but sit around and feel anxious. I decided to go out for one beer, just to ease the tension a bit. Hours later, I was in the bathroom of a bar on Cannery Row, snorting lines, with my friend Mike.

"I'm running a marathon tomorrow," I said to him as I dusted off my nose.

"The fuck you are."

"Yup. I have to be in Carmel at five thirty to catch a bus to the start."

He looked at his watch and his eyes got big.

I looked at my watch. "Shit." It was 2:00 a.m.

I rushed home, showered, brushed my teeth twice, and splashed my neck and armpits with cologne. I downed several glasses of water and some aspirin and made it to Carmel in time to board the last bus to the Big Sur start. The twenty-six-mile ride along the hilly, twisting coastal road nearly killed me. My stomach was doing backflips, my left ankle was throbbing and purple—I must have wrenched it during the night—and I desperately had to pee. What was worse, the guy next to me insisted on making small talk all the way. It was all I could do not to vomit on him. When I finally stepped off the bus, wearing only a singlet and running shorts, I realized I was underdressed for the forty-degree morning air. Now I was nauseated, scared, intoxicated, *and* freezing.

Over the years, I had mastered the art of the strategic puke, and I decided that this was a good time to use my skills. I went into some bushes and let loose. I felt better and was able to force down a banana and some Gatorade at the snack table. I wandered around a little, then heard the national anthem being played over a loudspeaker. I joined the race workers around me standing at attention. As I was finishing a second cup of Gatorade, I heard a gunshot. On instinct, I ducked. But nobody was shooting at me. Apparently, the race had begun. I was nowhere near the start line.

I sprinted up the road and caught the slow-moving back of the three-thousand-runner pack. When the logjam of runners loosened, I picked up the pace. The sun broke through the fog as we emerged from the redwoods and headed out into the broad green hills. I could smell the booze on my skin and imagined everyone around me could, too. At mile nine, I crossed a long bridge, then started the two-mile ascent to Hurricane Point. Jay had warned me about this climb. The wind was blowing thirty-five, maybe forty miles per hour—right into my face—and my stomach was a hard-balled fist. I struggled up the long hill and crossed another bridge. When I reached the half-marathon mark, I stopped to barf again. A guy running by asked me if I was okay.

"No. I'm so hungover. Got a beer on you?"

He laughed.

"Highlands Inn. Mile twenty-three!" he yelled back, as he pulled away. "Always a party there."

He thought I was joking about the beer, and I guess I had been, but by mile twenty-one, a cold beer was all I could think about. I started looking for the Highlands Inn. At last, I rounded a curve and spotted a group of about a dozen people sitting in lawn chairs, with coolers by their side.

"Three miles to go," one of them yelled. "You might as well start drinking now."

A few of the racers whooped and waved; most of them kept their eyes forward and ran by without acknowleding them.

I stopped. "Who's got a beer for me?" I yelled.

Someone passed me a can and I tipped it back and drained in. The group cheered. I gave a small appreciative bow. I accepted another, drained that one, and belched. High fives all around. Then I ran again, and for the next mile I felt fantastic—better than I had felt all morning. The road was so beautiful—the rocky headlands, the twisted cypress trees, the long curves of dark sand. The Pacific was an exceptional blue all the way to the horizon, where it disappeared in a blurred bank of cotton-pale fog.

The road turned inland and I passed a band playing in front of a gas station. Groups of people were cheering and waving signs. Kids on the side of the road were smiling and holding out trays of sliced strawberries for the runners. I smelled the ripe berries and felt a sudden wave of nausea. My legs buckled and I lurched to the side of the road, doubled over, and my stomach let loose again. I stood up and took a few wobbly steps forward, wiping the mess from my chin. The kids stood staring at me with their mouths open. "Gross," one of them said.

I was wrecked, completely spent. But I was going to finish this damn thing. I walked, then forced myself to run again. My feet were on fire, my quads were screaming. I saw the MILE 25 sign. I passed a field with horses behind a barbed-wire fence and swaths of orange poppies bent nearly horizontal in the wind. I kept moving, up a short, steep hill, then across the Carmel River bridge. At last, I glimpsed the finish line. I willed myself to stand tall, lift my knees, pump my arms. *Bring it in strong, Engle, with some style. Bring it in as if you are an athlete, not an asshole.*

I crossed the finish line in just under three hours and thirty minutes. A race worker put a clay finisher's medal around my neck. All around me, runners were whooping, pumping their fists, hugging friends. Some were crying. And I felt, what? Some satisfaction, yes. I had done it; I had shown Pam and my friends and myself that I could follow through on something. And relief, definitely, that I had finished the goddamned thing and would never have to do it again. But something else overshadowed the other feelings: crushing despair. I had just run 26.2 miles. A fucking marathon. I should have been flying. Where was my joy? Where was my runner's high? As soon as I got home, I put in a call to my drug dealer.

- - - -

Several months after Pam and I moved into our new house, my father-in-law, Horace, came for a visit. He was a North Carolina country boy with a wonderfully corny sense of humor. He was warm and gregarious and I liked him a lot. Horace had been a heavy drinker, but he'd cut way back after he had a quadruple bypass. I decided not to drink or use drugs at all during his weeklong visit.

On his last night in town, Horace said he wanted to treat us to dinner at the Monterey Plaza Hotel, overlooking the bay. I had sold two cars that day and collected $200 in cash bonuses. Before I left work to meet Pam and Horace at the restaurant, one of my fellow salesmen who was also my drug connection mentioned he was "holding." I did feel like celebrating, but . . . Horace was still here. I decided the smart thing to do was to buy some coke while I had the opportunity, but hold off dipping into it until after Horace went home.

Five minutes later, I pulled over on the way to the restaurant and did two quick lines. Then in the parking lot, I did two more. By the time I walked in, I was wide-eyed and jabbering. I think Pam knew I was high, but she kept it to herself.

Cocaine is not an appetite enhancer but I forced myself to eat my dinner. I smiled at Horace, commented on the exquisite food, wiped my mouth delicately with the cloth napkin, agreed with Pam that the view of the bay was spectacular. I was aware of the clinking of glasses, the tonguelike flicker of the votive candles, and the murmur and laughter of the other diners. I wanted to scream, *You are all fucking up my high!*

"I'll be right back," I said when I couldn't stand it one more second. "Men's room."

I headed toward the restrooms, then veered off to the bar, where I ordered a double shot of tequila. Once I was in the bathroom stall, I did a quick bump. I knew I could make it through dinner now, even if Pam and Horace ordered dessert.

When we got home, I made a big show of yawning and saying I was going to turn in early. I stared at the ceiling and waited for Pam to come to bed. She'd had her share of wine and fell asleep right away. When I heard her rhythmic breathing, I crept out the back door and walked toward a bowling alley about a mile away. That was the closest bar. I knew that I was screwing up badly. I could see myself on the road in the dark, going where I knew I should not be going, but I couldn't stop it from happening. Drunks and addicts live like that; in their own shitty movie, they are both the star and the audience.

A little before 5:00 a.m., I staggered home, relieved that I had made it back before anyone would be up. When I got close to the front door, I was shocked to spot Pam and Horace sitting at the kitchen table. I detoured to our detached garage and slipped inside. I noticed a pile of my dirty running clothes next to the washing machine. Eureka. I stripped off my jeans and shirt and put on running shorts and a tank top. Then, I went to the sink and splashed water on my head and my shirt. I jogged in place for a few minutes until I was suitably winded, then went outside and walked into the kitchen from the back patio.

"Good morning!" I said with all the faux invigorated cheer I could muster. I grabbed a paper towel to mop my face and stood there, breathing hard.

Then I saw the way they were looking at me.

"We've been up since three waiting for you to come home," Pam said evenly. "I told Dad everything."

- - - -

In January 1991, I agreed to go to Beacon House, a rehab center in a rambling Victorian mansion on landscaped grounds not far from our house. I did it in part to appease Pam and my family, and in part because even I could admit that I would benefit from practicing a little *moderation*. I partied hard the night before I had to report for my twenty-eight-day stay. I stumbled up the front steps of the treatment center as Pam drove away. She had left my suitcase on the sidewalk.

After I filled out paperwork, I was sent to get a physical at a medical clinic a few blocks away. I walked to the clinic and sat in the waiting room surrounded by regular people—mothers with kids, elderly couples, a pregnant woman—feeling as if I had a big flashing sign over my head that said DOPE FIEND. I fidgeted in the chair, flipped through an old AARP magazine, and picked at my cuticles. Finally, my name was called and I was shown into an examination room.

The young nurse was pleasant enough while she asked me questions and checked my vital signs. I was relieved that it seemed I was going to get through this without a lecture. When it was over, I thanked her and turned for the door.

She grabbed me by the arm and spun me toward her. "You know you could quit if you really wanted to. You're just weak and you lack character."

So there they were: the very words I had said to myself a thousand times. It was as if she had heard them through her stethoscope while she listened to my heart. I had suspected I was deficient; now I had confirmation from a medical professional. I bolted from the exam room and out the clinic door, blind with shame.

I had been told to return immediately to Beacon House. But I felt the lure of the beach a few blocks the other way—and the pull of a windowless dive bar called Segovia's, where I'd spent many hours. A walk along the water, one beer—I needed those things now.

But I knew that taking off would be a colossal mistake. Pam and my boss would be furious. They had both made it clear that if I didn't follow the treatment-center rules and complete the full twenty-eight-day rehab stint, I would not be welcomed back. I had to do my time even if I was, as the nurse had made clear, a lost cause. I trudged back up the hill to Beacon House.

Now I had to get through detox. I was used to stopping cold

turkey—I'd done it many times before. I knew what to expect—the shakes, the anxiety, the agitation, the sweating, the brain fog—and a part of me welcomed it all. I deserved it. I spent the weekend lying in bed, pacing, or paging through *The Big Book of AA*—which had been left on a table in my room. I emerged only for meals, and I attacked them with strange gusto, stuffing myself with stews and rolls and cookies as if somehow food could tamp down the pain.

On Monday, I had my first counseling session. I had never talked to a therapist in my life and I dreaded it. I walked into his office, a high-ceilinged, wood-paneled room in the front of the house. Sunlight streamed in from the big windows that looked out on the green half-moon front lawn, planted with lantana and pines. My counselor was a thirtysomething, clean-cut guy in glasses and a button-down shirt. He introduced himself as John and I shook his hand. He was wearing one earring, a brown stone set in gold that looked very much like an eye. I sat down on a couch opposite him, poured myself a glass of water out of a pitcher, and downed it.

"So, a little about me," he said. "I've been sober more than five years. I got started with drinking and drugs as a kid. Spun out of control in college. DUIs, dealt, all that."

I was surprised he offered me this information. I had assumed I'd be required to do all the talking. I relaxed a little and said, "Sounds familiar."

We talked about where I was from and what I did for a living, and how long I had been using.

"Do you think you are an addict?" John asked.

"I'm not sure. I know that when I start drinking, I can't stop."

"Do you want to be sober?"

"I think so."

"Why?"

"Because I know I need to change if I want to save my marriage and keep my job."

"Okay, but do *you* want to be sober? For you? Forget marriage or jobs."

"I like to drink and I like how I feel when I do cocaine. But lately,

I need to drink more and do more drugs to get to the same place. I'm worried. It takes more for me to escape."

"Escape what?"

"I have no idea." I laughed nervously.

He waited for me to go on.

"People always tell me what a great life I have. I have a wife who loves me and a job that I'm good at. But I don't feel happy. I don't feel anything. It's like I'm trying to be what other people think I should be, checking boxes to meet some requirement."

"What do other people think you should be?"

"Someone better than I am."

"Who thinks that?"

"Everyone. My dad. My wife. Me."

"Are there things that make you happy?" John asked.

"I don't think I know what happy is."

"Do you feel happy when you sell more cars than anyone else?"

"No, not really. I just feel relieved."

"About what?"

"That I have been able to continue the charade. I have put off for another day people discovering the real truth about me."

"Which is?"

"What?"

"What is the real truth about you?"

"That I see people crying or laughing or filled with joy—and I think, 'Why don't I ever feel like that?' I don't have feelings. I only pretend to have them. I take cues from how people look on the outside to figure out how I should feel on the inside."

John smiled at me.

"Fucked up, isn't it?" I said.

"No, not at all. That's pretty much what every addict thinks."

"Really?"

"So, we manufacture feelings with drugs and alcohol."

I felt a flood of relief and gratitude. "Yes, exactly. I do that, for sure."

"What's the closest you think you come to having authentic feelings?"

I thought for a minute. "I would say it's when I'm running."

"Tell me about that—how you feel when you are running."

"It's like I'm scraping out my brain and my guts. Things settle down. My mind stops wandering. I can focus, you know? Just tune out the bullshit."

"That sounds like a good thing."

"Yeah."

"So you feel happy when you are running?"

"Happy? I don't know. I guess so. I feel strong. More in control."

"And you like feeling that way? Strong? In control?"

"Yeah, I mean I almost never experience that in the rest of my life. I feel like I'm weak, just unbelievably weak, with no backbone, you know? If I was strong, I could quit drinking, quit everything."

"This isn't about some flaw in your character," John said.

"It absolutely is."

"No. It's not. You have to know that. Addiction is a disease. It's not all your fault but now that you know that, what happens next is up to you."

I looked him in the eyes. No one had ever said that to me. That I was not entirely to blame.

- - - -

Over the next four weeks, in groups and one-on-one counseling sessions, I came to understand that whatever was in me that demanded appeasement with drugs and alcohol was not of my own creation. There was no logical reason why I was destroying myself. Some secret combination code existed inside me—and when those tumblers fell into place, the craving took over. Science couldn't define it, love couldn't conquer it, and even the promise of a certain death didn't deter it. I was an addict and I would always be an addict, the counselors told me. But—and this was the key—I didn't have to *live* like one.

On the final Saturday of my stay there, I was allowed to leave the center with a friend to run the Sky Climb, a 7.5-mile trail race to the top of Ollason Peak in a beautiful park outside Salinas. I had run only once while in treatment, and I was feeling fat and out of shape. When the gun went off, I zoomed to the front of the pack and stayed there for about a mile. I felt great until the trail started up a steep hill and I realized I was in trouble. I tried all the tricks—looking ahead, not at my feet; shortening my stride; pumping my arms—but it was no use. Lactic acid built up in my quads and I gasped for air. There was nothing I could do. I slowed to a jog as runner after runner passed me. Finally, I had to walk.

But instead of feeling defeated or humiliated—even as a woman old enough to be my grandmother trotted by and said, "Keep it up!" and "You can do it!"—I felt something else, something new. I felt clean. My body was free of drugs and alcohol. Nothing was masking the pain or clouding the effort. The course leveled off at the summit and I could run again. After I crossed the finish line way back in the pack, I stood in the breeze and looked out across the yellow and gray-green hills toward Monterey Bay. It had been a dry winter; the blue lupines were still weeks away. But that land had a beauty that suited me at that moment: barren, stark, on the cusp of coming back to life.

CHAPTER 4

. . . drunk with the great starry void . . .
I felt myself a pure part of the abyss,
I wheeled with the stars,
my heart broke loose on the wind.
                    —PABLO NERUDA, "Poetry"

I got out of Beacon House at the end of my twenty-eight-day stay and dedicated myself to sobriety. I went daily to AA meetings. I also threw myself into running, not so much because I loved to run—that would come much later—but because it gave me and everyone I knew tangible proof that I was doing well. I entered the Napa Valley Marathon, partly to see how it felt to run that distance as a sober person and partly to see if I could qualify for the Boston Marathon. My mother was there to see me run a 3:07, and five weeks later I was on the starting line in Hopkinton, Massachusetts. About a week after that, I ran the Big Sur Marathon again—this time as a sober person and a member of a thirteen-person bungee-cord-connected "centipede" team. Centipede groups were common sights at short, fun races such as the Bay to Breakers 12K in San Francisco; we decided to be the first centipede to run Big Sur. Three of the team members dropped out, but the remaining ten of us finished under 3:30, which had been our goal. We had even stopped for a group pee twice along the way. A photo of our centipede appeared inside the back cover of *Runner's World* magazine. My friends cheered me on, and even my dad seemed impressed by my running and my commitment to staying sober.

Sobriety was awesome. In forty-five days, I had run three marathons—all in respectable times. I was in good standing at work and at home. I was sticking with the 12-step program. I went fifty days, sixty days, eighty days. Picking up my ninety-day sobriety chip felt like a turning point. I misconstrued it as a graduation, of sorts, as if it confirmed that I had this sobriety thing in the bag. Then, for reasons I will never understand, I let it drift away. I stopped calling my sponsor and I quit going to meetings.

Instead, I focused on money. We'd just gotten the devastating news that Fort Ord was shutting down. The servicemen and their families had been the engine of the local economy. Without them the value of our house would plummet and Toyota sales would tank. I had to find another way to make a living. My friend Joe, a guy I knew from Gold's Gym, told me about a new thing called automotive paintless dent repair. This technique saved car dealers and insurance companies money by eliminating the cost of painting cars that sustained heavy hail damage. Joe was going to Oklahoma City to learn how to do it and asked me to come along. Pam and my father were against it.

"You finally found something you're good at," my father said. "Why screw it up?"

Pam reminded me that making a big change such as this wasn't advisable in early sobriety. As usual, I assumed conventional wisdom didn't apply to me and left with Joe for Oklahoma City.

At the end of every day of training, most of the guys in my class went out drinking—but I went straight back to the motel. On our final night, the guys convinced me to come out to celebrate our graduation. I figured there wouldn't be any harm in tagging along. I could just drink water. I sat down at the bar and someone slammed a shot of tequila in front of me. I looked at it for a few seconds. I wanted it. I really wanted it, but I knew I couldn't have it.

On the other hand, was this not the perfect opportunity to demonstrate my ability to drink like a regular person? To show off the new me, the one who now recognized his limits and maintained control? I picked up the drink, tossed it back, and felt that beautiful warmth pass through me, a fast-burning fuse that started in my head and sparked right down to my feet. I called for another shot and a beer and another beer and another shot, and then, shit, I don't know what happened. The next morning, I woke up hungover and bewildered by how easily I had picked up that first drink. I had thrown away six months of sobriety without a fight. I was ashamed of my behavior, but the good news was that I had done it in relative privacy. Pam didn't know I had relapsed and neither did my father, and I wasn't going to tell them. I didn't plan to keep drinking, so there was no reason to share my secret.

Back in California, I was eager to try out my new dent-repairing skills, and I began calling on dealers. One day, I talked my way into the office of the manager of the largest Honda dealer in central California. I told him I had a service that would save him money and I wanted to give him a free demonstration. He was intrigued enough to hand me the key to a car with a dent in its door and point me to a vacant corner of the lot. I had requested privacy; the technique I was about to use was a closely guarded secret.

I went to work. It only took a few minutes to realize that two weeks of dent-repair training had been about three months too short. There was no way I could reach the dent by sliding my hand tools down the window opening. I'd have to take the door apart. Before long, the door was in pieces on the ground. I finally wedged a tool in behind the dent, but my lame attempt at fixing it left it worse than it was when I began.

When I saw the manager coming out to check on me, I hurried over to talk to him before he could get close to the car. "Almost done! I'll bring it around in a bit."

I didn't know what to do. I felt sick. I headed for the men's room, and on my way I passed the manager's office and noticed the keyboard just inside the door. I knew that a code matched each key to every car on the lot. That gave me an idea. I walked outside and wrote down the key number to one of the burgundy Accords identical to the one I had been trying to fix. I reassembled the car I had mangled and parked it as far from the showroom as possible. With the keys I swiped, I pulled the new car around to the front of the dealership—just as the manager was walking out the door.

"Okay, here she is!" I said as I got out of the car.

"Hey, that's fantastic. I can't believe it. Looks brand-new." He shook my hand and asked me if I wanted to fix more cars right away.

"I'd love to, but I'm swamped."

He offered to pay me but I told him this one was on the house. I went home and never returned his phone calls offering more work.

Joe had discovered he was equally inept at dent repair, so we called the guys who had trained us and complained. They invited us to meet them in Rapid City, South Dakota, where they were headed to repair a fleet of hail-damaged cars. They promised us we would really learn how to fix dents this time, and—this got my attention—we'd get paid while we learned. I packed up and drove straight through for two days.

After several weeks, my skills improved. The cars really did look as good as new when I was done with them. I was proud of that and of the way I had avoided trouble in Rapid City—except for that one night I went to a Merle Haggard/Clint Black concert with the guys. I remembered draining a flask that someone handed to me. Then things went black. I came to the next morning, barefoot, inside a giant cement irrigation pipe with a Native American named Cactus Feather and several members of his tribe—all of whom had their own bottles of wine, apparently purchased by me. And one of them was quite happily wearing my shoes. I was, it seems, a generous drunk. Once again, I had carelessly tossed aside whatever sobriety I had accumulated. And once again, I decided the best course of action was to keep this latest relapse to myself. I felt guilty, but who was it hurting if I blew off some steam from time to time? I rationalized it by congratulating myself for not doing drugs.

I stayed in Rapid City for another few weeks until we got the news that Denver had just been hit by one of the biggest hailstorms in history. One hundred thousand cars were pocked with golf-ball-size dents. Joe and I packed up the next morning and headed for Colorado. We worked long hours and made huge money. I was pocketing about $1,000 a day, but rather than making me feel happy and secure, this windfall made me anxious and irritable. Cash had always meant coke to me. I was vulnerable when I was in the money. *Why not do just a little?* I'd say to myself. *It doesn't have to turn into an all-night thing. Have a little fun. You've been humping it so hard. Take a break.*

After work one Friday, I told the guys I was going back to my hotel. But that was a lie. I went straight to a bar. After a few shots, I told the bartender that I was visiting and asked him where I could find some fun. He mentioned a nightclub nearby and even told me about a party in his neighborhood that I could come to later that night. As I was paying, I asked him if there was any part of the city I should avoid.

"Stay clear of Colfax," he said. "A lot of bad shit goes down there."

I thanked him for his sage advice.

Colfax Avenue ran through the heart of the city for more than twenty miles, so it took a while to find the section he had warned me about. Finally, in Aurora, I hit some blocks with boarded-up windows, short-stay motels, liquor stores, pawnshops, and clusters of guys hanging out on the corners—just waiting for a putz like me to roll through. Bingo.

There was an art to getting coke—good coke—from a stranger. If I just pulled up and straight out asked to buy some, it would almost certainly be lousy—cut with laxatives or even rat poison. What I needed was some local talent, someone who could hook me up and keep me from getting robbed or worse. I drove around for a while until I spotted a petite young woman dressed in jeans and a tight T-shirt. She looked safe, as if maybe she were just enjoying a nice evening stroll.

I pulled up next to her and caught her eye. She gave me a slight lift of her chin that told me she was willing to find out what I was looking for. I rolled down the passenger-side window and said, "What's happening?"

She said her name was Jasmine. I told her I was looking for coke and asked her if she wanted to drive around with me. She got in the car and directed me through a series of turns that took us deeper into the neighborhood. She kept looking back, as if she was expecting to be followed. Dusk became dark and I felt myself getting anxious.

"Almost there?" I asked, trying to sound relaxed.

"Keep going. There. Up there. Pull over behind that dumpster."

I did as I was told, and moments later a huge black man emerged from the shadows and knocked on my window. He was holding a gun. What had I gotten into? I rolled down the window. Just then, Jasmine reached over, grabbed my balls, and squeezed hard. I wanted to scream but I held it in. The big guy seemed amused that I hadn't reacted to having my nuts in a vise. He said something that sounded like "Whassupmothafuckafuckinkillyouassholewhatchoowant?"

Trying to not to let my voice shake, I said that I was hoping to buy some coke, an eight ball, please, if he could get it.

"I thought maybe you was a cop, but no cop would be stupid enough to ask for powder down here." He nodded at Jasmine and she released my balls. "Here's what I got." The big man opened his hand and showed me a dozen yellowish rocks.

Jesus. Crack. I had never smoked crack, had never wanted to. But I was in no position to negotiate. I handed him $250 and he passed me the drugs. I started rolling up the window, but before it closed completely, he stuck the barrel of his gun in the opening. I thought he was going to kill me.

"Come back and I'll give you a better deal next time."

I drove away and, with my heart hammering, turned to Jasmine. "I told you I wanted coke. I didn't ask for crack. I don't smoke fucking crack."

"If you like coke, you gonna like this better. You don't love it, I'll take it off your hands and we can negotiate something . . . you know?"

I pulled over and parked under a broken streetlight. She took a little glass pipe from her bag. It was charred and had what looked like a clump of copper Brillo pad stuffed in one end. She held out her hand and I gave her a rock. I was mesmerized by the length of her fingernails and the dexterity with which she loaded the pipe. She held a lighter under the rock and it sizzled and popped as it melted. Then she brought the pipe to her lips and, holding the flame to the dope, inhaled the swirling white smoke that had collected in the chamber.

When she could no longer hold it in, she exhaled and, eyes closed, threw her head back. "Fuuuuck . . ."

She held the pipe out to me. I hesitated. I had snorted cocaine for nearly nine years. I liked it. I knew how to do it. There were downsides, but I could manage them. Fear and ego had kept me away from crack. Lowlifes did crack. I was a marathon runner, for God's sake. I was not smoking crack.

"Just try it. Going to make you smile like nothing else."

I took the pipe from her. I wanted desperately to be high. "Maybe just a little one."

I picked out a small rock and loaded it into the pipe as she had. Then I held the lighter to it and pulled the smoke into my lungs. In that instant, my head exploded with some otherworldly, incandescent orchestral wind—audible light, visible sound. With coke, I was used to waiting for the high to arrive. But this, this was entirely different. There was only the now of it, the insanely glorious, blazing now. It was bigger and better than anything else I had ever felt. It was my big bang, my rebirth. It would be my unraveling. All I could think about was doing more.

When we ran out of the first batch, we went back to the dumpster. We scored four more times in the next twenty-four hours. The big dude and I were best buddies now. He knew he didn't need to rob me because he was well aware that, sooner or later, he'd get all my money.

Day two, I was running out of cash. Jasmine was getting antsy. She asked if I had any credit cards. I said, yeah, but I couldn't get cash on them, not without going to a bank, and I sure as hell couldn't go into a bank in this condition.

"We ain't going to no bank," she said cheerfully. "We goin' to the mall!"

I let Jasmine drive. She pulled up to a corner where a few kids were hanging out. One of them flashed a gun. Another gun. Christ, everybody had a gun. I had been buying cocaine for years and I had never seen even one handgun. Jasmine got out of the car and went to talk to the boys. They all turned to look at me. I got nervous and edged over toward the driver's seat. Then Jasmine walked back over, with the kids trailing behind her.

"Okay, all set. They're coming with us. You gonna buy them all Starter jackets and they'll hook you up."

The boys climbed into the backseat and we drove to the Cherry Creek Shopping Center, a fancy mall where I had bought pants the week before. They knew what store to go to. I pretended to be browsing for socks while the boys argued about who got the jacket with the Oakland Raiders logo. Eventually, each had picked out a jacket, and I brought them to the counter and handed over my gold American Express card. The kids put on their new duds and strutted out of the store. One big happy family. When we reached my car, the boys bickered with each other about who should pay me off in dope. In the end, they handed over about $1,000 worth of crack—enough to last several days.

By dusk, I'd smoked it all. Even Jasmine was alarmed. She kept telling me to slow down, take a break, save some for later. But I knew there was no later for me. I knew that I had fucked up badly. I was now missing my second day of work. I hadn't talked to Pam in days. I wanted to keep my high going for as long as possible because when this was over, I wasn't sure what I would have left.

- - - -

I opened my eyes. My mouth was dry, my lips cracked and swollen. I sat up in bed and realized Jasmine was gone. I went to the window and looked out at the motel parking lot. It was snowing hard. I didn't see my car. Shit. I pulled on my jeans and patted the pockets. Empty. No keys, no cash, no rock. Light-headed and nauseated, I sat back down on the stained bedspread, which sparked with static electricity. I leaped to my feet. I had to get out of here. I looked around for my jacket. That was gone, too.

I left the room and in heavy, blowing snow headed down East

Colfax wearing only a short-sleeved shirt, jeans, and sneakers. After a few blocks, I came to a pay phone. Perfect. *I'll call the cops and tell them my car was stolen. They'll find it for me and I'll be on my way home.* The booth smelled like urine but at least I was out of the wind and snow. I picked up the receiver and pushed 9 and then 1, but held my finger over the last 1 button. I hung up, stared at the phone, picked up the receiver, dialed 9 and 1 again, and then slammed the receiver back down. *Guess what, asshole?* I said to myself. *You can't call the cops. No one is calling the cops.*

I walked out again into the storm. After several blocks, I spotted a familiar red-and-white sign. When I got closer, the smiling, freckled girl on the Wendy's sign made me tear up. I went in and looked at the menu on the wall behind the registers. I hadn't eaten in, what, four days? A couple with two kids sitting at a booth stared at me as I grabbed a fistful of napkins and used them to dry off my face and arms. When I went to throw them away, I noticed a plastic salad plate in the trash barrel. I pulled it out and wiped it off with the wet napkins. Then I walked up to the salad bar and started to load up the plate with lettuce, pale tomatoes, shredded cheese, and croutons.

"Hey!" A guy in a Wendy's shirt was waving his fat arms at me. "Get outta here."

Humiliated, I slunk back out to the sidewalk. With the snow stinging my face and bare arms, I looked up and down the street, wondering what to do. I could flag down a car. I could call Pam, but she couldn't help me. No one could help me. What if I just lay down right here and let the snow pile up over me? Maybe my family would think it was an accident, that I had somehow lost my way. A tragic loss.

I willed myself to keep moving. I came to an intersection and shielded my eyes from the blowing snow. To my left, about half-way down the block, I saw a white Toyota 4Runner just like mine. A cloud of exhaust blew out of the tailpipe; the car was running. I stumbled toward it, sure it was mine, and then sure it couldn't be mine. All I could think about was how warm it would be inside that car, how much I wanted to be inside it. I moved faster, feeling scared, suddenly very aware that I was walking down a street I shouldn't be on. A white guy in the hood wearing a T-shirt in a blizzard.

As I got close, I saw that the roof rack on the car looked just like the one I had on mine. Then I saw the North Carolina license plate. I started to run toward it, and a big woman struggling with a shopping cart in the deep snow looked up at me. I opened the driver's-side door and saw the CDs I'd flung on the passenger seat and the sunglasses I thought I'd lost. It was my truck. The woman yelled as I scrambled in. I backed up, heard empty beer cans rolling on the floor, then slammed the truck into drive and pulled away from the curb, swerving in the snow.

"Yes!" I shouted.

I couldn't believe my incredible luck. I made a quick turn, then another, hoping to find the highway. I was in my car. I was warm. I was free. Then I heard a high-pitched cry behind me, like that of a cat. I cranked my head around and looked in the backseat. A baby, maybe eighteen months old, in a blue snowsuit, was staring at me with huge dark eyes, mouth open, wailing.

I had to go back. I looped around to the street where I'd found my car.

"It's okay," I said to the crying baby. "It's okay."

I saw the woman standing in the street with her back to me and her hands on her head. When I got closer, she turned around and we made eye contact. I drove up and stopped. She ran to the car, opened the back door, reached in, and yanked the kid out.

- - - -

Pam didn't even ask me about my disappearing act because she could guess what had happened. She didn't need to know the details. Instead, she came to Denver and stayed with me while I finished the hail job. She had even more reason to try to keep me from coming off the rails again—and I had a new reason to try to stay clean: Pam was pregnant. We had only recently stopped using birth control, thinking that we wanted to start a family eventually. I'm sure Pam believed that my becoming a father would be a powerful impetus for change. I liked the idea of being a dad; I just didn't think it would happen so soon. I was terrified. I knew I couldn't afford to screw up anymore. In February 1992, we sold our house, despite the depressed real estate market in Monterey, and we moved back to Atlanta. Two months later, a buddy of mine in the dent-repair business called me from Florida. A storm had dropped baseball-size hail on thousands of cars in Orlando, and he'd landed a big repair job at a Cadillac dealer there. He had more work than he could handle and asked me to come down and help. Pam encouraged me to go. We desperately needed the money, and she probably wanted some time away from me.

I was ready for a little getaway, too. I needed to escape the constant guilt I felt about my drug use and drinking. With a baby on the way, I tried to stay clean, but every couple of weeks I would spin off for a few days. Based on no tangible evidence, I hoped that a change of venue would straighten me up for a while. But I couldn't get away from myself. As I worked long hours repairing hail dents in the stifling Florida heat, the lowlight reel of my life played on a continuous loop. I was an addict. I was a terrible husband. I was going to be a terrible father. I had no business bringing a child into this world. I was an addict. I was a terrible husband. I was going to be a terrible father. . . .

For the first week or so, all I did was work and go back to my room. But my anxiety and self-hatred escalated, and finally I felt I had to find some release. No drugs, I told myself, just a couple of beers. An excellent plan, except for one simple fact: I had never, ever, gone home after only a couple of beers. Sure enough, a few hours and many drinks later, I was shitfaced and steering my 4Runner through a seedy section of the city.

My first mission, as always, was to make a friend. It didn't take me long to spot her: a tall, gaunt light-skinned black woman in tight shorts and stiletto heels.

I rolled up next to her and leaned toward the open passenger-side window. "What's up?"

She peered in at me. "What's up with you?"

"Anything good happening around here?"

"You a cop? You look like a damn cop."

"I'm not a cop. I'm just looking for something to do." Even though I already knew the answer, I asked her if she knew where I could score some coke.

She leaned in through the open window. "This look like Beverly fucking Hills to you? Ain't no powder in this neighborhood. Maybe some rock."

I shook my head. If I started smoking crack, I knew things were guaranteed to get very bad. I hesitated for a second, but even in my hesitation I knew what I was going to do.

"What'll a hundred get me?"

She pulled a glass pipe and a lighter out of a pocket, took a small cream-colored rock from her mouth, placed it in the pipe, and held it out to me. "I gotta see you hit this first."

I knew she was testing me to see if I was a cop. They always thought I was a cop. A part of me got a little rush from that—even though my bearing was more Barney Fife than Sonny Crockett.

"This isn't part of what I'm buying." I took the pipe from her. "This is on you." I held the lighter to the pipe, heard the familiar sizzle and pop, and smelled the burnt-plastic odor as the rock melted. Then I held it in my lungs as long as possible before letting out an involuntary "Ahhhhhh" as dopamine pinballed into my brain.

"Aight. I think we can do some business." She climbed into the passenger seat. Her name was Monica. She smelled like booze and flowers and something else that made me think of a carnival midway. "Down there." She directed me through the neighborhood. "Turn here. Pull over."

On the corner, seven or eight young guys were passing things among them, looking up and down the street, doing the dealer shuffle. I stopped the car. Monica leaned out of the window and talked to one of them while two others walked slowly around my truck, making sure I spotted the guns tucked in their waistbands. After a few minutes, I had what I was after—a nice fat eight ball of crack. Monica and I drove around the block, pulled over, and did a couple of hits. Then we cruised. Life was beautiful. My worries had disappeared.

That eight ball should have been enough dope to last us through the night. It was gone in less than three hours. We scored again on another street corner and got a dark-paneled room on the fourth floor of a dive motel where all the doors opened to an outside landing that ran the length of the building. Monica and I kept partying, chipping away at my dope.

During the night, another woman showed up. She talked too fast and bounced around the room in a way that nauseated me. When she sat, both her knees jackhammered so hard that the TV shook on its stand. Every time she came near me, I got up and moved. Finally, to get away from her, I went into the bathroom. Monica and the other girl started talking in a ridiculous stage whisper that I heard perfectly through the thin door.

"How much cash he have?" the fidgety one asked.

"Tapped out," Monica said. "Just some rock."

Monica sounded as if she were protecting me, but I was not fucked-up enough to believe that this was actually the case. She didn't want to have to share.

"Let's get him to take a killer hit and see if he passes out or croaks. Then we take whatever he got left," the new girl said.

I opened the bathroom door and stood in the doorway. Both women looked at me.

"You looking like you need this," the new one said, and gestured for Monica to give me the pipe. I took the massive hit they had prepared and made a big show of sucking every last bit of smoke into my lungs. Who did they think they were screwing with? I was superman.

"Damn . . . ," Monica said.

"You some crazy-ass motherfucker," the friend said, slowly shaking her head. Then she got up and left.

I was high out of my mind but I still wanted more.

"Maybe you ought to slow down," Monica said to me a few times, which just spurred me on. I was not a person who slowed down. She even stripped down in front of me one time, making it clear that sex was available. But all I wanted to do was smoke.

When the drugs were gone, we ventured out to buy more. We

repeated that pattern for the next few days. Sometimes we went out in bright sunlight, sometimes in the dark. A few times, Monica went out alone to buy booze. I was a wreck while she was gone. I alternated between sitting motionless on the bed and staring at the door, certain it was about be bashed in, and peering through the curtain, looking for the bogeyman who was no doubt lurking at my door. I turned the television volume up, but still I heard footsteps, sirens, shouting, motors racing, a weird shrieking bird that surely wasn't a bird at all, but a signal of some sort. I stared at the peephole in the door, certain someone was outside looking in. When Monica finally returned, I nearly cried with relief. She handed me a bag with a toothbrush and toothpaste in it, which surely was for her own benefit. I hadn't brushed my teeth in days.

On the third or fourth day in the room, a special news report came on the TV to say that the white cops who had beaten Rodney King had been found not guilty. Riots were breaking out in LA and in cities all over the country—including Orlando. A local news crew was on the scene in one neighborhood: shop windows had been broken and the streets were filling with angry mobs.

"Hey, that's my street!" Monica said. "Couple of blocks from here."

Suddenly, someone pounded on the door. I nearly shit my pants.

"Monica!" It was a man's voice. "Monica. Open up!"

"Crap," she said, and then, to my great horror, opened the door. Two of the biggest men I had ever seen entered. In my fog, I could only guess that Monica had told these guys to come if they had anything to sell. But something seemed wrong. They were giving off a terrible vibe, ruining my high. I wanted them out of the room. I bought some of their dope, hoping that would get them to leave. When they finally took off, we smoked what we had gotten from them, and right away I knew I'd been ripped off: it was terrible—absolute shit.

"Assholes," Monica said, but I was certain she'd set me up with those guys. There was only one way to feel better. I needed more drugs. Good drugs. We drove back to the neighborhood where we'd scored before. Things had changed. Hundreds of people were out on the sidewalks and down one side street; a car was in flames. I felt the dangerous energy of it. We got what we needed and hurried back to the room. Now a TV news report was showing a white big-rig driver being dragged out of his truck in LA and getting his head smashed in. Monica and I sat on the bed, staring at the TV screen.

The only way to deal with all of this was to stay as high as possible. Eventually, we ran out of dope and I must have passed out. The next thing I knew, the phone next to the bed was ringing. I reached over to the table and knocked over a glass of water as I fumbled for the receiver.

"What?" I croaked.

"Get the fuck out of there!"

Monica. I was barely able to process that she wasn't in the room but was, instead, screaming at me over the telephone.

"Leave now. I mean it. Those guys that sold you the fake shit last night, they are coming up there. Going to rob you and kill you, man." She dropped her voice. "Sorry."

I bolted up in bed. My whole body was trembling. I needed a hit so I could think. I tore the room apart. I emptied the drawers in the bedside table, crawled around patting the stained carpet looking for crumbs, went through all my pockets. I didn't find dope, but amazingly, I did find my car keys. I rushed out of the room, looked over the railing, and spotted my car under the only working light in the parking lot.

I ran down the metal stairs, then stopped in the shadows at ground level when I heard angry male voices. I peered around the corner but saw no one, so I slipped between cars and hurried to my 4Runner. Even in my stupor, I remembered that my car would chirp and the headlights would flash when I clicked the unlock button on the key. There was no way to open the doors quietly.

I heard the voices again and looked up. Moving up the left stairwell were the two big guys from the night before, and they were carrying baseball bats. In the still night air, their words were clear:

"This white boy so damn stupid, he ain't gonna know what hit him. I bet the dumbass just opens the door and invites us in, like last time. We get a free pass tonight thanks to Rodney King."

I watched them walk to my door. I had left the lights on, and the edge of the curtain was still pulled back from my peeking out. One of them peered in the window while the other guy turned around to scan the parking lot. *Chirp-chirp!* My headlights flashed as the four door locks shot upward. I had flinched and involuntarily hit the unlock button on my key. It was as if my car were screaming, *Hey! Down here!*

My two pursuers looked over the railing. I froze as we locked eyes, then I pulled the door handle. But I'd waited too long; the alarm had automatically reset itself. Now it was blaring, cycling through a dozen different sounds, each more obnoxious than the last. The two men sprinted for the stairwell.

I scrambled into the car, jammed the key into the ignition, and turned it. Nothing. The car wouldn't start. The men had reached the ground and were heading for me, bats poised to do damage. Somehow, I remembered that I needed to turn off the alarm before the car would start. I pushed the alarm button and tried the key again. At last the engine turned over, and when it did, the stereo came on so loudly that I thought someone was screaming at me from inside the car. It was Nine Inch Nails singing "Head Like a Hole."

I slammed the car into reverse and turned the wheel hard. My bumper scraped the car backed into the space next to mine, then snagged and yanked off its front bumper. I shifted into drive, and as I hit the gas, the rear window of my 4Runner exploded from the impact of a baseball bat. I screamed and pulled away, tires squealing, then turned back to see the two guys running behind me. One of them threw his bat at my car but it came up short and bounced toward the curb.

In my rearview mirror, I spotted the men getting into their car—the very one that I had just stripped of its bumper. It was still hanging on from one side, and their car was essentially trying to run it over again and again, like a speed bump that wouldn't quit. Their car lurched forward, spraying sparks. I cackled the way one can only cackle at the end of a four-day crack binge and sped down the road.

As I drove, I kept glancing in the mirror half expecting the car to come flying up behind me, like a scene from *Miami Vice*. No car appeared. The immediate danger seemed to have passed. I turned the music down and looked around. My rear window had a big hole in it—sure to rouse suspicion from any cop on the predawn beat. But I could hide that by rolling the window down to get it out of sight. I pushed the button and the window groaned and descended about halfway before jamming to a stop. Even when I released the button, the motor kept whining and pulling.

"Goddamnit!" I yelled.

The motor continued grinding away. I smelled smoke. Finally, the racket stopped, as if the rear window had accepted that it wasn't going any farther. A few seconds later, my headlights turned off and the hazards came on. Next came utter silence. The engine had stopped. I was like a glider losing altitude. I turned the wheel hard to the right, trying to get off the road. The steering wheel locked up and the brakes became stiff. Useless. The car rolled to a slow stop at about a forty-five-degree angle to the guardrail.

I had wanted to hide my shattered window so I wouldn't attract attention. Now I was sticking out in the road. Each time my car's hazard lights flashed, they illuminated the gaping hole in my back window. I had been smoking crack and drinking for four days. It was four in the morning and I was probably the only white person in a ten-mile radius on a day when much of the country had erupted in racially charged violence and mayhem. And now I was on foot.

Before I started walking, I decided that it was a good time to do a little housecleaning, as if having a tidy car would make me look more respectable to whatever helpful officer happened along. I tossed beer cans and an empty vodka bottle—*When did I drink that?*—into tall weeds alongside the road. Then I spotted my glass pipe in the driver's seat. *So that's where that went!* A black hole about the size of a quarter was burned into the upholstery under the pipe. I reached back and felt a hole in my pants that matched up exactly with the one in the seat. Then I poked my finger into my pants and discovered a painful burn on my skin.

After making certain there was nothing left to smoke, I tossed the glass pipe into the brush and started walking in the direction of lights. My plan was simple: keep my head down and my feet moving. After about ten minutes, an SUV slowed and pulled up alongside me. I glanced over and saw the passenger window coming down. In the driver's seat was an obese, bare-chested white man. I had a sickening feeling that he was naked below the waist, too.

"Need a ride, sweetie?" he said in a high-pitched voice.

I ignored the man and walked faster.

The car continued to cruise alongside me. "Sweetie?"

I refused to make eye contact.

"Asshole," he yelled in a much deeper voice, and sped off. Immediately, I went from scared to indignant. Who was the pervert calling an asshole? *You come back here and I'll kick your fat ass, you fat fuck.* I kept walking, jangling with adrenaline. I had to get off the streets. I had to get some sleep—and I had to think of a story to explain away my four-day absence.

As I walked, I started throwing out what I called Santa Claus prayers—the ones that promise, "If you get me out of this mess, I will never, ever, screw up again." The universe pretty much always came through for me, even as I failed, over and over, to hold up my end of the deal.

After a few minutes, I spotted a big lit sign in the block ahead: MASSEY CADILLAC. I couldn't believe it. Somehow I'd ended up in front of my workplace. It seemed like colossal good luck, luck I didn't deserve—but later, after all of this was over, I came to believe that some higher power, some benevolent, all-knowing super-Santa, had led me to the one place that would help me get to safety.

I finally knew where I was. From here, I could get back to my hotel. Two days later, I picked up my car in a tow yard, paying two traffic tickets and the towing fee, more than $600 total. My car had about $1,000 in damage.

Pam pretended it didn't happen because denial was the only way she had left to deal with my relapses. My boss forgave me. He knew I had a drug problem, but I was also his best technician and I made him a lot of money. My poor battered 4Runner, which so often took the brunt of my bad behavior, also seemed to forgive me.

- - - -

I watched in awe as my son, Brett, emerged into the world. I felt transformed, as if I had gone a lifetime with diffuse emotions that had been looking for a place to light—and now here it was. Brett. I knew what I felt. I loved him. I was happy.

I would never drink or use drugs again. I was certain of that. Now that the hollow place inside me was so thoroughly filled, how could I possibly even consider putting poison into my body? I stayed home with Pam and Brett for a wonderful week before returning to Wichita, Kansas, where I was in the middle of a huge hail-repair job. By then, I had started my own company and had several guys, including Garrett and Shayne, both of whom had been sober for about a year, working with me. We were sharing a furnished apartment in Wichita.

I loved the physicality of the work and the satisfaction I felt from a job well done. I talked about Brett all the time, and the more I talked about him, the more I knew that I would stay sober. I was so grateful to have that dark part of my life behind me.

On July 10, Pam and Brett came to visit. I had reserved a suite in a hotel and took a few days off from work. I remember lying on the bed with Pam, Brett between us, his arms and legs swimming in the air, like an upended turtle. I felt overwhelmed with love, wanting to do everything in my power to keep my little family safe and secure.

So I was astonished to find myself driving down the tenement-lined streets of northeast Wichita after dropping Pam and Brett at the airport. The car seemed to be making turns on its own. I knew I didn't want to do what I was about to do, but I knew I was going to do it anyway. *So much work. Such a great dad. Give yourself a little treat.*

Six days later, I was sitting on the ground in a parking lot numbly watching police search my 4Runner, which now had several bullet holes in it. I know there had been a dealer and a gun and the *pop*,

pop, pop when he fired it at me. I know I had floored the gas and fishtailed down the street to get away. I remembered stumbling out of my $15-a-night motel, which I could no longer pay for, and realizing my car was missing.

The funny thing was, I had called the police myself to report my car stolen—and they had found it. Now they were pulling out the things I assured them the thieves had left behind, including my crack pipe—the sight of which caused such a seismic jolt of *want* in me that it took all of my strength not to leap up and rip it from the cop's hand.

When I had gone through treatment at the Beacon House eighteen months earlier, I had embraced every aspect of the program except for the "higher power" part. I was an atheist and I figured that higher powers and Gods were for people too weak to help themselves. I didn't need that kind of outside aid. I was a strong guy. Just point me to the goal and I would get there myself.

But at last I could see that my way had not worked. My beautiful new son could not keep me clean. Nor could my wife or my father or my business or my ego. I was twenty-nine years old, and I was sitting in a gutter, in filthy clothes, my fingers black and blistered. For the first time in my life, I put my head down and said a prayer. It wasn't one of my save-my-ass-just-this-one-time bargaining prayers. It was a real prayer, a simple prayer. I asked to have this craving for drugs and alcohol taken away. I asked to not die.

The police actually sent me on my way. I was dazed and exhausted but I knew something important had happened. I had felt the prison gate of addiction swing open. I don't understand how it happened, but I stepped through that door.

I found an AA meeting that night. Most of the speakers recounted the usual blackouts and family betrayals.

Then a man got up and started to talk about passion. He said we had to find a spiritual connection to something that we loved. He said to think about all the time we spent using and planning to use and recovering from using: "Now fill that time with something else. Something meaningful."

In the morning I got up and put on my running clothes. I walked out of the apartment complex and felt the heat rising off the city streets. I turned down a side street, pushed the timer on my watch, and started running. My legs felt shaky and weak, my breathing labored. I began to sweat profusely. My entire body itched as poison oozed out of my pores. I ran for twenty minutes, then turned around and battled a hot headwind all the way back. By the time I got close to my apartment, I was nauseated and oddly chilled. I doubled over in pain, gasping for breath. A woman in a minivan stopped to ask if I was all right.

"Just overheated," I replied, thinking about what I could have said: *Just coming down off a six-day crack binge.* "Thanks, though." I waved weakly.

I went to three more AA meetings that day, and for the next six months I sat in on at least one recovery meeting a day. I found myself a sponsor who forced me to work the 12 steps. John didn't take crap from me. He told me that if I didn't do what he told me to do, I'd have to find another sponsor. I followed his rules—and when I felt shaky and desperate at 2:00 a.m., I called him.

I flew home every couple of weekends to see Pam and Brett. Pam understood that this was how I had to do it. I had to be removed from my life while I went about the hard work of saving it. I spent my time working, going to meetings—and running. I ran along the river, I ran through cornfields. I ran alone and in a group. Every day, I looked forward to getting out there, to losing myself in the rhythm of it. As I ran, I remembered what that man had said at that first AA meeting about finding a passion—something that would matter so much that you would do anything not to lose it, something so precious and powerful that it would override any impulse to use again.

Gradually, I saw that I already had it. Running. I loved running. I needed running. Nothing else made me feel so clean, so focused, and so happily spent. In those six months of recovery, I never missed a day. Garrett and Shayne teased me about switching addictions. They laughed at me when I came back from a run, pumped up, talking fast about my latest epiphanies about my relationships or my sobriety or my business. But it wasn't a matter of simply trading addictions. The high that I experienced after a long, hard run—that effervescence of endorphins that had eluded me for so long—was purer and sweeter than any pleasure I had ever felt on drugs. Drugs and alcohol had been my way out. Running would be my way through.

CHAPTER 5

In the space between chaos and shape, there was another
chance.

—JEANETTE WINTERSON,
The World and Other Places: Stories

In the three years after my day of reckoning in Wichita, I ran marathons
in Jacksonville, Des Moines, Pikes Peak, Dallas, Calgary, Guadalajara,
Monterrey, Cancún, Maui, Honolulu—the list goes on. I celebrated
Thanksgiving at the Atlanta Marathon, Carnival at the Mardi Gras
Marathon in New Orleans, St. Patrick's Day at the Shamrock Marathon in Virginia Beach, Patriots' Day in Boston. Any event near a hail
job, I jumped on it. Through it all, I stayed sober. Race after race, I
forced myself to bypass the tempting beer tents—a finish-line fixture—
and go back to my room, shower, change, and head out to an AA meeting. Nothing about it was easy; everything about it was necessary.

At home, I pounded out miles on the broad trails along the Chat-
tahoochee River or on the single track that veined the hills above it.
Sometimes I drove out to Stone Mountain Park, ran the perimeter of
the mountain base, then went full throttle up a steep trail to the mountain's bare rock summit. My runs kept me—and probably Pam—sane.

My training philosophy was to run as hard as fucking possible
every time I went out. I craved depletion; anything less left me anxious.
I knew nothing about the benefits of speed work or aerobic thresholds
or hill repeats or tapering. *Pacing* was not in my vocabulary. My results
reflected my ignorance. I'd run balls out during the first three-quarters

of a race, then find myself breaking down in the final miles. I felt helpless—that freight train of hurt coming on: the lactic-acid burn, the rubber legs, the slow-mo crash.

The more I raced, the more I cared about my times. I started to obsess about breaking three hours in the marathon. I got close, but race after race, I found myself lurching across the finish line several minutes over. The San Diego marathon nearly did me in. Pam and Brett were there to greet me as I came in at 3:01. Three. Oh. One. Unbelievable. They were bouncy and excited. I was pissed off.

"The headwind," I said. ". . . And this huge blister on my heel . . ."

Brett asked to sit on my shoulders, so I hoisted him up even as I continued to rail against the factors that had conspired against me.

Brett tapped me on the head. "Daddy."

"If I hadn't started so far back in the pack . . ."

"Daddy!"

"I should have . . ."

"Daddy. Daddy!"

"What?" I said sharply.

"Daddy, did you have fun?"

His question brought me up short.

"Did you have fun, Daddy?"

"Fun? Yeah, I had a great time."

I said it because that's what he wanted to hear. But I knew it wasn't true.

I thought about Brett's innocent words while I showered and, later, when I was lying in bed, unable to sleep. Maybe I was doing something wrong. I had been running compulsively, without thought or intention—and certainly without joy. I ran when I was sick and I ran when I was injured, which seemed to be most of the time. I ran after spending twelve straight hours doing the difficult physical labor of fixing hail dents. I ran in rain and cold and heat and humidity, all so that I could give myself a gold star for the day. Missing a day of training terrified me. If my commitment to running wavered, didn't that suggest that my commitment to sobriety was in jeopardy, too, that my willpower had a dangerous chink?

This wasn't working. I had to find pleasure and reward in the running itself. It had to be about how I felt while I was doing it, not just how I felt when I was done. And I had to listen to my body. It was time to make adjustments, come up with a new plan. I started mixing in easy runs each week with hard ones. I figured out roughly how much mileage I needed to log to race well at a certain distance—and I kept it at that. I even allowed myself days off. I stopped obsessing about breaking that three-hour mark. If it happened, it happened. I was making myself nuts trying to force it. Besides, I had more important things going on. Kevin Engle entered the world with ease on November 29, 1994. He was peaceful and curious from the very beginning. Now I had two sons, a successful business, a happy wife, and more than two years of sobriety.

It took more than a year, but that three-hour barrier finally fell. In October 1995, I ran a 2:59:02 at the Twin Cities Marathon in St. Paul, which qualified me for the hundredth Boston Marathon, a special event that I was aching to run. From then on, I broke three hours almost every time I ran. I had found my groove—and I'd done it by giving myself permission to relax.

Several weeks after the Twin Cities race, I got a call from the manager of a Brisbane, Australia, auto auction. His huge fleet of cars had been pummeled by a massive hailstorm, and he wanted to hire me to do repairs. In late November 1995, just before Kevin turned one, my crew and I boarded a Qantas flight for the long trip back into summer.

Right away, I found a local AA meeting to attend. I also started training with a group of runners who met daily at a sports shop. One day, after a run with them, I noticed a flyer on the store's bulletin board for a 5K trail race in a state forest. It sounded appealing—a chance to get out of the city, add to my race T-shirt collection, do a little postrun sightseeing, maybe even spot my first kangaroo. I tore off the directions to the event and marked my calendar.

On race day, I got up early so I could make the two-and-a-half-hour drive out to Nanango. I thought 7:00 a.m. seemed a little aggressive for the start of a fun race, but maybe that was the way the

Aussies did things. I didn't mind. Dawn broke over the scrubby, dry grasslands. I was driving through what I had been told was kangaroo country, so I was paying close attention to both sides of the road. Nothing. They were probably still asleep.

And then I saw one—right in front of me. I slammed on the brakes, but too late. There was a sickening thud. I pulled over, turned on my hazard lights, and got out, expecting to see a mangled marsupial. Instead, I found a slightly dazed looking but otherwise intact kangaroo staring at me accusingly.

I apologized in what I hoped was a calming voice and took a step toward him. He started to panic, so I backed off. Then I heard something in the brush and looked up just in time to see a dozen or more kangaroos crossing the road. Illuminated by the car's strobelike red flashers, they looked like a troupe of alien disco dancers. I watched them bounce away, then turned back to check on my victim. He was gone.

Rattled but relieved, I continued on to the East Nanango State Forest. I parked and found the race registration table.

A cute blond girl handed me my race number, but no T-shirt. "You only get one if you finish."

I walked away, chuckling to myself. *If* I could finish a 5K? I dropped my backpack near a pile of bags and surveyed the field of runners while I pinned my number on my shirt. They were not the lean and wiry road-race warriors I was used to. Some men had ponytails and some women had buzz cuts. Some were overweight. I overheard two guys near me talking while they stretched.

"Gonna be a hot one," one said.

"Don't know if I'll finish before dark," his friend replied. "Just give it a go."

I smiled to myself. These guys were worried about finishing a 5K?

"You ever run fifty-two K before, mate?" One was looking at me.

My face flushed. *Fifty-two* K? Uh-oh. I mumbled something in response, did a few lunges, and then walked, as casually as I could, back to the girl at the registration table. I asked her for a map of the course. She picked up a flyer and handed it to me. My eyes locked

66

on the symbol at the top. *Nanango Forest Foot Race 52K.* Holy shit. Thirty-two miles instead of a little more than three. I thought the marathon was the ultimate distance. Did people really run beyond 26.2 miles? And if they did, why?

I weighed my options. I could walk back to my car and drive away. No one would ever know. But I'd driven all the way out here, nearly murdered the Bambi of Australia, an innocent kangaroo, and paid the race fee. I studied the map again. The route was three loops of about 17K, 10.5 miles each. *Oh, what the hell*, I thought, *I'll do one lap as a training run and call it a day. I won't get the cool T-shirt, but I'll have a good story.*

A loudspeaker announced it was time to gather on the starting line.

Five minutes later the whole group started shuffling down the trail, and I shuffled along with them. There had been no starting pistol, not even a loud yell, but we were off. The course followed a red-dirt road and then became a narrow trail as it climbed through stands of feathery hoop pines, some draped with streamers of gray-green moss. We crested a hill and then headed down, bottoming out in a forest of giant ferns. Jungle-bird sounds I'd never before heard told me I was far from home. In a while, we started up again. I was soaked with sweat, breathing hard. It went on that way for more than an hour: long climbs, knee-punishing descents, the relative relief of a canopy of broad-leafed trees, then out into the open again.

At last, I came to the top of a long hill and could see the start/finish banner in the distance and a handful of runners spread out ahead of me. I was almost done. I'd be heading for breakfast with the AC cranking while these guys were still busting their asses in the forest. I could hear the loudspeaker; names and hometowns were being called out as each runner approached.

"And here comes Charlie Engle. Crikey, I didn't think Yanks could run that fast."

Great, now I was representing all of America. Too bad I was quitting. I pulled up after crossing under the banner and helped myself to some cookies and water. I could relax now. I watched runner after runner come through, grab some food and water, and continue. One was a young woman, maybe nineteen or twenty years old, who was limping badly. She had blood running down her legs from mud-caked scrapes on both knees. I figured that was it for her. But she wasn't stopping. She just smiled and kept running. Wasn't anyone going to wave her off the course? She must be delirious.

"Heading back out?" someone at my elbow said. It was the girl from the registration table.

"Short break," I said, my mouth full of cookie.

"Good luck."

The way she was looking at me, I knew I had to pretend to start running again. I figured I could begin the second loop, veer off near my car, and split. No worries, mate.

I sheepishly acknowledged the cheering spectators as I returned to the course. When I was close to the parking lot, I looked around. Perfect—no one nearby; I could escape. But as I headed for my car, I remembered my backpack—which contained my keys, which was in a pile of runners' bags right at the feet of the announcer. Now what? I could feign an injury, limp back to retrieve my pack, and pick up some undeserved sympathy. I could go back and fess up to misunderstanding the race distance. Or maybe I could just keep running and see what happened.

Approaching the start/finish area at the end of the second lap, I heard the announcer's voice again.

"Here comes the Yank, here comes the Yank! He's gaining ground. This guy is for real. He could win this thing!"

I passed a clump of cheering spectators and gave them a wave. I had covered twenty-one miles—eighteen more than I had expected to run when I got out of my car this morning. I was sunburned, blistered, dehydrated, and seriously chafed. But I was still going. Twenty-three miles, twenty-six, twenty-seven—this was new territory. Now every step was the farthest I had ever run. Twenty-*eight*, twenty-nine, thirty. Something remarkable was happening. I was suffering, yes, but this was not the kind of pain I was used to, the kind that implored me to stop. This pain told me to go on. Feel the pain, welcome the pain, use the pain, transcend the pain.

At a little after noon, under the blazing Queensland sun, I crossed the finish line. Someone put a sash around my neck and slapped me on the back. I had won the men's division. I'd run 32.3 miles in five hours, three minutes, and ten seconds on a tough, hilly course—and I had done it with little preparation. I was shocked that I'd done so well—and even more surprised that I felt pretty good after all those miles. I would never have entered the race if I had known how long it was. *Sometimes the universe does for you what you are unable to do for yourself.* I remembered that line from AA. And now I wondered, *How much farther could I go?*

CHAPTER 6

It is not down on any map; true places never are.
—HERMAN MELVILLE, *Moby-Dick*

I returned from Australia feeling that inspiration was all around. On a chilly February day, I ran the Charlotte Marathon, a race that was the US men's qualifier for the Olympics. I was thrilled to be in the company of the country's best runners, especially Bob Kempainen, a twenty-nine-year-old medical student from Minnesota, who won the race despite vomiting six times during the final five miles.

Two months later, I was part of the biggest field ever to run the Boston Marathon. I relished every minute of it. I high-fived kids along the course, snapped pictures, and upheld a Boston tradition by stopping to kiss a few cheering coeds as I passed Wellesley College. Near the finish, I searched the crowd for Pam. I spotted her in the front row shouting and clapping for me. I was touched by her pride. It was the happiest run I ever had—and while I was having all that fun, I even managed to finish in less than three hours.

That July, the Summer Olympics came to Atlanta. I'd grown up watching the Olympics on television and, like a lot of kids, dreamed about competing in them myself. That was never going to happen, I knew, but I still felt a deep connection to the Games, maybe because my grandfather had coached many Olympians in his day.

I bought a ticket that allowed me to attend every track-and-field event and parked myself in Centennial Olympic Stadium. I saw Donovan Bailey break the world record in the 100 meters, Michael Johnson scorch the 200 and 400, Carl Lewis win his fourth long-jump gold, and Haile Gebrselassie, one of the greatest distance runners of all time, take the 10,000 meters. The last event was the marathon, which started and finished on the track. After the start, the crowd followed the action on a JumboTron TV. The stadium erupted when the three lead runners came off the city streets and onto the oval for an epic fight to the end and the closest marathon finish in Olympic history. I left the stadium in awe of what I'd seen and inspired to train harder, push myself farther, and seek out bigger challenges.

Not long after the Olympics, I turned on the television to watch the Discovery Channel's *Eco-Challenge*, a five-part series about a three-hundred-mile, nine-day team adventure race in the backcountry of British Columbia. The opening footage was of snow-covered peaks and fast-moving rivers, set to a slow aboriginal drumbeat and wavering eagle-bone-flute music. *Eco-Challenge* founder and producer Mark Burnett would use the same kind of introduction when he went on to create *Survivor* for CBS four years later. Slow-motion shots showed competitors pushing themselves to the limit as they rappelled, rafted, cycled, and ran through the wilderness. And a member of the First Nation Lillooet tribe spoke in his melodic native tongue, with this voice-over translation:

"Push yourself until the pain comes, until you feel you cannot survive, and then go on. Here the ego will let go, here you will be purified."

I felt as if he were talking directly to me.

That episode and the ones that aired the next four nights riveted me. What those competitors were putting themselves through—the danger, the exhaustion, the breakdowns, the puking, the disorientation, the fear, and the sleep deprivation—it looked like absolute hell. Sold.

I requested an entry form for the next event, which was being held in Australia in mid-1997. But when it came in the mail, I discovered you could register only if you had previous adventure-racing experience—and paid part of a $10,000 team entry fee. I could come up with the money, but the experience requirement was a problem. I had never ridden a mountain bike, been in a kayak, or rappelled off a cliff. And I had never navigated anything other than my way home from the gym or the grocery store—and that hadn't always gone so well. I could run and swim, and I had proven many times that I could go for days without sleep, even without chemicals in my bloodstream, but if I was going to compete in one of those races, I had a lot to learn.

I bought a mountain bike and started riding the trails near my house. I studied books about map and compass navigation. I went kayaking a few times and eventually figured out how to stop the thing from spinning around in circles. Clearly, though, I needed some expert help. I found an *Eco-Challenge* four-day training camp in Los Angeles, but the week after I signed up, it was canceled.

I had to put my adventure-racing ambitions on hold then because the hail season had begun. I hit the road, setting up jobs and shutting them down when the damaged cars stopped coming in. I filled my limited time off with running and AA meetings and, when I was home, hanging out with my boys.

Though I was making good money, the pressure of running my own business started to feel overwhelming. Eventually, I decided to partner with a large dent-repair company in St. Louis. Pam wasn't happy about moving again, but she agreed it was for the best.

One day not long after our move, I was reading a magazine and I noticed an ad for the Presidio Adventure Racing Academy in San Francisco. They were holding a camp for aspiring racers, coached by elite competitors. I signed up that day.

- - - -

Twenty of us gathered late in the afternoon for orientation in an old Army building in the Presidio, overlooking the Golden Gate Bridge. Among us were two San Francisco–area cops, a firefighter, a navy fighter-jet pilot, and several type A businessmen. I got the sense as we chatted that most were there because they thought the camp sounded like a cool way to spend a long weekend. A few thought they might try some short local races. Not me. I was there to become a bona fide adventure racer. I couldn't wait to push myself to the kind of extreme limits I had seen on TV. I felt certain it would be powerful and life altering and illuminating—and would scrape away that last scuzzy layer of my past.

After we signed a long release form, we were welcomed by the director of the academy, Captain Duncan Smith, a charismatic, square-jawed retired Navy SEAL and ex–investment banker. Smith had been a top finisher in the Raid Gauloises, the world's premier adventure race, which was held annually in different remote corners of the world. After his introductory remarks, he told us to grab a jacket and a headlamp. Our first task would be a navigation hike in the woods above the Army base. I practically jumped out of my chair with excitement. I couldn't wait to get started. Climbing that trail in the dark, with the smell of the ocean and the eucalyptus trees in the damp, cool air, I felt I was right where I was supposed to be.

My primary instructor was Michael Lucero, one of the racers I'd watched in the *Eco-Challenge* British Columbia broadcast, who was also a successful hip-hop music video producer. In our first classroom session the next morning, he drummed into us the importance of choosing your team wisely. Watch out for muscle-head warrior types, he said. One of his teammates in British Columbia had been a yahoo who listed as a hobby "boar hunting with a knife." Soon after the race started, he dropped out.

"Remember," he said, "you are only as fast as your slowest team member."

We spent several hours learning how to use compasses and altimeters, discussing group dynamics, and taking notes on practicalities such as how to seal a flapping blister with Super Glue, how to duct tape your nipples to prevent chafing, and, my personal favorite, how to use a condom as an emergency water bottle.

"Go with unlubricated," he advised, trying to keep a straight face. "No aftertaste."

Michael mentioned that he had a team entered in the upcoming Raid Gauloises, which this year was being held in Ecuador. I decided that I had to get on his squad. I started dropping not-so-subtle hints to him about how much I wanted to do that race. It was ridiculous to think I might have a shot at joining his team—it was as if I expected to win a starting position on a Super Bowl team without having played a single peewee football game. But my desire to do it made me bold.

On the second day of camp, I was paired in a kayaking exercise with Austin Murphy, a senior writer on assignment for *Sports Illustrated*. After an hour of drills, the group paddled out into San Francisco Bay, fighting chop, headwinds, and a powerful ebb tide. We whooped as we made our way under the Golden Gate. The Pacific was wide-open to us. Then we realized that we'd all paddled into the path of a massive Hanjin container ship. The freighter narrowly missed us, but its wake flipped several of the kayaks like bath toys. The Coast Guard had to rescue them. Somehow, Austin and I had stayed calm and kept our boat upright. I hoped Michael had noticed.

Later, we were divided into groups of five for a twenty-four-hour practice race. We would start on Angel Island for the hiking/running leg, then we would kayak across the bay in the dark and finish on mountain bikes in Mount Tamalpais State Park. Physically, my team was tough, but we had little confidence in our orienteering skills. We agreed that I might be the least lousy at navigation, so I became the compass handler and de facto leader.

Michael shadowed us to ensure our safety. I had learned from him that the navigator must make firm decisions. Confidence was key.

We got through the hiking leg fine, then we did okay in the kayaks—despite the fog and strong currents. Somehow, I got us to Sausalito, where we would be getting on bikes. As the sky started to lighten, I spread the map on the ground, placed the compass on the map, and tried to get my bearings.

"That way," I said.

Michael gave me a slight smile. I interpreted this as approval of my decision. It was not.

We started pedaling. Periodically, we stopped so I could look at the compass. During one of these breaks, Michael suggested that I take a few minutes to be certain about where we were. I felt something was off. Once more, I got out the map and the compass. This was strange; we seemed to have exited the map. I looked at my compass and at Michael. Then it hit me. I reached down, picked up the compass, and spun it around. It had been upside down. Michael grinned at me and nodded.

"Shit," I said.

My team laughed and I had to laugh, too. We turned around and pedaled back onto the map. Despite our detour, our team finished second. Michael even complimented me on my leadership and teamwork. I went home fired up about my performance, in love with adventure racing—and convinced that I had found my calling.

Later, Michael and I talked on the phone and I told him again how much I wanted to do the Ecuador race. He was polite and said I had great "potential." That was not what I wanted to hear. Still, I kept training. I focused on becoming a better navigator, especially while kayaking and biking. I spoke to Michael a few more times, telling him all the things I had been working on. He remained noncommittal. I hoped he'd come around, that he'd call one day soon and tell me I was in.

Then, in early May, I got terrible news. On his way to a race in Colorado, Michael Lucero had been killed in a car accident. I couldn't believe that someone so strong and fearless was gone. How senseless and unfair. I could only imagine how devastated his family was.

With a heavy heart, I continued to train. About six weeks after Michael's death, I got a call from Tony Green, one of Michael's Raid teammates. He said that Michael had been impressed with me, but didn't think I was ready for the Raid. Still, they needed to fill Michael's slot with a fifth team member right away. Did I want to do it? Without hesitation, I said yes. It wasn't how I wanted to get on my first team, but I felt sure Michael would have urged me to go. I said a silent thank-you to him and vowed to make him proud. Then I pictured him giving me a nod and saying, "Be careful what you wish for."

- - - -

I had planned to sleep on the flight from San Francisco to Quito, Ecuador, but had been too amped up to even close my eyes. It had been a dizzying couple of months. I'd completed certification courses in sea kayaking, canoeing, and white-water rafting; practiced ice climbing with cleats and mountaineering in roped progression; and taken the requisite hours of riding lessons—even though horses scared the hell out of me. I'd gotten vaccinations and filled our den with piles of new gear. I'd also undergone a hypoxia test to determine if I was prone to altitude sickness. I wasn't: excellent news, since one stage of the race required scaling Mount Cotopaxi, a 19,347-foot active volcano.

The baggage claim was swarming with Raid Gauloises participants in team jackets, shouting at each other in languages I didn't understand. The Raid had been started by a French journalist and most of the forty-nine teams were European. My team was known as Team Charles Schwab thanks to being underwritten by the brokerage firm. We elbowed into the throng as a steady stream of backpacks, duffel bags, and huge plastic trunks started moving along the conveyer belt.

Tony was our team captain. Though his orienteering skills were limited to what he had learned many years ago as an Air Force Academy student, he still had the best credentials to be our navigator. The rest of the team included Scott Williams, a former all-American collegiate swimmer who coached a top masters swim team in San Francisco; Steve Hilts, a superb kayaker who worked for a vegetable packing company; and Nancy Bristow, a mountain guide and Mammoth Mountain ski patroller. Steve and Nancy were highly accomplished adventure racers. Tony and Scott were almost as green as I was.

We also had a two-man support crew, who would handle our equipment during the race and take care of us at transition points: Rolf Dengler, a former US Navy diver and ex–New York nightclub bouncer whom I had met when he worked at the Presidio Adventure Racing Academy; and Kurt Lawrence, Scott's easygoing, athletic brother-in-law. The last member of Team Schwab was Rebecca Ranson: my mother.

After running it by my teammates, I had asked my mother if she wanted to accompany us to Ecuador as our team reporter. Raid organizers encouraged journalists to follow teams. My mom was a great writer and had always talked about traveling to exotic places. I was sure she would jump at the chance. I warned her that we wouldn't have much time together. She'd be traveling by truck and I'd see her only at race transition points. She'd probably be wet and cold and miserable—and the altitude could be a problem. I also told her that she might be seeing me in distress.

"Remember how upset you got when I went into shock after the Napa Valley Marathon?" I asked her. "There could be that kind of thing—or worse."

She promised me she would be all right and said she had been craving a challenge. I was happy I could offer her this opportunity and that she would get to see me doing something big. I also hoped this might motivate her to get healthy. I had been trying for years to get her to quit smoking and start exercising. We planned to meet at the Raid headquarters hotel in Ibarra, forty-five miles outside Quito, in time for the pre-race orientation.

Earlier in the week, I'd said good-bye to Pam and the boys. I felt guilty leaving them; we were getting ready to move again—this time from St. Louis to the Monterey Peninsula, where I was going to go back into business for myself. Pam would be handling the boys and the movers by herself. She didn't complain. I knew she was excited for me—and much preferred this version of her husband to the one she had lived with before I got sober. But I felt uneasy as I drove to the airport. I'd left my family many times—for work, for marathons—but this time, I was intentionally putting myself at risk in a way I hadn't since I had gotten sober. In recovery, I'd built a safe and comfortable life. I had two great kids, a nice house, and a supportive wife. Why didn't that feel like enough?

As hard as it was to admit, a part of me missed something about those addict days—not the drugs themselves, but the pulse-jacking danger of that life, knowing that every day I could be teetering on the edge of a rusted blade. I felt happiest and most alive when I was in peril.

- - - -

Before we boarded the flight for Quito, I'd spent a few days with my team in San Francisco, going over official checklists and sorting through our gear. Right away, I was alarmed by how disorganized and stressed-out Tony seemed to be. He'd get everything packed, then pull it all out looking for something he'd "lost"—only to realize the thing had been sitting in front of him the entire time. When we offered to help, he snapped at us. At the airport, he came unglued when we were charged $1,500 in excess-baggage fees. Scott and I moved some things around and quietly talked the airline representative down to $500. As I boarded the plane, I wondered just who I was following into the wilderness.

- - - -

"Do we have everything?" Tony shouted. We'd landed and Tony had to raise his voice to be heard above the airport din.

We all said yes. He looked down at a crumpled piece of paper in his hand.

"Our driver is . . . Alejandro. He should be outside waiting for us. White truck, blue tarp. Got everything, right?"

"Yes," we said again, and started for the exit.

"Wait." Tony stopped short. "I'm missing a bag. Damnit. They better not have lost it. It's all my mountain gear."

Nancy pointed to an overstuffed duffel gliding by on the carousel. "Isn't that yours?"

Dozens of white trucks, all with blue tarps, lined the curb. We found four Alejandros before we found ours. Our Alejandro hugged us all like old friends and started helping us load our gear. In only a few minutes we saw that we had too much stuff and too many people to fit in the truck. After much discussion Scott, Nancy, and I decided to hang on to the back of the truck, with our feet on the bumper and our hands on the frame over the truck bed; Rolf and Kurt would sit on top of the gear. Tony and Steve would cram into the cab with Alejandro.

Whooping like kids on a carnival ride, we headed north on the Pan-American Highway. The novelty of hanging on to the back of the truck began to wear off as the temperature dropped and the roads narrowed. We finally arrived in Ibarra and checked in to the Hosteria

Chorlavi, an old hacienda that had been converted into a hotel. That evening, along with the other Raid teams, we dined on cauliflower soup, grilled trout, pastries filled with rice, and *helados de paila,* the ice cream the waiter said the town was famous for.

Finally, we could hit the sack. I was with Nancy, in what I hoped would be a nonsnoring room. As I closed the door, I heard Tony saying, "I can't find my room key. Has anyone seen my key?"

Early the next morning, I got a cup of coffee and stepped out into the cobblestone courtyard. The air was clear and cool and scented with cedar and roses. Before me, a massive mountain, green and brown and cut with deep, shadowed clefts, loomed above the wide valley. A kite tail of clouds streamed off its broad conical summit. I'd read about this mountain: Volcán Imbabura. The Incas considered it a god, and the locals thought of it as a sacred protector: *Taita*—"Papa"—Imbabura. I could see why: it emanated great power. I stood completely still, as if movement might make the mountain disappear. I inhaled and exhaled slowly and deliberately. This is what I had come for. This was why I had worked so hard to be sober: to be able to breathe this air and stand before this mountain.

"Charlie," someone said in a loud whisper. I looked up. Rolf was sitting on the tile roof.

"Hey," I said.

"Beautiful, isn't it?"

"Amazing."

I waited for Rolf to climb down, and together we went to find Team Schwab. Raid organizers required all competitors to do three days of progressively more difficult acclimatization hikes; today would be our first, a seven-hour trek to eleven thousand feet. Besides getting us used to climbing at altitude, the hikes were meant to wear us out—the idea being that if we were fatigued when we started the race, we would be less likely to go out too fast and risk altitude sickness or injury. I thought that theory was flawed—wouldn't being tired increase our chances of getting hurt?—but was not in a position to question it.

After a morning gear check, we headed out. I was so excited. I was about to compete in the Raid Gauloises against the best adventure racers in the world—guys I'd seen on TV when I first dreamed of doing something like this. I couldn't wait to attack this first hike.

A little before ten that night, I staggered, half-dead, back into the hotel. The hike had been brutal, partly because I'd behaved like an idiot. I'd been so anxious to show my teammates that I was not the weakest link that I had rushed to the front of the group and stayed there—even when I got so light-headed I started seeing black spots. Michael Lucero, I was certain, would not have been seeing black spots. Thankfully, just when I thought I might collapse, Scott had spoken up from the back and asked the group to slow down.

All I wanted to do now was fall into bed. I turned toward my room—then spotted my mother by the lobby fireplace. She was wearing a knit hat, the black fleece top I had sent her for her birthday, jeans, and black Converse high-tops. I had to laugh. There was no doubt who the fifty-five-year-old chain-smoking playwright was in the group. I hugged her hard. She felt so small in my arms. I had a deep pang of regret. What had I been thinking suggesting she come? I helped bring her bags into my room, trying not to let on how exhausted I was. I offered her my bed, but she insisted on sleeping on the floor.

"You two need to get a good rest," she said. "I'm fine."

I lay there, wide-eyed, head pounding, worrying about my mother and wondering how the hell I would ever get through the race if I was this wasted from a practice hike. Maybe I wasn't ready for this. Maybe Michael had been right.

Things improved over the next two days. I calmed down about trying to impress my teammates. My mother made friends with some of the other teams' crews. My headache faded. We found a pace that worked for us all and took turns carrying one another's pack in case one of us faltered during the race. We even managed to laugh. We kidded Tony about his habit of losing things. I was teased about having to bring my mom with me.

In between the hikes and inventorying of gear, I found a quiet time to take a walk with my mother through the whitewashed colonial town. We were trailed by several mangy, emaciated dogs.

"Poor things. I wish I could bring them home with me," my mother said, holding out her hand to one particularly pathetic-looking mutt.

She had always been a rescuer of strays. She was afraid of heights and going to the dentist, but she would try to pet any dog, no matter how big or fierce. And the dogs would invariably give in and allow themselves to be loved.

"I think I'm going to write a play about the Raid," she said to me. "It's all so inspiring!"

"That would be great. But we should probably survive it first."

"Oh, that doesn't matter. Most of my plays are tragedies."

I laughed. We walked past an ancient-looking gray-stone church and into a manicured green park.

"Want to sit?" I pointed at a green slat bench under a tree heavy with bright pink flowers.

"I'm so proud of you. The way you go after what you want. You have such an adventurous spirit."

"I get that from you."

"I don't know." She looked pleased. "Maybe a little."

We sat in silence looking up at the peaks visible in the distance beyond the red tile roofs of the town.

"It's strange," she said. "I had such vivid dreams about you right before I left to come here . . . about that night you put your hand through the shower door and you were bleeding and crying. . . ."

I looked at my feet. "That was bad," I said quietly.

"I was so scared for you."

"I'm sorry."

"You don't have to say you're sorry."

"But I am sorry. I'm sorry I put you through that. And . . . I'm . . . I'm also sorry I moved in with Dad." I couldn't believe I had finally said those words.

"What? No."

"I was so excited about California, you know? And I thought you would be happier without me; you'd have your freedom."

"Let's face it. I wasn't exactly mother of the year."

"You were, though."

"I understood."

"But it must have been really hard."

She leaned into me and put her head against my shoulder. I put my arm around her. "It was. It was hard. Thank you." She looked up at me and smiled.

We were both in tears.

"I'm just so happy," she said. "I'm here with you now. I get to witness this."

- - - -

Later that day, all forty-nine teams and their crews crowded into a stuffy school gymnasium in town where stone-faced race officials sat at a long table on the gym floor. Some of us were given headphones so we could hear a rough English translation of what was being said by the French-speaking organizers. When Patrick Brignoli, the race director, began to speak, the PA system squealed with feedback.

"Welcome to lovely and exciting Ecuador. This is the most difficult and the most beautiful course in Raid history. You will have a wonderful adventure, but it will be hard. You will suffer. You will have pain, but you will see beauty. You will give up on your body and then it will come back for you."

He pointed at a map on an easel. The unmarked 593-kilometer—368-mile—course would trace a semicircle around Quito from the northern Andes to the Pacific. We would start at 13,100 feet and navigate our way on foot for two hundred kilometers, bushwhacking south through the *páramo*—high-altitude grassy plains just below the snow line. Then we would ride horses and run to snowcapped Mount Cotopaxi. After climbing the peak using ropes and ice axes, we'd head west through the cloud forest on mountain bikes. The final 151 kilometers would be on water—in rafts, canoes, and finally sea kayaks—through the tropical lowlands to the ocean.

Forty checkpoints would be along the way. At each one, we would have our team "passport" stamped. Miss a checkpoint and you were out of the race. Have one team member drop out and your whole team would be disqualified. Arrive at a transition point after the designated cutoff time and your team would be bumped from the official race. You would have the option to continue—but it would be purely for the experience.

"You will love this course as much as you hate it," he said. "Now we must talk about the dangers. They are very real."

A French doctor stood up to tell us what we might encounter. Through the static in the headphones, I heard "snakes, rabid dogs, alligators, pulmonary edema, leptospirosis, avalanches, currents, helicopter rescue, possible death . . ."

I looked at my mother and smiled. She smiled back. She hadn't been given headphones.

Brignoli took the microphone again and began introducing each team by number. We were team #7, and when he got to us, he raised his hand for quiet. "This team from America would have been Michael Lucero's team. Many of you knew and admired Michael. He was a good man; a strong competitor. He lost his life recently in a tragic auto accident. We would like to dedicate this race to him."

The audience applauded and got to their feet. I felt all eyes upon me, straining to see who had replaced Michael. I knew that even if I had the best race possible, I could not begin to fill his shoes. But I would give it my best. More than a thousand AA meetings and dozens of marathons had taught me that I could control my effort but not the outcome. I would try to remember that when things got dicey.

– – – –

"Where's my headlamp?" Tony said, alarmed. "Did someone take my headlamp?"

We were up before sunrise, getting set for the start. We all joined in the search for the missing light. Tony thought he might have left it in the truck, so we pulled everything out of it, but still no luck.

"Hey, Tony!" Scott called from the room the two had shared. "Come here. Does this look familiar?"

The headlamp was hanging from the doorknob in his room. Tony shook his head in disbelief.

We thought we were ready to go—until a button popped off my

pants. I called my mother in from the courtyard and asked her if she could help. Then I sat on the bed in my underwear while she sewed the button back on.

"You know I'm not good at this." She bit the thread in half with her teeth.

I laughed. "Just make it so my pants won't fall down."

She was almost finished when my entire team came through the door looking for me. They took in the scene and doubled over with laughter. I laughed, too, and knew they wouldn't let me live this down.

We made it, at last, to the starting area on a grassy flank high on Cayambe, a cone-shaped peak topped with snow. Though the equatorial sun was bright, the morning air was frigid. I stamped my feet and blew on my hands, as much out of nervousness as cold. The French team next to us was laughing and smoking cigarettes and passing around a bottle of champagne. In the crowd of spectators—a mix of curious locals and team officials, media and crew members—I spotted my mother, with a camera hanging around her neck. Her pants were covered with mud. She must have fallen on the steep, slippery trail. I called to her but she didn't hear me.

Two officials lifted flags—one for Ecuador and one for the Raid—to signal the start. We were off. Some of the teams took off at a full sprint as if they were running a 100-yard dash. Team Schwab fell in behind several groups moving at a saner pace. I tried to take in the scene so I would remember it forever; the high white peaks, the green farmland in the valley, the line of brightly clad runners moving through feathery yellow ichu grass. I was shoulder to shoulder with Scott and we looked at each other and grinned.

"We're doing the Raid!" we said, and high-fived each other.

We made it to Checkpoint #1. It felt great to get that first passport stamp. Maybe this wouldn't be so tough after all. Maybe Team Schwab would surprise everyone. We descended into ravines and then scrambled up the oddly spongy open scrublands.

Several teams were visible just ahead of us. Even so, Tony insisted we stop frequently so he could check the map. I felt slightly annoyed. Why stop when we had other teams in sight? We couldn't *all* be going in the wrong direction, could we? Every time we stopped, the other teams got farther away—and I got more irritated.

By the time we got to CP #2, our beautiful day was gone. Clouds had rolled in, the temperature had dropped twenty degrees, and it had begun to rain. It was challenging enough to plot a course in fair weather; now, with visibility shot, we had real problems. Many hours—and many map-studying stops later—we stumbled into CP #3. While we were getting our passport stamped, an official told us that three racers had already dropped out—two with sprained ankles and the other with severe stomach problems. I could only imagine how bad it must feel for their race to end before it had even begun.

It was raining harder as we set off. We could see one team ahead of us on the ridgeline, but we would have to hustle if we wanted to keep them in sight. Tony called for another map check.

"Come on," I snapped. "Let's just catch up to the team in front of us and stick with them. It's going to be dark soon."

He glared at me. "I need to be sure that I know where we are so that I can make the right decisions."

By the time we got moving again, the group ahead of us had disappeared. We were on our own. Fog rolled in as darkness fell. When we turned on our headlamps, the light bounced off white vapor.

"This way," Tony said, and we followed him up a long rocky slope. We plodded along in silence, breathing hard in the thin air. Tony wanted to stop again. In the light of our headlamps, with rain pelting us, we watched him muttering to himself, turning the maps this way and that. I caught Steve's eye. He knew what I knew, what I think we all knew—that less than twenty-four hours into the Raid Gauloises, we were freezing, we were wet, we were exhausted—and we were lost.

"That way." Tony pointed into the swirling fog.

Over the next several hours, we passed the same rock formations three times—always from a different direction. We knew we had to be near CP #4 but had no idea how to find it. I imagined all of the other teams waltzing through the checkpoints and hearing about the American team who hadn't even made it to CP #4. I thought about asking Michael Lucero for divine guidance, but then hoped he wasn't watching.

According to the map, CP #4 was about five miles from CP #3; we'd probably already walked twenty trying to find it. After another hour of wandering in the cold rain, Nancy suggested that we set up the tent and try to get some rest until daylight. Tony grumbled a little, but finally agreed this was sensible.

We got out our lightweight and expensive "five-person" tent. It was the first time we'd set the thing up, and it looked laughably small. One by one, we crawled in. There was so little room by the time Scott squeezed in that his hips and legs were left sticking out of the tent. Of course, we hadn't brought ground pads—no extra weight for the amazingly fleet Team Schwab!—so the floor was instantly wet and cold. Sleep was impossible. Steve couldn't stop coughing. If one person needed to turn over, we all had to roll at the same time.

To see the first light of dawn was a relief. We wormed our way out of the tent, groaning and rubbing our necks. The fog had lifted a bit and we could actually see more than ten yards in front of us as we started walking again.

Nancy stopped abruptly and held up her hand. "Shhh."

I heard it, too. The sound of voices. We headed toward the sound and, cresting a hill, saw a bright red Raid tent lit with flashing strobes in a clearing. We looked at each other in disbelief. We had been so ridiculously close.

Sheepishly, we presented ourselves to the French race officials at CP #4.

"Ah, *bon* . . . one of our lost teams has arrived. Now we are missing only nine."

So, we were not the only ones. That cheered us up. I went behind some boulders to pee, and when I came back, my team sang "Happy Birthday" to me. They presented me with a squashed, candle-topped cupcake and a damp, bent card from my mother. I had forgotten all about it; I was thirty-six. The brief break gave me time to say a silent prayer of gratitude for six years of sobriety, for my beautiful healthy kids, and even for the chance to be cold, wet, and lost in the mountains of Ecuador.

I stood above Tony while he placed the maps on the ground and plotted a route to the next checkpoint. I wasn't a stellar navigator, either, but I wanted to watch what he was doing. He clearly didn't appreciate my looking over his shoulder.

"There," he said.

"Are you sure?"

"Charlie," he said sharply, "I got it."

Eventually, we did make it to CP #5. From there, we descended through a forest of gnarled trees, whose trunks were sloughing off strips of dark red bark. Moss and lichen and giant bromeliads dripped from the branches; birds and frogs warbled and trilled in the ghostly mist. It felt primeval and otherworldly. It seemed entirely possible that in the tangled green canopy, I might just spot the slit reptilian pupils of a *Tyrannosaurus rex*.

- - - -

We slipped our way down the slick hills and emerged from the woods on a muddy road that, according to our map, would lead us to CP #6 in the village of Oyacachi. We passed tin-roofed huts and sulfurous hot springs. Women in bright shawls and long skirts called to us to buy bangle bracelets and wool felt fedoras. When we found the Raid official, Tony handed him our passport.

"What position are we in?" Tony asked. I winced. Did we really want to know that?

"You are . . . number thirty-five," the official said, looking at a clipboard. "The fastest teams came through in twelve hours."

It had taken us twenty-eight hours, but at least we weren't last. We decided to take a few minutes to organize our gear and have something to eat. Steve and I sat on a log. He suddenly doubled over in a coughing fit.

"You okay?" I asked.

"The pace is too fast," he said before he started to cough again.

"We can back off," I said.

"Let's go!" I heard Tony shout. "Let's move!"

"Shit," Steve said.

We shouldered our packs and started walking again. A few emaciated dogs padded along for a while, then gave up as we crossed plank bridges over swampy flats and began to climb. The fog enveloped us once more and obliterated any hope we had of gaining on the teams ahead of us. We were walking blind.

It took another thirty sleepless hours to get through the next three checkpoints. It was almost comical. Tony had once looked up from the map and said, "That way," and we had marched off into the soup, only to come upon a checkpoint and realize that we had left that one hours earlier.

- - - -

Steve's cough was getting worse. My feet were in agony—something was digging into my ankle bones. Nancy had gone quiet. Scott let out exasperated sighs every few minutes. We slogged on in the damp cold. Late in the afternoon on day three, from a hillside above a boggy plain, we spotted trucks, tents, and a corral full of horses. We all cheered. We had finally arrived at CP #10, our first transition point.

We found the camp Rolf and Kurt had set up for us.

"Where's my mom?" I asked Rolf.

"Asleep in the tent. She wanted us to wake her as soon as you got here."

I decided to let her sleep while I got myself cleaned up a little. I didn't want to freak her out.

I limped over to Rolf's tent. "Something's up with my feet." I lay down in the tent and Rolf helped me get my shoes off. The pain was excruciating.

"Jesus," Rolf said. My socks were soaked with blood. He carefully rolled them off and grimaced. My ankles looked like butchered meat. Rolf picked up my shoes and looked inside. "The plastic has worn through the padding." He showed me the exposed heel counter. "The edge has been rubbing against your ankle bones."

"Charlie!" My mom peered into the tent. Her face looked puffy and her hair was lopsided. "Are you okay?"

Rolf tucked my bloody socks behind his back.

I scrambled to my feet and hugged her. I could smell cigarette smoke on her clothes, and for an instant the smoke reminded me of being in a bar, and a thought zinged out: A *beer would taste great right now.*

"I'm fine," I said. "Couple of blisters. How are you doing?"

She looked spent. Her clothes and boots were caked with mud. "Well, it's been quite an adventure. Ecuadorian mud treatment. Good for the skin."

I gave her another long hug.

Then I heard Tony hollering, "Schwab, let's get our gear together and head out ASAP!"

I stepped out of the tent barefoot.

"Did you hear?" Tony said. "We're in fourteenth place! We have to get our horses and get going!"

"We can't go now," I said. "We can only ride the horses until seven. Dark Zone rule, remember? We'd have to camp with them in a couple of hours."

"But we're in fourteenth place."

"We are tied for fourteenth, Tony—with twenty other teams. Look around—no one is leaving now. They're being sensible and waiting for morning."

"We came here to race, Charlie, not to sit around camp with our mothers."

"Nobody is leaving tonight," I said slowly. "Steve is sick. My feet are trashed. We are all fried, including you. We need to sleep. It's the smart thing to do. We can take off as soon as it starts getting light."

Tony stomped away. One by one, he called each team member into the tent to try to convince him or her we should get going. Nobody was budging. Tony had been overruled.

At dawn the next morning, we got up and dressed. My ankles felt a little better now that Rolf had bandaged them and cut off the plastic ridge that had been chewing them up. Nancy, Steve, and I walked to the makeshift corral. The rules said that each team would select three horses and we'd take turns riding them. Veterinarians stationed at upcoming checkpoints would make sure the horses were staying healthy. We walked up to the poncho-clad vaquero, and he handed us the reins of three saddled horses.

He motioned for us to leave.

I pointed at another horse in the corral. I thought that one looked calmer than the one I had been given. "That one? *Puedo tener este?*"

"No. You go," he said.

"These are fine, Charlie." Nancy and Steve started leading their horses back to our camp. Mine, however, refused to move. I gave her a strong tug and she pulled back even harder. One of the horse wranglers came up, smacked her hard on the rear, and she took a few steps and stopped again. He hit her again and she stomped her feet and whinnied.

The vaquero raised his hand once more.

"No," I said, putting my hands up. "*Que está pasando?*"

"*Ella es una nueva madre*," the wrangler said.

Even with my limited Spanish, I understood that he was telling me that my horse was a new mother; the baby in the corral was hers. No wonder she didn't want to leave. I asked again for another horse.

"No. *No es posible*," the vaquero said.

Now I was pissed. I told him that we would just take two horses then and leave the mother.

"No, no. *Descalificado*." He shook his head.

Steve came back to see what was going on. I told him we were being forced to take a mother horse away from her baby.

"*Por favor?*" Steve asked, pointing at another horse.

"No. *Descalificado*."

"Okay, okay." I threw my hands up. "*Vamos con el bebé!*"

We'll go with the baby.

The horseman shrugged and went to get the foal. I took the mother's reins and the baby fell in behind her without hesitation. I wasn't sure if I had just solved a problem or created a bigger one, but at least we were moving again. Tony and Scott shook their heads when they saw us coming back with a baby.

"Are you kidding?" Tony said.

"It was the best option," Steve said.

"It was the only option," I added.

We said good-bye to our crew and left camp, along with a handful of other teams. It was cold, but visibility had improved greatly. Patches of blue sky broke through the clouds. Tony seemed to have gotten past being overruled by the team the previous night. He even let me look at the maps with him, though it was obvious where we needed to go. Ahead of us—some twenty miles across the lunar rolling plains—loomed our next destination, the perfect cone of Cotopaxi. I felt it drawing us forward, like a powerful magnet. I imagined how it would feel to be standing on its summit. Then, I noticed a massive black bird overhead, riding the thermals.

"Look," I said. "Is that a condor?" I'd been told they were so endangered that the odds of seeing one were slim.

"Wow," Nancy said. "Yeah, it is!"

"Gotta be a sign," I said. "Our luck is about to change."

"You do know that condors are vultures, right? They eat dead flesh," Scott said. "They picked the right team."

We found out quickly that if the condor was indeed a harbinger of something, it was not of good fortune. For starters, the foal stopped every ten minutes or so to nurse. And all four of our horses were so afraid of water that they had to be pushed and pulled over even the narrowest irrigation channels. By midmorning, all the other teams had passed us. At CP #11, we switched riders. We had decided that no one should ride the mother horse—she got so agitated when her baby was near her, she was nearly impossible to control. Tony got on one horse and Steve on the other, and we headed out again.

As we gained altitude, the wind picked up and the temperature nose-dived. After a few hours, Nancy and I noticed that Tony had stopped talking. He was riding with his head bowed, and his body was bouncing limply with each step of the horse.

"You okay, Tony?" Nancy said, walking alongside him.

No answer.

"Tony?"

"Yeah!" he said with a start, and sat up in the saddle.

"You okay?"

He looked at Nancy blankly. "Okay. I have to pick up the kids."

He slumped over again.

"Tony!" Nancy grabbed his knee.

He mumbled something about maps and school buses.

"Look at me, Tony," Nancy said.

He fumbled with the zipper on his jacket as if he were trying to take it off.

"I think he's hypothermic," Nancy said. "We need to get him warmed up."

"We need to get out of this wind," I said.

We looked at the barren plains ahead of us. I pulled out the maps and compass and went through the steps Michael had taught me many months earlier. I saw a river on the map that, if I was right, should be over the next long climb. I thought the river valley would provide some shelter. It would be a good place to set up our tent and get Tony warm. My teammates looked at me expectantly.

"That way," I said.

We crested the hill, but found no river and no trees—only another long, exposed ridgeline.

"If the valley isn't over that next hill," I said, "we'll stop and put up the tent. Is everyone on board with that?"

I strode out ahead of the team, and the extra effort made my heart hammer. When I got to the top of the hill, I yelled with relief. The river was there. I could also see tents, people, and horses. Other Raid teams had stopped here for the night. As soon as we got down to the riverbank, we got our tent up and helped Tony into it. Then we covered him with Mylar space blankets and a sleeping bag, and I went to secure our horses.

The vaquero had told me that when we camped, we should pull the saddle off the mother, put it on the ground, and tie her to it. The other horses, he said, would stay with her. I did what he said and then went back to the tent.

Tony was not getting better. His shivering had escalated into full-body convulsions. Nancy and Scott lay down and sandwiched Tony with their bodies.

"If he doesn't improve soon," Steve said, "we need to think about using the emergency radio."

We both knew that would mean disqualification from the race.

"If he doesn't get better soon, we'll call," I said.

I went back to check on the horses. They seemed to be happily grazing. Then I walked over to see if any of the other teams had any information to share. I found a woman who spoke some English, and she told me that all the French teams here were traveling together. The Raid officials had told them that the cut-off times to get to the next transition point had been extended because of the bad weather in the trekking section. This was excellent news. I went back to tell my team. Steve was standing outside the tent.

There was more good news. Tony was coming around. I suggested we get some sleep, and if Tony was feeling up to it, take off at 4:00 a.m.

We all crammed into the tent; this time *my* ass and legs were sticking out the door. I was awake for a long time, shivering, listening to the wind and the whinnying horses and my snoring teammates. I knew now I wasn't going to star in the "triumph of the rookie" story I had written for myself. We'd be lucky to stay in the race. I was cold and hungry and tired. But I was grateful to be here, grateful to be feeling it all. I had lost too many years being numb.

My watch alarm went off and I woke the others. I went to check on the horses and scanned the area with my headlamp. They weren't there. Maybe I was looking in the wrong place. I shone my light all around. No horses. Had someone stolen them? Was another team playing a trick on us? Not funny. I went back to tell the team that our horses seemed to be gone.

"What do you mean, gone?" Steve said.

"Like gone, gone. I tied one up to a saddle. The others were supposed to stay with her."

"Is the saddle still there?" Scott said.

Steve and I walked back to look again.

My headlamp shone on the saddle, sitting by itself in the dirt.

"Shit," I said. "She must have pulled loose."

Unless we found our horses, we would be disqualified and it would be my fault. The only thing we could do was wait until the sun came up, then go out and hunt for them. Maybe they hadn't strayed too far. When it got light enough, Nancy, Steve, and I went out to look. From the top of a hill, we could see other teams making their way along the river. I felt terrible; we should have been right there with them.

"Look." Nancy pointed into the valley. "There are horses down there."

I saw them, too. It wasn't unusual to spot horses—we'd seen several wild herds in the past few days. But this appeared to be a foursome, and one of them looked to be much smaller than the others. Steve and I hurried down the trail. As we got closer, I could see that two of the horses had saddles on.

"Yes!"

Now all we had to do was catch them.

Steve and I split up, hoping that we could close in on them from opposite sides. The horses were having none of it. As soon as we got close, they spooked and ran farther down the valley. We decided to see if we could get behind them and at least get them running back toward our camp.

As we got close to the horses, I heard a loud whistle and looked up to see a man on horseback riding toward me. He had on a striped poncho and a brimmed hat. He spoke to me in rapid-fire Spanish.

I shook my head. "*No comprendo.*"

He climbed down from his horse and unzipped my bright yellow team jacket. I thought he was stealing it. Okay, fine. I wasn't going to fight him for it. But when he had pulled it off me, he balled it up and threw it on the ground. He motioned to Steve to do the same. Then he pointed at the horses.

"Oh, it's the yellow!" Steve said. "That's what's freaking the horses out."

Without the bright jackets on, we were able to walk right up to the horses and pick up their reins. We waved and said, *"Gracias,"* to the vaquero and started back to our camp. Our teammates cheered when they saw us. We packed up and headed out.

– – – –

While I had been getting our passport stamped at CP #15, I had asked the official what time we needed to get to the transition at CP #16 to stay in the race as a ranked team. He told me we had until 4:30 p.m. I looked at my watch. It was 2:00 p.m. If we hustled and didn't get lost, I thought we could get there.

A little after 4:00 p.m., we spotted the checkpoint. After all we had been through, we were still going to make it. When we arrived, we said a quick hello to our crew and I hurried up to the French official with our passport. It was exactly 4:23 p.m.

He looked at his watch, clucked his tongue, and gave me a sad smile. "Ah, well, eet's a good effort, but you have missed the cutoff time." He tapped his watch. "You are eight minutes late."

"No! We were told that we had until four thirty. We made it. You see? On time. We are on time."

"Eet's too bad for you, yes? They apparently do not have the updated information at the last checkpoint. You have missed the cutoff and nothing can be done. But do not worry, you can still climb the mountain if you wish. Or you may skip the mountain and continue to the bicycles. Or you may simply stop. Your choice."

I wanted to strangle him. "My choice," I said with calm intensity, "is to continue as a ranked team since the mistake was made by your official and not by my team. I want to file a protest."

He stood there with his arms crossed, looking at me with bemused disdain, as if I were an American tourist who had just requested ketchup for my escargot. "It is not possible," he said stonily.

"I bet the French teams can roll in whenever they want, right? This is bullshit! We are still in the fucking race!"

Nancy came up, grabbed my arm, and stepped in front of me. She spoke to the official in French. He shook his head and answered her, speaking rapidly.

Nancy nodded and replied, then turned back to me. "We're out of the official race. We are in the Trans-Ecuador group now. That's it."

Nancy, Scott, Steve, Tony, and I sat in a circle on the damp ground. Mom, Rolf, and Kurt stood around the edges, listening. We had to decide what to do. We talked about how great it was that we had gotten this far and how good it would feel to take a hot shower and sleep in a real bed. We talked about skipping ahead to the bicycle leg; that would get us out of the altitude, and maybe then we'd all feel better and be able to finish strong. It made sense to bypass the volcano.

Finally, Nancy, who had been quiet during the conversation, spoke up. "People come from all over the world just to climb Cotopaxi. We're here. I would really like to go to the top."

We turned and looked up at the peak in silence. Nancy was right. We might never have this chance again. My stomach churned with indecision. The choice was clear: comfort or pain.

After a minute, Steve said he wanted to try. Tony and Scott said they did, too.

"Let's go," I said.

Our crew helped us get our mountain gear together. I said a quick good-bye to my mother. I knew she was worried about what lay ahead for us. "I will zee you at *les bicyclettes*," I said to her in my best Inspector Clouseau French accent.

Our next destination was the Refugio José Rivas, the mountain hut at nearly sixteen thousand feet that was serving as CP #17. The Raid had stationed doctors there to make sure everyone was healthy enough to try for the summit. Steve's cough worsened as we climbed. By the time we arrived at the hut, we all knew it was bad. He was coughing up blood and seemed disoriented. We took him straight to the doctor. The news was terrible. Not only did he have severe bronchitis, he also had a blood oxygen saturation level in the high fifties—dangerously low. The officials told him he had to be helicoptered out immediately. He was crushed by the news, but we all knew there was no choice. I hugged Steve, sharing in his sadness.

Now we were four. We had to start for the summit at 1:00 a.m. so we could be off the mountain before the sun made the snowpack unstable. We had a few hours to rest, but as usual, I couldn't sleep. My head ached, my chest felt congested, and I had developed a dry cough. I just wanted to get going. Finally, it was time to gear up and pass a final medical check. I fought to suppress my cough because I didn't want the French doctor to listen to my chest. I cracked a couple of jokes that he did not find amusing, then he waved me along.

In darkness, we started up the exposed face on slippery volcanic scree. After about an hour, we reached the snow line and switched to heavy boots with crampons. We pulled out our ice axes and roped up. I was at the lead; Nancy was at the back. The sky was cloudless and the stars were hard white points as bright as I'd ever seen them. We climbed slowly, each step a project. Lift the foot, move the foot, place the foot.

It was difficult enough to climb at this altitude under normal circumstances, but we had started out exhausted, dehydrated, hungry, and oxygen starved. We forced ourselves to push on, following a circuitous route that crossed snowfields, skirted crevasses, and passed wind-sculpted ice formations that, when illuminated by our headlamps, looked like breaching white whales. Several hours into it, I sucked on the hose connected to my hydration pack and got nothing. I realized I hadn't cleared it after taking my last drink, and the water line was now frozen solid. I couldn't believe I had forgotten something so basic. There was no point in saying anything about it to my teammates. I would simply have no water from here on out.

At about seventeen thousand feet, we took a break. On the eastern horizon, the dark sky was shot with broken shards of orange and gray. Wind swirled around us. Sitting in the snow, I felt oddly detached from my body, as if I were looking down on myself from above. I breathed deliberately and slowly, trying to focus on where I was and what I was doing. Everything was blurry. And then I heard music. Beautiful echoes—a guitar and a flute playing a lilting, intricate melody. I

closed my eyes to listen. When I opened them again, I half expected
to see a small Ecuadorian band marching up the trail. I caught Scott's
eye and pointed to my right ear. He gave me a puzzled look.

"Do you hear that?" I asked.

"Hear what?"

Nancy and Tony looked at me with quizzical expressions.

Maybe it was some atmospheric phenomenon, an upwelling of
sound from a village far below, like smoke curling away from a fire;
maybe it was in my head. When I first got sober, I was told that if I was
patient, if I kept trudging the road of Happy Destiny, as they said in
AA, I would be amazed by the gifts that would come my way. I thought
this music, wherever it was coming from, might be one of those gifts.

I looked up at the summit and thought of tough races I had run;
those last excruciating miles when you didn't think you could go on.
This was so much harder. But it was not harder than quitting drugs.
It was not harder than staying sober. I knew I had already done the
hardest thing. I knew I could make it to the top.

"Ready?" Tony said.

"Ready," we all replied.

And then, somehow, we were on the summit. It had taken us
almost seven hours, but we had done it. We cheered and hugged
each other and turned to take in the view. Snowy peaks seem to float
above a layer of silvered clouds. To the north, I recognized the silhouette of Imbabura, the majestic volcano from that first morning
in Ibarra. I pulled out a photo of my boys from inside my jacket and
kissed it twice, with tears in my eyes. I loved them and I had been
away from them so much.

We stayed on top for about ten minutes, foggy brained, elated,
freezing, pummeled by wind. Then we started the long, slow
descent. When we finally reached our crew, the reunion was joyous.
We told Rolf, Kurt, and my mother about the climb, and when we
were done, I asked them how they were.

"Good," Rolf said. I saw him glance at my mother.

I took a long look at her. Her eyes were swollen and her color
was off.

"Great," my mother repeated in a tone that I recognized meant not so great.

"What?" I said.

Rolf said he had found my mother shivering uncontrollably in her tent the night before. She'd been hypothermic and unable to speak. He had covered her with every warm thing he could find and made hot-water bottles to put in her sleeping bag. Then he had gotten into the sleeping bag with her.

"She came out of it," Rolf said.

"Mom, you should have told them you felt bad."

"I don't know what happened. I was so cold, and the next thing I knew I was waking up from this strange dream."

"With this strange man," Rolf said.

My mom laughed.

I felt sick that my mother had gone through this. I knew hypothermia could kill strong people. My mom was tiny, nearly sixty years old, and smoked and drank too much. I had brought her to Ecuador for an adventure; I never imagined she would be anything more than uncomfortable. But she could have died.

"I'm sorry, Mom."

"I'm fine now, Charlie. Perfect. Now, Rolf has to tell you something."

"What else?"

"The officials said you have to bypass the biking section and go directly to the river."

– – – –

The air got more humid and more deliciously infused with oxygen as we drove toward the jungle. By midafternoon, our truck had reached the banks of the muddy, fast-moving Río Toachi. The Raid staff stationed there said we had to hurry—that if we didn't launch immediately, we would not be allowed to continue.

We changed clothes and flung our gear into the blue raft. I was at the back, trying to remember what I had learned in my paddling certification course as we bounced and rolled through Class III and IV rapids. We were soaked and nearly flipped several times. Through it all, I couldn't stop smiling—none of us could. Even Tony, who had been subdued since we had gotten off the mountain, brightened up. To be moving fast with little effort and to know there was no chance of getting lost—it was bliss.

The Raid rules said we had to get off the river before nightfall, so we beached the raft at twilight. Sitting on big, round river rocks, we watched the sky go dark, swatted at mosquitoes, and listened to the night noises of the jungle—rasps, whines, shrieks, and clicks.

We had studied the map and knew we were close to the finish. This was likely our last night together.

"How good will a shower feel?" I said.

"And a bed," Nancy said.

"First thing I want is a cheeseburger," Tony said.

We sat in silence for a long time.

"I feel so bad for Steve," Scott said. "Missing this."

"I know," I said. "It's been fantastic. Even the parts that completely sucked."

At dawn, we slipped the raft back in the water. Within a few minutes, we came upon the next checkpoint, where we would trade the rafts for inflatable canoes. After we beached our boat, Scott and I started inflating two limp canoes with foot pumps. Hissing sounds came from both boats. We looked over at the race official, who shrugged, as if to say, *This is what you deserve when you are so slow and arrive at the back of the pack.*

We used patch kits to fix the holes and pushed off. Tony was noticeably shaky.

"You don't have to paddle," I said. "Just enjoy the ride."

The current carried us through a high-walled canyon, past terraced farms and ramshackle villages. Women were doing their wash on the riverbanks. Dogs barked, children waved and shouted. It was humid and hot, with no breeze at all, even on the water. A fish jumped ahead of us and left a circular wake.

"Something stinks," Tony said. The farther we went downriver, the fouler the smell. Clumps of raw sewage floated by.

"What's that?" I pointed at what looked like a dead body. When we got close to it, we saw that it was the bloated carcass of a pig folded around the trunk of a submerged tree.

We abandoned the idea of using our water purification tablets; nothing was strong enough to make this river potable. Instead, we decided to go ashore at a village to see if we could buy drinks. I had been in charge of the team money, but realized that in my rush to change clothes before the water leg, I had left most of the cash in my other pants—which were now with our crew. We only had a few sucres among us. I started up a muddy trail, and when I came upon a small boy, I said, *"Tienda?"*

He led me up to a tiny shop. I smiled at the shopkeeper and pointed at Fantas, Cokes, bottled water, and a big box of Ritz crackers. Then I put my money down. She shook her head. I took off my digital watch, laid it next to the money, and pushed it toward her. We had a deal.

Revived by my loot, we took to the river again. At last, we spotted the checkpoint where we would switch from canoes to sea kayaks for the final forty-mile stretch on the Río Esmeraldas. We went ashore and I handed our passport to a race official.

"You cannot continue," he said without making eye contact.

There would be no negotiating. We were done. We were told to get into a motorboat that would take us the rest of the way. The boat chugged down the murky river through low green hills until we reached the broad delta, where it emptied into the Pacific. From here, we turned south along the coast, slamming through teeth-jarring waves. We saw container ships and high-rise hotels and smokestacks. At last, we spotted a group of people on the Same Beach in Esmeraldas. It was the finish line of the Raid.

The boat captain cut the motor. "Now, you swim."

We all laughed. Then we saw he wasn't joking.

"Swim?" I said.

Nancy spoke to the man in French. She listened and nodded a few times.

"He says that if we want to experience crossing the finish line, the only thing we can do is swim ashore. Then we can walk the last bit."

Okay, we were going to swim. We all slid over the edge of the boat fully clothed. The water was clear and warm, and I felt it washing away ten days of grime and tension and struggle. When we reached shore, we walked together on the dark sand toward the white banner that marked the end of the race.

Steve was there cheering, and so were Rolf and Kurt and my mother. I saw that she was crying, and I teared up, too. I had done all I could do. We all had. The weather had been horrendous and the course had been difficult and we had suffered. I'd asked for help and been a leader; I'd gotten angry and pissed people off. I'd doubled over in pain and in laughter. Now that it was over, I knew one thing for sure: I had to find a way to do it again.

- - - -

A few days after I returned from Ecuador, Pam and I loaded up our cars and drove with the boys, three cats, and two dogs from St. Louis to our new house on the Monterey Peninsula, not far from where my father and stepmother were living. It was more than a little disorienting—going from the summit of Cotopaxi to a corner booth in an Oklahoma City Applebee's just off the I-40. I told my family some stories about the race, but I understood that although Pam was proud of me for being sober and chasing my dreams, I should keep the more harrowing tales to myself. I hoped I impressed upon my boys the importance of perseverance and commitment. I wanted them to be proud of me; they mostly wanted to know where I had gone poop.

Once we were settled in Salinas, I knew I should get busy calling insurance companies and lining up dent-repair technicians for the spring hail season, but I couldn't get myself to pick up the phone. I didn't feel like doing much of anything. I got to a few AA meetings, though I went to fewer than I knew was good for me.

It wasn't just fatigue or culture shock. I felt unmoored, adrift. I had been fixing dents for eight years—working in dusty body shops, living in motels, eating crappy road food—and the thought of starting yet another seven-month cycle of chasing storms put me in a funk. I told myself I should be happy that I was successful at it; I'd bought houses, nice cars, even a horse for Pam, which she adored. But I felt trapped by what I had created. The more I earned, the more we spent, the more I had to make.

Something else, though, something deeper than just the prospect of another hail season, was at the heart of my dark mood. I felt it more every day: Pam and I were drifting apart. I had thought this move might be good for us—that old addict belief that everything would be fixed with a fresh start. But being back in Monterey only made it more obvious that our relationship had changed. I had been a drug addict and alcoholic when we met, and our marriage had been built on Pam's taking care of me, cleaning up my messes. I was grateful for all she had done. But I was a different person now, walking a different path. I loved my boys, but I wasn't sure I loved my wife—and it didn't feel as if she loved me. I wondered what it would be like to fall in love as a sober person.

- - - -

One Sunday, my friend Gary invited me to join a bunch of guys at his place to watch a 49ers game. I had been moping around the house, and Pam encouraged me to go. At halftime, I wandered into the kitchen.

Gary was mixing a round of screwdrivers. "Engle, something to drink?"

"Just OJ would be great." I dipped some chips into a bowl of salsa.

"Second half's about to start," someone yelled.

Gary handed me my drink and headed back into the living room, balancing three tall glasses.

My mouth was on fire from the spicy salsa, so I took the juice and downed more than half of it in one gulp. Instantly, my face flushed and my throat started to burn. Vodka.

I gripped the glass. I couldn't believe I had just taken a drink— my first in more than six years. *At last,* I heard a voice inside me saying, *things are getting interesting.* I didn't know what to do. I stared at the glass. *It's no big deal. You might as well drink the rest of it. One drink. You've been good for so long. You deserve a little break.*

My whole body went on alert. I heard laughter in the other room; no one knew that I was waging an all-out war in the kitchen. Where were those brilliant words of wisdom that I had stored away for just this moment? Everything I had learned in recovery seemed to be just out of reach—as if someone had tied a string to them and were jerking them away from me each time I got close.

I tried to slow my breath and calm my thoughts. I had taken a big swig of vodka—but I had done it without intent. It was an accident. I was still a sober person. What mattered was what I did next. If I chose to take one more drink from that glass, then all I had worked for would be lost. I would have to start again. I knew that if I relapsed, I would not survive it. One more sip—an *intentional* sip— wouldn't just mean the end of my sobriety. It would likely mean the end of me.

My hand was shaking as I put the glass down on the kitchen counter. I walked directly to the front door and left without saying a word. I drove in mist to Lovers Point, a beach park in Pacific Grove where I had started many long runs in the past. I threw on some running clothes that had been in the backseat of my car and took off.

I wanted it gone, out of me. I ran as hard as I could, in a blind panic, pumping my arms until my fingers tingled and my chest heaved. I was on pavement, then kelp-strewn sand, then a boardwalk, then pavement again. I ran past twisted cypress trees and an empty golf course and dunes covered with spiky grass. I ran until I couldn't take another step, then I stopped and doubled over, gasping. When I caught my breath, I stood up, looked out at the chaotic gray surf, and screamed into the wind. I didn't care who heard me.

I stood there for a long time, letting the wind batter me, watching the waves explode on the dark rocks. Finally, I turned back the way I came, walking at first, then running. The wind was at my back now, like a hand pushing me home. Tomorrow, first thing, I would start making those calls to the insurance companies and begin lining up those jobs. I had to, for my family. And I'd work on things with Pam. Maybe we could find a way back.

I got in the car, turned the key in the ignition, and flipped on the windshield wipers. In the rhythmic scrape and whine of those rubber blades, I felt my addict slink back into the foul bunker where he lived. I knew he wasn't gone forever. He would sit quietly, waiting for me to stumble. He was patient. He had all the time in the world.

- - - -

Several weeks later, Scott Williams called. He still had Charles Schwab sponsor money and was putting together a four-man team for the Southern Traverse, a world-class 450-kilometer adventure race on New Zealand's South Island. Did I want in? I talked to Pam about it and she encouraged me to go. With a race on the calendar, my mood instantly improved.

In May, my team, which included two veteran racers, Chris Haggerty and Rob Jardeleza, arrived in Nelson, New Zealand. Chris, a US Navy SEAL and our chief navigator, told us at a meeting the night before the start that he required one thing from us: trust. If he wanted our opinions, he would ask for them. Otherwise, he said, our job was to keep us moving forward.

I loved his forthrightness. Launching a kayak under a milky morning sky into the calm waters off Pohara Beach, I had a feeling this experience would be very different from Ecuador. I was right. Chris was a skilled navigator and inspiring leader. When tactical mistakes were made—we climbed the wrong mountain and had to spend the night anchored to the side of a steep cliff—no one launched arrows of blame. I felt privileged to be out there in that spectacular wilderness with these guys, working together to get through the difficult stretches, picking up the slack for whoever of us was struggling at that moment. Our cohesiveness paid off; we came in tenth overall and were the top American finishers.

The team got along so well that we decided to stay together, with the addition of Nancy Bristow, for the upcoming Raid Gauloises through Tibet and Nepal. On April 29, 2000, I was with them at fourteen thousand feet on the high Tibetan plateau looking up at a fortress-topped mountain, waiting for the race to begin. I felt confident that this team was destined for at least a top-ten finish.

The first leg, a short, steep trek up the mountain, took us directly through a thirteenth-century monastery. Children smiled and shouted as we passed them; the monks in their garnet robes looked on unperturbed from a prayer-flag-draped courtyard. I felt silly rushing by them in our high-tech gear; our urgency suggested we were doing something important. I wished I could stop for a minute, to try to tell them that the Buddhist philosophies that are so much a part of addiction recovery—the idea that suffering and cravings can be overcome through mindfulness, compassion, and wise actions—had saved my life. Instead, breathing hard and drenched with sweat, I muttered a few sheepish *Namastes* and hurried past them.

By the time we reached the ruins of ancient walls near the peak, the altitude had slowed our pace to a plod. Step by step, we worked our way to the transition point, where we would switch to mountain bikes. From the top, we could see the white summits of Everest and Cho Oyu floating above rolling dun-colored hills to the south. Nancy, Chris, Scott, and I paused to take in the view. Rob was bent over with his hands on his knees.

We started out on the bikes, but the strong headwind and soft sand track made pedaling almost impossible. Several times, we had to get off and walk. The only consolation was that the teams ahead of us were doing the same thing. In the thin air, I was rubber legged and light-headed, but Rob seemed to be in real trouble. He simply stopped pedaling and tipped over. Chris convinced him to let him carry his pack for a while.

"He says he can't see," Chris said to Nancy, Scott, and me when Rob was out of earshot. "Everything is blurry. I don't know—maybe he just has sand in his eyes."

As the hours went by, we could all see that it was much more serious than that. By the time we dropped off the bikes and started a long trekking leg, Rob was disoriented and having trouble walking a straight line. We knew we had to go back for help.

We backtracked to the previous checkpoint, and the race medics tested Rob's oxygen saturation levels. Their faces told us what they discovered; his readings were shockingly low. He was suffering from severe pulmonary edema. Rob was quickly placed into a portable hyperbaric chamber. I felt sick seeing him lying in that coffinlike contraption; Rob was one of the toughest guys I'd ever known. After about an hour, his condition improved, and he was told he had to descend immediately to thicker air. He would ride a donkey and be accompanied by a local Sherpa guide. We watched him ride down the trail.

"Stay out of the bars," Chris yelled after him.

Rob raised one hand without looking back.

"Now what?" I asked when Rob had disappeared from view. We knew we were out of the race since we had lost a team member, but as in Ecuador, we were allowed to continue for the experience.

"I'm going to go down, too," Chris said. "Make sure Rob is okay."

I understood his desire to be with his friend. But Chris's departure meant that what was left of our team no longer had a navigator. The three of us had to decide if we should go on. I was exhausted, and I could see from the strain on Nancy's and Scott's faces that they were, too. I could have said, "We've worked so hard to get here. Let's keep going." I could have volunteered to take over the navigation. I could have tried to convince Scott and Nancy that we should not let the opportunity to see this magical place slip away. They could have said the same to me. Instead, we kicked the dirt and shrugged and loaded our packs into the Raid SAG wagon for the long drive to the finish area.

I have never regretted a decision more. Every time we passed teams who were still out there, giving their all, I slid down in my seat to avoid being seen. Bumping along in that bus of shame, I vowed to myself that I would never quit a race again.

CHAPTER 7

We wanderers, ever seeking the lonelier way,
begin no day where we have ended another day;
and no sunrise finds us where sunset left us.
Even while the earth sleeps, we travel.
We are the seeds of the tenacious . . .
we are given to the wind and are scattered.

— KHALIL GIBRAN, *The Prophet*

By the start of 2003, I had added three *Eco-Challenges* (Borneo, New Zealand, and Fiji), another Raid Gauloises (Vietnam), the Discovery Channel World Championships (Switzerland), and a handful of other events to my adventure-racing résumé. I'd been chased by pissed-off crocodiles, chewed up by leeches, and showered with bat shit. I'd fallen asleep on a bicycle, woken up with a tarantula in my sleeping bag, capsized in Class V rapids, and hung off a cliff tangled in climbing ropes. I had contracted leptospirosis from swimming in a river tainted with pig urine; had my oozing, macerated feet mistakenly plunged into an acid bath by a race crew nurse; and developed several raging cases of an excruciating diaper-rash-like affliction called monkey butt. But I never quit another adventure race.

That's not to say the results had always been stellar. In fact, in about half of the events, my team finished with the "unofficial" designation because we'd lost one of our teammates to ailment or injury along the way. Adventure racing was cruel like that: bad things just happened—no matter how prepared or determined you were. I had yet to get a team disqualified, but I knew, if I kept racing, my turn would come.

By 2003, I was also, to my great surprise, being occasionally recognized in airports and restaurants, thanks to my appearance in a CBS *48 Hours* segment about the Borneo *Eco-Challenge*. Producers had asked me to shoot video for them while I raced, and even though they said they'd probably use less than a minute of what I gave them, I was excited enough about it that I didn't mind adding the weight of a camcorder and batteries to my gear. Plus, race director Mark Burnett had told the CBS guys no one could finish an *Eco-Challenge* while carrying a video camera, and I wanted to prove him wrong.

I spilled my guts to that lens; not just about my physical and mental struggles in the jungle, which were many, but also about my addiction and my sobriety. It was cathartic for me to have to put into words what I was doing and why I was doing it—to explain my belief that this kind of suffering led to enlightenment and personal growth. CBS ended up using about eleven minutes of my stuff and even brought me to New York to watch the premiere. When I walked into the editing booth, the guys who had sorted through my twenty-five hours of raw footage gave me a standing ovation. It was my first inkling that you didn't have to win a race to be considered interesting—and that I might have a talent for documenting my adventures.

After the show aired, reporters started contacting me for interviews. I also began receiving daily calls and letters from people who had been moved by my story. Some were athletes who had also gotten sober, but more often they were addicts or alcoholics searching for a way out of the hell they were living in.

It tore me up to hear their stories, but I had no foolproof answers for them. I could only tell them what addiction had been like for me, what had happened to me, and what life was like for me now.

- - - -

Besides, who was I to dispense advice? Like everyone else, I was a work in progress. Pam and I had continued to struggle. We went to counseling, but by 2002 our marriage was over. We were open with the boys about what was happening and did everything we could to keep them feeling secure. After selling the Salinas house, we drove across the country together and set up two adjacent households back in Greensboro, North Carolina, where real estate was more affordable—and Pam would be closer to her family and friends.

Shortly after our move East, I got a serendipitous call from Tom Forman, a former *48 Hours* producer I had hit it off with in Borneo. He told me he had a new show in the works called *Extreme Make-over: Home Edition*, in which volunteer construction crews built a house in one week for a deserving family. He wanted to hire me as a freelance cameraman and producer.

"You are completely unqualified for this job," he said, laughing. "But if you don't tell anyone that, I'll bring you on board."

I'm sure part of what he saw in me was my ability to function on little or no sleep. That served me well when I joined the *EMHE* crew; the shoots went round the clock for ten manic days. I loved it—and the schedule suited me. Between episodes, I had plenty of time off to be with my kids and to train.

Just what I was training for, though, I wasn't sure. The adventure-racing world was changing; Mark Burnett had decided to end the *Eco-Challenge* to focus on *Survivor*. The Raid had been shortened and streamlined. At the same time, my enthusiasm for team events had waned. I'd had my fill of the complicated logistics, the clashing personalities—and the constant hustle for sponsors, whose support could be jeopardized with one ankle sprain. I was hungry to succeed or fail on my own.

When my friend Mary Gadams called me in early 2003 to tell me about the Gobi March, a new running event she was organizing in northern China's Gobi Desert, I told her to count me in. The 155-mile race borrowed its format from the Tour de France; the winner would be determined by the cumulative time of six stages, which ranged from about six to fifty miles. But unlike the Tour, I wouldn't have a *domestique* to bring me supplies or guide me. Runners in the Gobi March carried all of their own food and gear on their backs and used a map and compass to navigate through some sections of the course.

But the Gobi March wasn't until September. I needed something else to focus on. I found it in the Badwater Ultramarathon. For years, I'd been hearing tales of this epic nonstop 135-mile race, which started in Death Valley at 280 feet below sea level and finished at 8,300 feet on Mount Whitney in the extreme heat of July. All runners had a support crew to keep them hydrated and fed—and to tend to them if they couldn't go on. Without their crews, runners would not survive. My teammate in Fiji and Vietnam, Marshall Ulrich, had won the race several times and held me rapt with his stories about it. I knew I wanted to do it someday. Badwater now had a new race director, Chris Kostman, who was actively recruiting athletes for the 2003 event. He invited me to enter. If nothing else, I figured it would be good training for the Gobi March.

A 1907 California newspaper ad suggested that Death Valley "had all the advantages of Hell without the inconvenience." The same, I was about to find out, could be said of Badwater. At 10:00 a.m., on July 22, 2003, with the temperature at 125 degrees and climbing, and the humidity an atypically high 18 percent, I stood shoulder to shoulder with some of the world's best ultrarunners including Marshall, Pam Reed, Lisa Smith-Batchen—and up-and-comer Dean Karnazes. In the weeks leading up to the start, I'd barraged Marshall with questions about pacing, foot care, and fluid intake, but now, looking east across the salt flats of the Badwater Basin shimmering in the heat, with a tinny recording of "The Star-Spangled Banner" being played over a bullhorn to signal the impending start, I went blank.

We got the go signal, and several runners shot to the front. Marshall hung back a bit and I stayed with him, trying to tamp down my nerves. The heat was beyond anything I had ever experienced; not just the suffocating air, but also the two-hundred-degree blacktop, which radiated like glowing embers through my rubber soles. I'd put in plenty of miles in hot and muggy North Carolina, but the only way I could have trained for this would have been to run on top of a lit stove.

My crew and I had decided that they would leapfrog ahead of me every few miles. But I noticed that most of the experienced runners had support crews with them almost constantly, offering fluids and ice packs and soaking them with big squirt guns. Before I started, I couldn't comprehend needing so much aid; now I wondered if I had made a mistake sending my team too far ahead.

Still, several miles into it, I was feeling okay—good enough that something inside of me whispered, *Why not go faster?* I moved past Marshall, lifted my hand, and said, "Good luck." Later he would tell me that he was worried when I charged past him like that, but he figured I would find out the hard way that pacing at Badwater was everything. I followed the molten asphalt ribbon as it unspooled across the baked sand, drawn forward by the promise of connecting with my crew—with their buckets of ice and cold drinks.

Though my crew did everything they could to keep me hydrated, by the time I connected with them again at mile seventeen, the Furnace Creek checkpoint, I was light-headed and nauseated. I downed drinks and dunked my head in a cooler of ice. I took off again in the savage heat. The wind had kicked up, but instead of offering respite, it created the effect of running into the mouth of a giant blow-dryer. I fought through it and maintained a decent sub-ten-minute-mile pace. When I reached the Stovepipe checkpoint at mile forty-two, I was in fourth placc.

The checkpoint had a motel with a pool, and like a lot of racers, I stripped off my shoes and shirt and jumped in. The pool might as well have been a hot tub. When I got out, I told my crew I was doing okay, but in fact, I was pretty sure I was in serious trouble. My legs were tender to the touch—not a good sign. My pee, when I finally had to go, was dark as tea. *Be careful, be careful*, I repeated to myself as I started the seventeen-mile climb to Townes Pass.

I alternated between running and walking. That's what I saw others doing. As I climbed, the sun dropped below the horizon and the temperature dropped slightly. After about three hours, I crested the peak in the dark. I had run nearly sixty miles. The next ten miles would all be downhill. This was my chance to push the pace. I stripped down to my briefs and took off my shirt. Then I turned off my headlamp. In the moonlight, I saw the dark silhouetted ridgelines of the distant mountains and the faint glow of the painted white line that marked the side of the road.

I knew my crew was out there waiting for me somewhere. I could see the red taillights of support cars in the distance. I knew runners were ahead of me and behind me. But for now, I was alone under a blizzard of stars. I inhaled the desert brine—so oddly oceanic—and let myself think about the first time I ever saw the desert. I was a kid, maybe ten years old. I had flown to California to visit my father during my summer vacation, and he was driving me back East to North Carolina. We were speeding along in his little Triumph Spitfire under the enormous Mojave sky—me with my arm out the open window and my hand rising and falling in the current of warm air, and my dad with a beer between his legs, laughing at something I'd said. We were having an adventure, the two of us. I had never wanted that trip to end.

I heard my feet hitting the pavement. I heard my breaths, each exhalation a small emphatic grunt. It hurt and I wanted it to hurt more, so I pushed harder. I peeled off miles, ignoring the searing pain in my quads and the fire on the soles of my feet.

Suddenly, my legs buckled and I struggled to stay upright. My muscles would no longer do what I asked them to do. I thought I might be having a seizure. I doubled over and vomited. I wiped my mouth with the back of my hand and willed myself to move forward. Then I vomited again. As if in a dream, I saw my crew approaching me, hands outstretched.

Somehow, with their help, I regained my composure and started moving forward again, using a strange hitching lock-kneed walk. Light leaked into the sky and the sun hit my face. I had fifty miles to go. I was not going to quit. I was going to get to that finish even if I had to crawl up the Whitney Portal Road on all fours.

I passed through Panamint Springs at seventy-two miles, then the Darwin turnoff at ninety miles, then Lone Pine, the tiny outpost town at the base of Mount Whitney, at 122 miles. At dusk, I turned up the Portal Road and saw the runners who had already finished being driven back down the road in support cars. The drivers honked their horns, and the passengers hung out the window and cheered. I tried to stand up straighter and look strong, at least for a few strides. The air was cooler and smelled of pine. When I looked back, I could see dozens of small white lights—the headlamps of racers on the long road behind me. This was my struggle; they had theirs. Everyone ahead of me and everyone behind me—and every member of every crew—would have his own story.

At last, I reached the switchbacks, and finally, thirty-eight hours after I had started, I crossed the finish line. Somehow, I had come in eighth place. I was met with a smattering of applause and a few cheers. I think someone called out my name. My crew hugged me and helped me sit down. I read their faces; I must have looked like death. But I had done it. With their help, I'd finished Badwater.

Next time—and I was certain there would be a next time—I would be smarter. I would remember that going out too fast always cost at least double any time you had gained. I would deal with problems as soon as they came up. I had felt small blisters developing on the soles of my feet early in the race, but I ignored them because I didn't want to stop to treat them. By the time I looked at them, they were the size of coasters and the pain was almost unbearable. I'd keep my crew closer to me and drink more fluids. And I would train hard for the downhills, not just the uphills. I had to prepare my body for the punishment of the descents. The pounding had done me in. I wouldn't let that happen again.

- - - -

Two months later, I checked my backpack one last time before the start of the Gobi March. I had packed all the required gear, including the minimum fourteen thousand calories, which I had satisfied with about seven pounds of freeze-dried meals, PowerBars, oatmeal laced with Ensure protein powder, Oreo cookies, Snickers bars, and baggies full of smashed Fritos and potato chips. The pack seemed to grow heavier the closer we got to start time.

Spectators had been arriving all morning on donkeys, camels, bicycles, and motorbikes, and now they lined the top of the weathered remnants of the Great Wall of China and stood along the ropes that marked the first fifty yards of the course. I looked out at the terrain we were about to cross. I had expected the desolate flats, but not what lay beyond them—high peaks forming a forbidding-looking wall. We were going to have to go through those mountains.

"So, remind me when the Sherpas come for our packs?" I said to a cluster of lean, fast-looking racers.

No laughs. Not even a polite smile.

The countdown began. I got in a ready position and looked at my feet. Three—two—one. I and the forty-one other racers took off. Almost instantly, I was engulfed in a suffocating cloud of brown silt the consistency of powdered sugar. It was in my eyes, my mouth, and my nose. I couldn't see or breathe. I stumbled and regained my footing, then fought to get out of the middle of the pack so I wouldn't be in the front guys' dust. I knew I was going out too fast, but I had to get to clear air. I chased down the lead group, my backpack thudding on my shoulders. I was going at a full sprint—not at all how I had planned to start out. My chest burned and I felt my quads start to seize. I thought I might puke. I was only minutes into a six-day race and I was in the grips of an anaerobic emergency.

I knew I needed to calm down. I'd been in this situation before: the all-out effort, the pain, then the rising of a wild, fluttering panic, like a bird flushed from a thicket. The only way out was to relax. Let your body do its job. Breathe. I started to feel a little better as I settled into a rhythm that I could maintain. At last, I was in clear air. Running shoulder to shoulder with the lead group, I waited to see what they would do. When they sped up, I hit the gas. When they slowed down, I eased off. We were testing each other, looking for that sweet-spot pace that would allow us to survive while keeping us out front.

I looked ahead, seeking out the small flags that we were told would mark the route. In the distance, I noticed a small dust cloud. It wasn't big enough to be kicked up by a support vehicle. An animal, maybe? I watched the puff move steadily forward.

"What's that?" I said to the guy on my right.

"What?" He matched me stride for stride.

"Out there. The dust. Something's kicking it up. See it?"

"Yeah. Got to be Kevin. Sub-two-thirty marathon. Guy's a rocket."

Kevin Lin, a five-foot-four-inch, twenty-six-year-old Taiwanese grad student, crushed me and everyone else on that first day. He also won Stage Two, a thirty-five kilometer canyon trek that included ten river crossings. Stage Three required some orienteering and I was able to make up time as Kevin got lost for a while. That seemed to scare him enough to make him dial back his pace. As he slowed, I sped up, and by the end of the day I had closed the gap on him to about thirty minutes.

Stage Four was forty-three kilometers across high plains. Kevin and I ran together for the first ten miles. His English wasn't great, so we ran mostly in silence. When we arrived together at a calm emerald lake at about fourteen thousand feet, we stopped to check it out. I dipped my hand into the frigid water and brought my fingers to my mouth. It was salty and bitter.

"Charlie," Kevin said. I looked up and he was smiling and holding over his head a set of yak horns he had found. I laughed and took a picture of him. Then he pointed at me and I handed him the camera, took the horns from him, and swiped on the ground with one foot like an angry bull.

After we had skirted the lake's edge, we started down a rocky slope and I saw a chance to make a move. After my experience with the downhill portion of Badwater, I'd put in months of training trying to get better at descents. Some of it was about foot placement and technique, but mostly it was about attitude, finding that happy medium between being on the brakes and being out of control. I knew if I was out of Kevin's sight, I would be harder to catch. And I knew I had better navigating skills than him. I pushed as hard as I could, rounding corners and scrambling over ledges. I imagined I was a mountain goat, sure-footed and fleet. It was one my best running days ever. By the end of that stage, I had taken the overall lead.

Kevin went out hard the next day, but I stayed with him. We seemed to have an understanding. We would run this stage together. We even waited for each other to pee or get a rock out of a shoe. Ed Poynton, a strong American runner living in Hong Kong, ran with us, too.

The final 10K stage began with a climb up and over a steep six-hundred-foot dune. Kevin was ahead of me as we struggled in the soft sand. When we finally crested the dune and made it down to a paved road, he sped out of view, as I knew he would. Even if he won that stage, though, I was pretty sure I had a big enough time cushion that he couldn't overtake me in the standings.

I chased Kevin past old beacon towers and through the streets of Dunhuang. Children in white shirts with red bandannas cheered and waved. Gongs sounded when I made the final turn into a court-yard of an ancient Ming Dynasty hotel. Kevin was waiting for me when I crossed the finish line. We high-fived and hugged. A Buddhist monk presented me with a medal. I had won the Gobi March. I had told my dad before I left for China that he could follow the race online. I wondered if he had checked to see how I was doing.

The following July, in another distant desert, Kevin and I went head-to-head again. This time we were in northern Chile for the 250K Atacama Crossing, a seven-day race that included a fifty-mile stage across the Valley of the Moon—terrain so desolate that NASA used it to test its Mars Rover vehicles. Stage One started out above the tree line at 13,500 feet in a tiny, abandoned village of clay-red houses. Kevin and I quickly put distance between ourselves and the rest of the pack. He was in superb shape and had kidded me about getting revenge for Gobi. I could feel him testing me, surging, then slowing down, then surging again to see if I would fold. I hung in there with him until he turned on the jets with a few miles to go. He beat me that first day by about forty-five seconds.

The second stage was across baked salt flats, a portion of which had a strange breakable crust. Kevin was fifty pounds lighter than me and seemed to dance across the fragile surface; I sank in with every step. When I finally got through the worst of it, I looked up and was surprised to see a figure in the distance. I got closer and saw that it was Kevin, standing there with his arms crossed.

"Why take so long?" he said, smiling.

We ran side by side again. There were no extended mountain passes or tricky technical downhills where I could use my expedition experience; all I could do was try to hang on. Nearing the end of the fifty-mile stage, Kevin surged ahead again. We both knew the only way he would lose the overall race was if he overslept or broke a leg. I could do nothing but enjoy the experience, shoulder to shoulder with my friend. We ran through cold slot canyons and past shallow lakes dotted with pale-pink Andean flamingos. We adopted a stray dog, who followed us out of a village one day despite our efforts to shoo him back. At night, when we stopped to camp, we gave him water and freeze-dried beans. "Arturo" stayed with us for the entire race.

On the final day, Kevin and I arrived together at the finish in the sunbaked town square of San Pedro de Atacama. He had beaten me by a little more than three minutes—but we both knew that he could have won by whatever margin he wanted. I was happy for him. A mutual friend had told me that the Gobi defeat had been difficult: Kevin was a superstar in Taiwan, sponsored by the state and under enormous pressure to perform. I understood how much this victory would mean to him back home.

We met again a few months later in the Jungle Marathon, a 220K stage race through the heart of the Brazilian Amazon. The race began poorly for me. I had planned to fly with Lisa Trexler, the woman I was dating, from North Carolina to Manaus. Lisa was attractive, with long chestnut-brown hair. She'd married at eighteen, had three children, and was divorced by thirty-one. Lisa hadn't traveled much, but she had an adventurous streak and was excited to be coming with me to the Amazon as a volunteer race worker.

Unfortunately, we missed our connecting flight in DC, which meant that we would also miss the steamboat that was ferrying racers and crew ten hours up the Tapajós River to base camp. I figured our Jungle Marathon was over before it began. I had already adjusted my thinking about the weekend—instead of wading with piranhas, I was going to be hanging out with Lisa and plowing through some pints of Ben & Jerry's and rented DVDs. Then the phone rang. It was Shirley Thompson, the race organizer, calling to say that if we could book another flight to Brazil, she'd find a way to get me to the starting line. Several hours later, Lisa and I were on a Manaus-bound plane.

Ten minutes before the race was scheduled to begin, the helicopter Shirley had arranged for us swooped low over the broad Amazon tributary and landed in a swirl of sand and debris on the riverbank beach. The only way I could have looked like more of a jackass was to have had "Ride of the Valkyries" playing as I stepped out of the chopper.

I spotted Kevin among the racers wiping sand from their eyes. He greeted me with a big hug. I said hello to a few runners I knew and introduced myself to some I didn't. One was Ray Zahab, a Canadian runner who was relatively new to the adventure-running world. He would tell me later, when we had gotten to be close friends, that on that first day when he shook my hand he thought, *Wow, this guy is a tool.* I didn't blame him. I would probably have said worse than that.

I adjusted my backpack shoulder straps and lined up with seventy-four other competitors under a starting-line banner. After that entrance, I felt pressure to have a strong showing. Kevin, Ray, and I surged to the front of the pack, along with several local runners who were fast even though they were either barefoot or in sandals, and carrying their race gear slung over their shoulders in plastic trash bags. I was embarrassed to be in my slick formfitting tank top and shorts and my expensive running shoes.

We came to a wide stream and had to swim. Once we scrambled up the slick riverbank on the other side, we were plunged into hilly, dense jungle. This was not a run; it was more of an obstacle course, with obstacles designed to maim. Trees sported thorns as big as knitting needles. Menacing roots seemed as if they might suddenly coil around your ankles as you tried to pick your way over them. Snakes slithered in the foul swampland ooze, and tarantulas dropped like hairy paratroopers from broad-leafed trees. It was the hardest first day of any ultra I had ever run. Somehow, though, I won the stage.

Day after day, we slogged our way in the saturated, overheated air through the jungle muck. At night, Ray and Kevin and I set up our camouflage hammocks near each other and cursed our fungal feet and the bugs and whatever mutant gene drove us to do these things to ourselves.

"This is really pretty stupid," I said.

"Yes. Stupid," Kevin said.

"Very, very stupid," Ray said.

We all laughed.

– – – –

"Tell me about Atacama," Ray said one night.

I told him about the baked red hills and the lunar salt flats. "It's the driest place in the world."

"Dry," Ray said. "God, I love dry."

"Me, too," I said.

"Dry is good," Kevin said.

"The sky must be amazing," Ray said.

"It's endless," I said. "One night, some astronomers showed up in our camp with these huge telescopes and let me look through. You can't really wrap your head around what you're seeing, you know? You feel so small."

"I like feeling that way," Ray said. "Small."

"It reminds you that you have no control over anything," I said.

"Atacama. I've got to do that one." Just as I was falling asleep, Ray spoke up again. "What's Gobi like?"

I described the ruins of the Great Wall and the yurts and the luminous rolling dunes.

"Yes," Kevin said. "Very nice. Big dunes."

"I've really got to do that one," Ray said.

"You really do," I said.

We were quiet again.

"Charlie?" Ray said.

"Yeah?"

"Did I tell you about the Marathon des Sables?"

"Yes, Ray. But you can tell me again."

Finally, he stopped talking and we lay there listening to the symphony of jungle noises. Some of the other racers were snoring loudly, competing with the bellows of howler monkeys.

After a while I heard Ray say in a comical stage whisper, "You still awake?"

"Uh-huh."

"I was just thinking,"

"Yeah?"

"I wonder if anyone has ever run across the Sahara Desert?"

"You mean, like, the whole thing?"

"Yeah," he said, "the whole way."

"Huh. Probably not."

"Yeah. Probably not."

Tomorrow was the longest stage—the one that would likely determine the victor. I had fallen back in the standings, but I thought I could handle the jungle better than anyone else there, and I was pretty sure I could win. I was right about that. But instead of imagining that moment of victory when I closed my eyes, I saw desert: clean bright bands of sky and sand. And I saw the horizon, that horizon that was always pulling you forward, always receding. *That would be something*, I thought as I felt myself finally dropping into sleep. *Really something. To run across the Sahara.*

CHAPTER 8

Don't loaf and invite inspiration; light out after it with
a club, and if you don't get it you will nonetheless get
something that looks remarkably like it.
    —JACK LONDON, "Getting into Print: An Essay"

Back home, I did some research and found no evidence that anyone had, in fact, ever run coast-to-coast across the Sahara. That
just fanned the fantasy: "firsts" in the adventure world were almost
impossible to come by. I spent hours looking at maps, tracing my finger in a meandering diagonal line from Senegal through Mauritania,
Mali, Niger, Libya, to Egypt and the Red Sea. The more I studied it,
the more I became convinced that it could be done—and that Ray
and I were just the nutjobs to do it. The life-altering conversation I
had with him went something like this:
    "Hey, Ray."
    "Hey, Charlie."
    "So, you wanna run across the Sahara Desert with me?"
    "I would love to run across the Sahara Desert with you."
    And like that, the Running the Sahara 2006 expedition was born.
Ray and I wanted a third runner to join us—and we agreed it had to
be Kevin. When I reached him in Taiwan, Kevin said yes right away.
(Though his English had improved from when we first met, I wondered
if he understood exactly what I was asking him to do.) I calculated—and
seriously underestimated—the distance we'd have to run to be about
four thousand miles. If we aimed to complete it in about three months,

which I figured to be the longest amount of time that the runners or support crew could tolerate, we'd need to run about fifty miles a day for eighty days. If things went well, maybe we'd even get some days off.

I told anyone within earshot that my friends and I were going to run across the Sahara Desert. Lisa said she was excited for me, even though we both knew that my going off to Africa for three months was not conducive to a meaningful relationship. We had talked about marriage. Our kids got along great, and even Pam sometimes came over when both families were getting together. But I just wasn't ready—and I don't think Lisa was, either. We needed time. Still, we wanted to stay together and made tentative plans for her to visit at Christmastime, when I guessed we would be somewhere in Niger.

- - - -

Several colleagues said they thought the run would make a great film. A buddy of mine knew James Moll, a director who had won an Academy Award for a documentary he'd made with Steven Spielberg about Hungarian Holocaust survivors. He suggested I go talk to James and helped set up a meeting.

As I drove to Warner Bros. Studios, I rehearsed what I planned to say. I hoped James might be intrigued enough to connect me with some scrappy student filmmaker who wanted an adventure. I got lost on the huge back lot, dodged a studio tour tram filled with sightseers who looked disappointed that I was a nobody, and rushed in, late and apologetic.

James, a friendly, athletic-looking guy about my age, offered me a seat. Then I launched in. *The Sahara. Four thousand miles. Three friends. Top runners. Do the impossible. Dunes. Tuareg nomads. Land mines. Two marathons a day. Camels. Heat. Mirages. Sand. Oases. Pyramids. The Red Sea. Never been done. Because it's there! Our North Pole! Our Everest!* I took a breath. Sweat trickled down from my temples. James gave me a close-lipped smile and nodded while he waggled a pen between his thumb and index finger. Then he stood up. The meeting seemed to be over, so I stood up, too.

He extended his hand. "Okay. I'll do it."

"You'll . . . do it?"

"Yeah. If you do this, I'm there with cameras. Let me make some calls and set up meetings with production companies. I'll get back to you."

I walked to my car in a daze. An Oscar-winning director had just told me he wanted to make a movie about Kevin, Ray, and me running across the Sahara Desert. Which meant that—holy *shit*—we actually had to *run* across the Sahara Desert.

I called my mother to tell her about the meeting.

"That's wonderful, Charlie. Follow your dreams."

"Thanks, Mom."

"You really are going to see the whole world, aren't you? I love your passion, even though you are a little crazy."

"Well, I get that from you." I laughed.

"Me? No," she said quietly. "I . . . just . . ."

There was a long silence.

"Mom?"

Nothing.

"Are you okay?"

"I don't know," she said. "Today I . . ."

"What?"

"Today I got lost on my way home from the grocery store."

"Really?"

"Yes."

"You've always had a lousy sense of direction."

"No. This was different. I didn't know where I was. Nothing looked familiar, and it's the same route I've been taking for years."

My throat tightened. My grandmother—my mother's mother— had suffered from Alzheimer's for years before her death. "I'm sure it's nothing, Mom."

"Where did you say you were going?"

"The Sahara. I'm going to run across the desert."

"Good for you, Charlie. Follow your dreams."

- - - -

A little more than a week after our meeting, James called and said the production company LivePlanet was interested in partnering with him on our project. They loved the enormity of the physical and mental challenge—and the potential the film had to shine a light on the difficulties faced by the people living in the North African desert.

"Matt Damon and Ben Affleck own the company," he said.

"Uh-huh."

"Matt wants to produce and narrate the film—if that's okay with you?"

"Matt *Damon* wants to narrate." I nearly choked. "Well, I was hoping for someone better. . . ."

James laughed.

Armed with the Matt Damon news, I decided it was a good time to call my father. I hadn't mentioned the Sahara idea to him yet.

"What?" he said. "What about your job?"

"This is an incredible opportunity, Dad."

"How are you going to make a living?"

"I'll figure it out. This could lead to some amazing things for me."

"Shit, Charlie. When are you going to stop this nonsense?"

"Never, I hope," I snapped.

I did have to quit my job at *Extreme Makeover: Home Edition*—planning the expedition required my full attention—but I had money in the bank thanks to some real estate investments I'd made with profits from the hail business. I'd started in the mid-1990s with two vacant lots and a small house, which I renovated, at Sunset Beach in North Carolina. When their values started to climb, I sold them. I had great credit and enough money to keep rolling into the next property. When Mom moved to Cape Charles, Virginia, a small Eastern Shore town that seemed about to boom thanks to a big golf resort that was being developed, I bought two properties there. I figured I could sell one or both if I had to.

Marc Joubert, one of the LivePlanet producers, called and invited me to New York. Matt Damon, I was excited to hear, wanted to go for a run with me. I met them both on a street corner in lower Manhattan.

Matt looked like any other fit guy in a baseball hat and running clothes until he shook my hand and flashed his movie-star smile. "Take it easy on me."

I smiled back. "Don't worry, I promised I would return you unharmed."

I had no intention of running Matt Damon into the ground. We ran at a casual pace through the streets of SoHo. It was fun to watch people's reactions as we went by. Some lit up with recognition and elbowed each other. Some shouted, "Hey, Matt!" or "Jason Bourne!" We covered a little over ten miles, and after we finished, we stood and talked for a while. Matt said he had never been to Africa, but hoped to get there soon. He asked me if I had any races coming up. I told him I was doing Badwater again in July.

"Badwater?"

"One hundred and thirty-five miles across Death Valley. It's usually about 130 degrees. One of my favorite races."

"I don't understand how you do that." He laughed. "I can't run more than twelve miles. After that, my body starts breaking down."

"No, it doesn't. You could go farther. You just have to reconfigure your relationship to pain."

- - - -

I got busy meeting with potential sponsors and investors, building a support team and mapping out the daunting logistics. I was also training hard for Badwater, not wanting a repeat of the miserable race I had in 2003. This time I paced myself well, had a great crew, and finished third, an improvement of more than ten hours from my first try. I was getting the hang of this.

In October, I enlisted my friend Donovan Webster, a *National Geographic* writer, to accompany me on a scouting trip to Africa. With his professorial wire-rimmed glasses, close-cropped hair, and safari shorts, he was a kind of thinking man's Indiana Jones. Unlike me, Don had traveled in the Sahara and knew many people who could help us, including Mohamed Ixa, a prominent Tuareg leader and head of a top desert-guide company.

After meeting with Mohamed in Paris, we flew to Dakar, Senegal, and made our way a few hours north to Saint-Louis, a French colonial city at the mouth of the Senegal River. It had a New Orleans feel to it, especially at night: the jazz coming out of the small clubs, the smell of fish and delta mud, the weight of the air. A multi-arched steel bridge spanned the river. Cross it and you were on mainland Africa on the westernmost edge of the Sahara. As soon as I saw it, I had no doubt: our journey would start here.

We moved on to Agadez, Niger, where we got a promise of support from UNICEF, and then flew to Cairo. Without an appointment, we went to the office of Zahi Hawass, the famed archaeologist who was Egypt's head of antiquities. When his secretary told him Don Webster was here, Hawass invited us in right away. Don seemed to know everyone, everywhere. I was happy I'd asked him to help me direct the expedition—and floored when Hawass said he would allow our film crew access to areas not open to the public.

Throughout the scouting trip, Don and I talked about water. Keeping hydrated would be the runners' biggest challenge. Thanks to LivePlanet and sponsors, we would have the resources to do that. Gatorade came on board and planned to use Kevin, Ray, and me as test subjects. We laughed about sacrificing ourselves to the Sahara for the sake of science, but for most of the desert people, hydration was a serious concern. The struggle for water defined their daily lives. I learned dirty water and poor sanitation caused 80 percent of illnesses in Africa—and one out of every five deaths of children under the age of five was due to a water-related disease.

I wanted to use the Sahara run to raise money, and I knew now where we could put our fund-raising energy. When I got home, I, along with Matt Damon and LivePlanet, created H2O Africa, the charitable arm of Running the Sahara, with the goal of bringing clean water to some of the communities on our route.

- - - -

How do you prepare to run two marathons a day, mostly on sand, for three straight months, often in hundred-plus heat? We had no training manuals or guides *For Dummies* to give us tips. Kevin, Ray, and I had to devise our own plans. I did know that we were not training to get faster; we were training to stay healthy under extreme duress. I logged about a hundred miles per week, lifted weights, and did yoga to balance out my fitness. Most of my runs were between ten and thirty miles, but some days I did half a dozen shorter ones so I could get used to starting and stopping and starting again. If I was going to the store, I would run for half an hour before getting in the car. Then, after I got home and unloaded the groceries, I went back out and did a quick ten miles. I came back, made calls, threw a load of laundry in, and went out for another hour. I forced myself to run at all times of day—especially those times when I didn't feel like running.

Ray, Kevin, and I talked a lot about food: what to eat, when to eat, and how to eat. I had been a vegetarian for years and wasn't sure what foods would even be available in the desert. Like most runners, we usually waited awhile after a meal before heading out, but in the desert we wouldn't have that luxury. Nutritionists at Gatorade advised us to take in about ten thousand calories a day; most of those calories would have to be eaten while we ran. To train my body to digest on the fly, I forced as much food into my stomach as possible before I ran. I hated starting out with a full belly, but I knew I had to get used to it.

\- - - -

We planned to start the expedition in March 2006. Any later and we would bump into summer heat. I thought Ray, Kevin, and I could handle it, but I worried about our crew and the production team. Then, I got the bad news that some of the financing for the film had fallen through. We had to push the start date back to September, and then again to November, while the producers sought more investors. Even with Matt Damon as the executive producer, financing a film such as this was difficult.

My own financial situation was getting trickier as the weeks and months ticked by. I'd put up the money for the scouting trip and for other travel associated with the expedition, and though I was promised reimbursement by the production company, I was carrying heavy balances on my credit cards. I was also paying several mortgages and sending Pam alimony and child support every month. Plus, a home-renovation business I had invested in was not panning out the way I had hoped it would.

I took a trip up to Cape Charles to visit my mother and to talk to my real estate broker about putting one of my properties on the market. When I came back from my meeting with the broker, I found my mother sitting at the kitchen table, staring straight ahead. A pen and paper were on the table in front of her.

"I forgot how to spell *the*," she said before I even said hello.

"What do you mean?"

"I was writing a letter and misspelled the word *the*. I knew I had spelled it wrong, but then I couldn't think of how to fix it. Such a simple word."

"You're probably just tired. Don't worry about it."

But I knew she was worried. We both were.

Not long after my visit, Mom went to Emory University for tests. A doctor told her it was early-onset Alzheimer's. She was sixty-three years old. I told her I wanted to call off the expedition so I could spend more time with her, but she insisted that I go.

"I'll be fine. Go on now and don't worry about me. You've made big plans and commitments to people."

She was right. I had a contract with LivePlanet. We had investors and sponsorships. Ray and Kevin were counting on me. I was too far in to back out now even if I wanted to. My mom would have been pissed if she thought I was canceling the trip on her account. She had always encouraged me to be free and live my own life, and that's what I was doing, even if my heart was aching to stay close to her.

Just before I left for Senegal, my broker called to say she had an offer on the condo—but it was for roughly $100,000 less than what I had paid for it. I didn't understand how it could have lost so much value. Maybe the appraisal I'd gotten when I purchased the property had been wrong. Something was off, but I didn't have time to deal with it. I signed power of attorney over to my accountant,

David Johnston, who said he would get answers from the lenders—and try to negotiate a restructured deal in my absence. In the meantime, I made the difficult decision to stop making payments on the properties—not because I didn't have the money, but because the values of both were plummeting. I felt uneasy; I had never missed a payment or gotten behind on paying for a property since my first house in Monterey. But I believed David would come up with a plan and everything would work out.

CHAPTER 9

When you go far, far beyond, out across the netherlands
of the known, the din of human static slowly fades away,
over and out.

    —ROB SCHULTHEIS, *Fool's Gold: Lives, Loves, and*
      Misadventures in the Four Corners Country

On November 1, 2006—two years after Ray and I had first joked
about running across the Sahara, our team gathered at a picnic table
at Zebrabar, a campground and rustic resort on the sandy east bank
of the Senegal River. It was the first time we were all together: Don,
Mohamed, James, Ray, Kevin; Jeffrey "Doc" Peterson, a sports medicine physician, and Chuck Dale, a massage therapist and friend
who had crewed for me at Badwater. We had a map unfolded on a
table and were going over the plan for the next morning, when we
would begin the run. Except for the big green bottles of Gazelle
beer on the table and the pervasive smell of dead fish, the scene
reminded me of an AA meeting. "One day at a time" would be our
mantra, too.

James had once asked me what I thought this film would be
about. I said I didn't know, but I was certain that if three guys ran
across the Sahara Desert, some shit would happen. We had laughed
about that, but it was the truth. There was no storyboard to follow;
no script to consult. We agreed it was best to keep contact between
the runners and the production crew to a minimum. We would run.
They would follow us in trucks and film.

"If you miss a shot of us running over a dune," I said. "We aren't going to do it again."

James assured me he wouldn't ask us to do anything that wasn't organic to the expedition.

That night, I lay sweating under mosquito netting in a tiny, airless bungalow. I could hear big river crabs bumping up against the outside walls, and workers banging pots in the restaurant. After a few more sleepless hours, I heard the film production crew get up. I knew it was time. I sat up in bed, swung my feet down to the sandy floor, and took a deep breath. I rattled off the Serenity Prayer in my head, something I did every morning.

When I was using drugs, people were always telling me I was crazy. I could stay up later and do more drugs than anyone else they knew. *Hell yeah*, I used to think. *Crazy!* I loved being crazy. Why would I want to be a run-of-the-mill addict? I wanted to be different, to be extreme. I liked putting that pipe to my lips and watching people's eyes get big as I inhaled. I got a rush thinking about the risks of the next hit and the next. When I got sober, a part of me worried that my life would be intolerably boring. Where would I get that kind of marrow-deep thrill? I found it first in marathon running, and when marathons became routine, I found it in adventure racing and in ultras. The more "out there" the challenge, the more people told me I was *crazy*, the happier I felt.

But, sitting there on that low bed, listening to the voices of the people I had convinced to join me in this particular insanity, I felt queasy and anxious. I was a champion salesman, and this was the biggest deal I had ever closed. I had assured Matt Damon—Matt fucking Damon—that three men could run across the Sahara Desert. I'd promised Kevin and Ray that the financing was there and the support crew was prepared and that James Moll would not make us look like jackasses. But I didn't know if these things were true.

Plus, one big hole remained in our itinerary. We did not have permission from Libyan officials to enter their country. Don had been working on it for months, but still had no answer. What if we reached the border and couldn't continue? Or, what if something awful happened en route—one of us was kidnapped—or even killed? Why had I conned these nice people into following me to their doom in the desert?

– – – –

A helicopter hovered overhead while James, wearing a safari hat and vest, shouted directions. Ray, Kevin, and I walked to the water's edge on a garbage-strewn Saint-Louis beach shared by fishermen and cows and feral cats. We waded knee-deep into the Atlantic and gave each other high fives. After we had posed for snapshots, we dried our feet and put on our running shoes. I pushed the button on my watch as I had done so many times in my life and started to run. Mohamed and Don followed us in a red Toyota 4Runner, hazard lights flashing, as we made our way past honking taxis, horse-drawn carts, market tables piled high with green melons, and groups of women in bright dresses balancing bowls on their heads.

"Can you believe it? Can you believe we've actually started?" I shouted to Ray and Kevin as we headed across the long bridge to the mainland.

"Only 6,499 kilometers to go!" Ray said.

One of the production guys ran up to us. "Hey, Charlie. James wants you to run across the bridge again."

"Shit. *Seriously?*"

We went back and started again.

– – – –

Eventually, we ran away from the congested city and into the Sahel, the hardscrabble zone between the true desert and the humid grasslands to the south. Acacia trees and clusters of pale adobe houses dotted the brown expanse. Kevin, in dark glasses, ran straight-faced and silent. Ray and I were shoulder to shoulder, giggling like kids, waving and saying to everyone we saw, *"Bonjour, bonjour!"*

"Cairo?" I shouted to some construction workers sitting under a tree. I pointed east. "Cairo? This way?" They lifted their hands in a puzzled salute.

Our general plan was to run about twelve hours a day, heading out before dawn, then taking a break in the midday heat, and starting again in the afternoon. Our team would drive roughly five kilometers ahead of us and be ready with drinks, food, and first aid when we reached them. The goal was to get us in and out quickly, like a crew at a NASCAR pit stop. When we quit for the night, they would have camp waiting.

James and the full production team would be with us shooting for the first ten days, then they would rejoin us in the middle of the expedition somewhere around Agadez, Niger—and again at what we all hoped would be the triumphant end on the shore of the Red Sea. At least one cameraman would be with us the entire way—and I would supplement their footage with my own video camera.

We ran about twenty-two miles and reached a reservoir and cement tower that marked the border between Senegal and Mauritania. Thanks to our humanitarian goals, we had gotten the support of the United Nations before we left. We hoped that would ease our way across borders, but apparently these guards hadn't gotten the memo. The sight of the twenty of us—three runners and a half dozen support people, two camera crews and trucks loaded with gear—must have been overwhelming to them.

"What's going on?" I asked Don after he had conferred with the guards.

"Most of Mohamed's guys only carry their local ID cards. They're nomads who consider the entire Sahara their home and see no need for passports."

The Mauritanian government did not agree. We sat in the hot sun and swatted mosquitoes while Don and Mohamed made phone calls and talked to officials. Hours went by.

"This is torture," I said, as we watched other travelers being allowed over the border. We were already behind schedule.

It was dark when a Mauritanian guard lifted the red-and-white metal gate and allowed us to run through.

"*Merci!*" Ray said.

On our second day, with the ground temperature at a withering

140 degrees, Kevin, the smallest of us, showed signs of severe dehydration. We had to stop several times so Doc could hook him up to an IV. When Kevin felt better, we ran again. Then Ray cramped up and felt nauseated, and he, too, needed intravenous fluids. We got in thirty-five miles before we quit for the day.

Months before we stepped foot in the desert, I warned James and everyone on the expedition team that the runners would likely appear to be on death's door, especially in the first days of the expedition. That was the way it went with long runs: you had to tumble into the pit of ruin before you could claw your way out. But when you got out, you would be stronger in every way. That was what endurance was all about. They said they understood, but now that we were in the middle of the breakdown phase, they were spooked.

- - - -

To be honest, I had some serious concerns about Kevin and Ray, too. They were both exceptional runners. I had seen their toughness and determination in the Amazon and elsewhere. I didn't understand why they seemed so beaten down after just four days. We had talked for hours about what it would be like. We knew it would be beyond anything else we had ever experienced—and that was one big reason it was worth doing. It seemed as if they weren't feeling what I was feeling: the exhilaration of being on the precipice, the rush of being pushed to the breaking point. I knew they could do this, but I wasn't sure they knew it.

On day five, when things should have been turning around for us, Kevin and Ray both felt worse.

During our lunch break, Doc pulled me aside. "You can't keep pushing them like this!"

"We have to keep moving. I'm already getting flack from Live-Planet about being behind schedule."

"I don't care about your production!" Doc barked. "You'll be running alone if you keep this up." I understood that it was difficult for him, as a doctor, to see us in pain. His instinct was to do everything he could to ease suffering.

"Look, I know this goes against your training, but this is what we all signed up for," I said firmly. "You have to adjust your standards."

We both took a deep breath and settled on a compromise. Doc asked me to at least alter the plan—run at night and sleep during the day. I agreed to try it for a few days, but we found it impossible to sleep in the savage afternoon heat. Harassed by mosquitoes and flies and scarab beetles, Kevin, Ray, and I sweated more lying on our thin foam mats in our tents than we did when we were running. Now we were dehydrated *and* sleep deprived.

We tried another approach: take a longer break in the middle of each day.

Both Kevin and Ray had developed tendinitis in their lower legs, and my right knee was hurting. (I'd had surgery on it earlier in the year, but I'd kept quiet about it. I didn't want anyone worrying about my ability to complete this expedition.) I was sure that most of our issues were because we weren't taking in enough fluids. To accommodate our injuries, we adjusted our gaits, which slowed our pace. By day six, we had run just 136 miles—less than half of what we should have logged.

We had reached the paved Trans-Mauritanian Highway, a straight road that shot across the baked plains and disappeared in a shimmering mirage on the horizon. Trucks and cars barreled past at a hundred miles per hour, blinding us in swirls of sand and choking exhaust. The Mauritanian government had built a few wells in this area, and the water attracted nomads and their livestock. Fast cars and big animals were not a good combination. Every hundred yards or so, we came upon the stinking corpse of a dead donkey, goat, sheep, cow, dog, or camel. Vultures perched on the carcasses, or on the mangled and burned-out cars that hadn't survived the collisions, and eyed us as we went by.

"He thinks we look like lunch," I said about one massive buzzard that seemed to have drawn a bead on us.

"Not yet, buddy," Ray said. "Check in with us in an hour."

By day seven, Kevin was in such bad shape it seemed he might have to quit running. I felt terrible for him, but I had made it clear before the expedition began that we wouldn't be able to wait for anyone for more than a few hours if he was having serious issues. We had to keep moving. The LivePlanet execs implied they would pull the plug if we got too far behind schedule. I didn't think they would—not at this early stage anyway—but I was aware they were spending more than $3 million on the film. We had to suck it up and get in the miles.

– – – –

And then, after ten torturous days, we all started to feel better. It was as if our bodies said, "Okay, I get it, you're trying to kill me. Time to make some adjustments."

On day eleven, we all ran well. Nobody vomited, nobody needed IVs, nobody looked as if he wanted to die—or strangle me.

"It's like a whole new expedition!" Don said with happy wonder during our midday break. "If we keep it up, we might actually be able to do this."

It was good to hear that. I needed his full support—and I needed him to project confidence to Mohamed and his crew. If they started to think we weren't going to make it, they might bail on us. If that happened, we were done. I also needed Don to assure the producers that we were making good progress. More than anything, I wanted him and the others to trust me. I believed we could run across the Sahara Desert—if we just stuck to the plan. I needed everyone else to believe it, too.

One afternoon, after a solid morning run, we stopped to tour a United Nations Development Programme water project being built to supply a thousand people with water for drinking and farming. In Mauritania and other sub-Saharan countries, decades of severe drought and overgrazing had led to the desertification of what had once been arable land. Herders were forced to abandon their livestock and settle in cities, where they almost always fell into extreme poverty. With water projects such as this, which we learned cost about $10,000 each, the nomadic people had a shot at survival.

Through a translator, I asked a man how much he was being paid to work in the fields.

He looked puzzled. The translator asked him again. He smiled. "No pay."

"Then, why are you working so hard?" I asked.

"He says it is to create a better life for his children," the translator said. "If the village grows enough crops, they can sell the excess and earn money to build a school."

I was humbled by the simplicity of his dreams. This man wanted a better life for his kids, same as me. But he wasn't hoping to buy them a bike or a video game; he wanted them to get an education — and water was the key to that. He gave a face to our mission and made me even more determined to help.

After we visited the wells, the locals threw us a little party in a Berber-style tent. We feasted on spicy couscous stew and olives and fresh-baked flat bread slathered in camel butter. Colorfully dressed women danced, and singers ululated for us. I was coerced onto a camel and bumped around in a circle to the howling delight of the crowd.

- - - -

At night, I looked at pictures of my sons. I had spoken with them a few times on the satellite phone since we'd left Senegal. They sounded good, busy, happy. We talked about how the Tar Heels were looking and what cool things my boys had planned for the weekend. They wanted to know if I had seen any scorpions. (Several had crawled over my feet while I was talking to them on the phone, but when I told them, they didn't believe me.) I said I loved them. It was important to me to say those words every time I spoke to my kids. I hadn't heard them from my own father until I was thirty years old.

- - - -

We continued across the barren, heat-blasted flats of Mauritania. The harmattans had come in from the east, the winds strafing the gravel plains and dimming the sun with dust. Though it was ninety-five degrees, we put on long-sleeved shirts, pants, gloves, and ski masks to protect ourselves. My nose started to bleed and wouldn't stop.

"I haven't had one of these since I stopped doing blow," I said with a laugh, my head tipped back, as Doc tried to stop the bleeding. He smiled and rolled his eyes. Everyone there knew my history.

Most of the locals we encountered were friendly. Some waved or turned their palms skyward as if to say, "What are you up to?"

"That's the Mauritanian version of WTF," I said to Ray.

"Cairo!" I shouted happily. "Pyramids!"

Sometimes, Ray, who was fluent in French, stopped to talk with villagers. I envied his ability to communicate with them.

"They have no idea where Cairo is," Ray said after one exchange. "Or what the Pyramids are." We were truly in one of the most isolated places in the world.

Occasionally, things happened that reminded us we were in a tumultuous region. Pickup trucks filled with armed men sometimes came alongside us and slowed to a menacing crawl. Political caravans rolled by with loudspeakers blaring. Mauritania was about to have its first free election since 1961. One group handed out pink armbands and we put them on, trying to fit in. We realized that was not the best idea when the green party drove past us and pelted us with chicken bones.

On the evening of November 15, we arrived in Kiffa, a city of about thirty thousand. Drifted sand all but obscured the narrow streets. We ran through a market, past carts piled with oranges and bananas. Men holding big butcher knives stood over fresh goat carcasses waiting to hack whatever animal part their customers requested.

We set up our tents under a shelter at an auberge on the far edge of town. I took a shower in a trickle of lukewarm, rusty-smelling water and shaved for the first time since Senegal. Then we all went to bed. It was impossible to sleep. The night was full of city sounds—grinding truck gears, yapping dogs, raised voices. Just before dawn, the call to prayer wailed over loudspeakers at the nearby mosque. I couldn't wait to get back out into the quiet of the desert.

The days went by in mind-numbing uniformity. Up at 4:00 a.m., coffee, breakfast, run until noon, lunch, rest, run until 7:00 p.m. It was the time after the running that I found most difficult. As expedition leader, I had to deal with logistics and problems that popped up during the day, and there was always something. An argument about whose turn it was to use the satellite phone. Ray needed more running shoes. Someone had gotten to use the computer just as the battery was dying. The constant back-and-forth with our producers in LA about the budget and schedule. By the time I crawled into my sleeping bag, I was wiped out. And I knew that, in just a few hours, I'd get up and do it all over again.

The good news was that Kevin, Ray, and I were getting stronger every day. Some of our injuries had healed as we ran—and some we had accepted would be with us for the duration. Doc treated our blisters and aches each night, but he had stopped thinking he had to make everything right. We were running roughly two marathons a day, every day. He got it: this would hurt.

The bigger challenge was dealing with the tedium of running. Besides several audio books, including biographies of Bill Clinton and Barack Obama, Khaled Hosseini's *The Kite Runner*, Cormac McCarthy's *The Road*, and Max Brooks's *World War Z*—all of which I listened to at least twice—I had loaded fifteen hundred songs on my iPod, everything from Eminem to Mariah Carey to Linkin Park. I put the music on "shuffle" and commanded myself to never skip a song. I believed the one that came on was the one I was meant to hear at that moment. I would not mess with the iPod DJ gods. Still, the "random" selections were exasperating; songs didn't seem to play with equal frequency. (When I was home, I checked the playlist statistics and found out that my suspicions were correct. Train's "Meet Virginia" came up nine times; Johnny Cash's "Ring of Fire" played forty-three times. No wonder I had that damn song stuck in my head.) Ray had only 250 songs on his iPod, so he had to face even more repeats. He told me one day he had listened to Led Zeppelin's "Stairway to Heaven" twenty-three times in a row. We never knew what Kevin was listening to, but he often put on his headphones at breakfast and kept them on until dinner. I sometimes wondered if he was listening to anything at all or if the headphones were just his way of saying, *Leave me alone*.

When we weren't listening to music, Ray and I talked in circles, cracking ourselves up. We quoted movies, and Ray bored me with talk of how good Canadians were at everything. We talked about what color our poop was that morning and how much we were farting. Ray went on and on about how much he missed his wife, Kathy. Kathy does this and Kathy says that. I had never seen anyone so in love. It drove me insane.

"You owe me a dollar every time you say her name," I teased him.

"Kathy, Kathy, Kathy, Kathy, Kathy," Ray taunted, and I sprinted away from him howling.

We also amused ourselves by teaching Kevin English curse words. We started with *motherfucker*, one of my favorites for its versatility and the way it rolls off the tongue. First, I made sure that Kevin understood that *motherfucker* was one word, not two, a common mistake made by rookies. Next, we worked on intonation, beginning with the cheerful "Hey there, what's up, motherfucker?" to the angry "Get your hands off me, motherfucker" to the slow, emphatic "Moth*erfffucker*"—so useful when you missed a flight or dropped your cell phone in the toilet. Kevin caught on quickly.

Some mornings Ray picked out what he called the word of the day—*perfect* was one—and used it so often that by the end of the day Kevin and I wanted to strangle him. And we told each other jokes, the same ones again and again. One of my standards was something I had heard long ago from an AA sponsor.

"Hey, Ray," I said. "You know how to eat an elephant?"

"No, Charlie. How do you eat an elephant?"

"One bite at a time."

One bite at a time. That was the only way to deal with the enormity of what lay ahead. Focus on the present: this footstep and this footstep and this footstep. When the morning miles accumulated, twenty-two, twenty-three, twenty-four, twenty-five, I allowed myself to think about lunch. After lunch and a rest, it would begin again.

This step, that step, this step . . . until we had logged our second twenty-five miles and we could stop for the night.

Some days, though, I commanded myself to see, really *see*, where I was, to not lose myself in music or mind games. To hear the high-pitched wind, feel the sand needling my shins, take in the bigness and the beauty of the Sahara. And, my God, it was beautiful: the crescent dunes in late-day shadow, the silhouette of a camel train led by men in robes; the red rocks that rose like citadel towers out of the dust and haze. Every day, I thanked my higher power for bringing me to this place.

- - - -

On day twenty-seven I could hear Kevin vomiting outside his tent. I looked at my watch: 3:30 a.m. He'd gone to bed saying he didn't feel well. We had all hoped he'd be better after he got some sleep. I heard him retch violently again.

By 5:00 a.m., everyone, including Kevin, was up. I could tell he didn't want to run.

"Let's just try," I said.

"I don't know," he said.

"Just see how you feel. Once you are moving."

We took two hours to cover five miles.

"You're doing great, Kev," I lied. But after another hour of watching him shuffling and wincing, I couldn't take it any longer. I knew he needed a break. We stopped and Doc gave Kevin two full bags of IV fluids. Then we all waited while he slept. At 2:00 p.m., he got up and said he would try again.

"You're a tough man, Kev," I said.

While Kevin was an experienced runner, this kind of suffering was new to him. From a young age, he was groomed to be a super-star. Many Taiwanese were surprised by his desire to go beyond marathon running. But I understood it. Kevin, like Ray and like me, had a void that could only be filled by pushing himself beyond his limits. I don't think Kevin fully recognized this yet, but I knew. I wanted him to dig deep, to see where this suffering would take him. But on that afternoon, he could not make himself go. I saw the pleading in his eyes. It was pointless to keep pushing him.

I asked Mohamed to find us a good place to rest. He set up camp on a nearby dune. I walked away from the others, laid out my small foam mat, and sat down. All around me was an immense sand sea, with waves pushed by the wind into nearly perfect parallel lines. In my hand, I held a small white seashell I had found earlier that day. I turned it over in my palm, studying its ancient whorls.

It was November 28 and we had been in the desert for nearly one month. We had run roughly one thousand miles and had three thousand more to go. Tomorrow was my son Kevin's twelfth birthday. I thought about him opening presents and blowing out the candles on his cake. I wondered if my mother had sent a card, then I pictured her alone and at her small kitchen table, holding a pen over a blank paper, unable to write. I felt sick with guilt. What was I doing on top of a sand dune in Mali?

I had no choice but to believe that what I was doing was making me a better person, a better father, a better son. And I hoped H2O Africa would improve the lives of hundreds, maybe thousands, of people. I wanted my boys to see me following my dreams. I wanted them to see that life was about finding your own passion. I knew my family was proud of me, but I also knew deep down that they probably just wanted me to be around more.

- - - -

In midafternoon, we crested a dune and there it was at our feet: Timbuktu—sprawling all the way to the horizon. Once a vital intellectual, religious, and trade center, the legendary thousand-year-old city had lured Western explorers for centuries with the promise of streets of gold. But what they found—and what we saw up ahead—was no El Dorado. It was a dust-colored maze of windowless houses and shops. As we ran along the edge of town, we were joined by a dozen young men holding trinkets and blankets and bags, shouting, "Buy, buy!" At first it was pleasing to hear English—we had been away from the tourist zone for so long. But then more of them arrived and they pressed in on us, shouting and waving their goods in our faces, and quickly we'd had enough.

I was happy to get to the sanctuary of the small hotel. After a brief shower under a trickle of cold water, local officials drove us out to a walled compound for a dinner show—a kind of Mali luau put on for tourists. The food was bland and the drinks were warm, but the band, playing a sort of bluesy reggae, was fantastic. We laughed and lounged on pillows at low tables, happy to forget about our schedule and our aches and pains. When I'd first envisioned the expedition, I imagined us doing this kind of thing everywhere we went—soaking in culture, getting to know the locals. But we just didn't have time.

The next morning as the haunting call to prayer went out from the ancient mosques, we got up, had coffee and breakfast, and ran away from the city. It struck me as funny that we had made it all the way from Senegal to Timbuktu—a place used as a metaphor for the ends of the earth—and now we were going *beyond* it.

Just as the sun came up, we reached the northern banks of the Niger River. Along its edges, rice fields and gardens glowed a jarring electric green against the golden desert sand. Fishermen tossed nets from low pirogues. We followed the river until the town of Bourem, where it dove south. We would continue east overland, through the open desert of the Gao region.

We had been warned about the dangers in this area. Two rival tribes were fighting; visitors had been robbed, their vehicles hijacked. But, Mohamed, as usual, had a plan. He knew the leaders of both factions, having fought side by side with them in Tuareg uprisings, and he invited them both to join us for the week. He guaranteed them each a "contribution" once we had safely passed through Gao. I had my doubts, but Mohamed was a calm and confident diplomat. Not only did these men show up to shadow the expedition, they also seemed to take pride in what we were doing. Most remarkably, they got along like old pals. At night, they shared camp chores and sat side by side laughing and telling stories. When we were through Gao, the two leaders, who Mohamed told me later were cousins, and who hadn't spoken to each other in years, hugged and walked into the desert in opposite directions. A short time later they resumed their fighting.

We were closing in on the Mali border. That was the good news. The bad news was that most of the team had been battling nasty intestinal ailments for several days. Somehow, though, I had escaped. I jokingly told everyone that all the drugs I'd loaded into my system in my twenties had made it inhospitable to viruses. After one particularly rough night, I let the team have some extra rest, but I couldn't give us the day off.

We started our run, but by midmorning Ray was lying in the open doorway of his tent, groaning and pale and holding his head.

"Poor Ray," Don said. "It's okay, Ray."

I stood over him and watched him writhe. "Hey, does anybody want any of Ray's stuff . . . if he doesn't make it?"

"Bastard!" Ray moaned.

After a few hours of rest, Ray got up and said he could go. I knew he was afraid—not of being sick, but of letting the team down. I felt awful for him, watching him puke and run and puke and run again.

"You are one tough dude, Ray," I said.

"Tough motherfucker," Kevin said.

- - - -

A few days later, Don and Mohamed went ahead in the truck to break trail for us. When we caught up with them at dusk, Don quietly pointed out a young boy who was sitting alone in the sand, a short distance from the truck. He looked tiny in his tattered T-shirt and worn pants.

"We talked to him," Don said. "He told us his parents have gone to get water. He's been out here alone for two days. He only has camel's milk to drink and a few bits of dried meat."

Don had given him a box of cookies, some bottled water, and a plastic bag filled with fresh dates. I peered around the back of the truck to look. Abadu, Mohamed's son, was talking to the little boy. When Abadu came back, I handed him a small flashlight with a push button. Abadu understood that I meant for him to give it to the boy.

"Can I say hello to him?" I asked.

"Wait."

Abadu walked back over to the boy and handed him the light. I could hear Abadu's voice, low and comforting, as he talked to him. In a few moments, Abadu turned and waved me over. I walked toward them. As I got closer, the boy whimpered and shied away from me. I squatted down to his level when I got near him, but he would not meet my gaze. Abadu touched the boy's head and then mine, as if to say, *See, he is just like you, only with light skin and funny hair*. The boy seemed to relax. He glanced up at me.

"It's okay," I said quietly. "It's okay."

I wanted to tell him we were nice people and that we would help his family. But what could I say or do to change his situation? He had been left like this before and he would be left again. That was the way of the desert. We stayed with him for a few minutes, then said good-bye and walked back to the truck. When I looked back one last time, I could see the little light going on and off, illuminating the boy's face. I felt so helpless; I would never know if he was okay, if his parents had returned with water.

I felt that same despair a few days later when we came upon a man who had been looking for us. He had heard a doctor was in our group. His wife and their newborn baby were both ill and needed help right away. We climbed into Mohamed's truck and followed the man to a large rectangular tent that was open in the front and on one side.

Doc examined the mother and baby. He said they were both severely dehydrated. With no simple way to treat the baby, he focused on the mother. He gave her electrolyte pills and salt tablets along with several bottles of clean water from our stock. He mixed Gatorade and handed the bottles to the husband and, with Mohamed translating, told him how to administer the pills and how much she should drink. I wondered what they must have thought about the bright green Gatorade.

"Will they survive?" I asked Doc when we had left the tent.

"Maybe. The mom needs to get stronger or the baby won't make it."

If we had been traveling a mile farther south or north, we would never have known of their existence. The mother and baby would probably have died. How many other people were we passing by that were in dire need? Like so many people who had come before me, I wanted to help. But what did that mean? The Tuaregs had lived in this desert for thousands of years. Who was I to say, "Let me help you"?

- - - -

At last, we crossed from Mali into Niger. Now we were focused on Agadez—the halfway point of the expedition—and the place where, if all went well, sometime close to Christmas Day we would rendezvous with Lisa; Ray's wife, Kathy; and Kevin's girlfriend, Nicole.

I was excited to see Lisa and I felt strongly that she deserved this trip. She'd lived through the difficult planning stages and been a big help to me at home while I was away. But I was also stressed by the thought of her being with me in the Sahara. For weeks, it had been just the guys. Our days were filled with bad language and bad smells. All we had to think about was moving forward, fueling our bodies, resting, shitting, running. Having her drop into the middle of it all felt a little like having your third-grade teacher show up at your bachelor party. I didn't know if I could speak to her like a normal person, give her the attention she deserved.

On December 23, I called her to make sure everything was set for her trip.

We talked about what to pack and what the weather would be like.

"Hang on," she said. "Someone is at the door."

I heard her talking to a man.

"Sorry," she said. "It was the mailman. I had to sign for a letter."

"What is it?"

She opened it. "It's from Countrywide Mortgage. . . . Oh. I'm sorry to tell you this, but it looks like your properties are being foreclosed on."

I had left North Carolina certain that everything would get sorted out with the lender while I was away. This was ridiculous. One of the properties had more than 100K in equity in it. How could Countrywide just take it? I asked Lisa to call my accountant to see what else we could do to fight it. I was sure I could get it all straightened out when I returned home. (I was wrong about that; my properties were gone.) For now, I had no choice but to put this mess out of my mind and just keep running.

- - - -

"You feel good, Kevin?" I said.

"Yes," he said.

"Are you happy you will see Nicole soon?"

"Yes." He smiled.

We were following our support vehicle's fresh tire tracks in the sand under a milky-blue sky. In the distance, mountains loomed above the scrubby, flat expanse. Kevin and I were running next to each other. Ray was ahead of us. So often, I wondered what Kevin was thinking about while he ran. He was silent most of the time, his mouth set in a straight, expressionless line, his eyes hidden behind dark glasses.

"Do people back home ask you why you are doing this?"

"Yes," Kevin said. "They ask."

"Me, too. I say I do it because I don't know the answer to that question. Maybe after I can tell you why I did it."

"I say, too. When I finish, if I finish, I will tell you."

"For now, the only reason I do it is because nobody has done it before. I want to see if I am strong enough, good enough," I said.

"Yes."

"And this is my ego. You understand ego?"

"Yes."

"This is because I want to be special. Maybe sometimes I don't

150

feel special, and so I have to do something to feel special and make myself different from other people."

"Yes."

"Because if I don't do that, then maybe I don't feel good about myself," I said. "But this is not a good reason."

"I think you want to do something in your life. Life is just maybe seventy years?"

"Yeah."

"So you have to do something," Kevin said. "To find mental happiness."

"Right. And we have to trust. You understand *trust*?"

"Yes, I know."

"We have to trust that we are on the path, you know, we are on the trail to something else."

"Yes," Kevin said.

"And whether you believe in God or Buddha or Allah, you know, we have to trust that we are doing this for reasons that we don't understand, and maybe this will take us to the next thing. Maybe when we get home, the phone will ring and it will be a person who says, 'Kevin, congratulations. Now I want you to do something else very special, very different, that will help many people.' And who knows what the opportunity will be? I think it's the ultimate in faith. You know the word *faith*?"

"Yes," he said. "F-E-A-R."

"No, not *fear*. *Faith*. *Faith* means 'to believe.'"

"Oh, F-A-I-T-H. *Faith*."

"Faith means to believe that something will happen."

"Yes," Kevin said.

"We have incredible faith because we are doing this for ten or twelve hours every day and we don't know why. You know, most people, for faith—they just go through their normal life and they think, 'Okay, I believe in God or I believe that something is going to happen to me,' but they don't really . . ."

"Do something," Kevin said.

"Right. They don't take risks. We risk everything."

"Yes."

"We risk our lives and we risk our jobs and we risk our family, everything. And we have faith. That is faith. We have faith that when we finish, something important will happen."

"Yes," Kevin said.

"It's like if you hold a book and you put it against your face, you cannot read it. You have to hold it away so you can read it. You have to have a different view, a different perspective, or you will never understand. And that's where I think we are now. Right now, we can't read the book, but later, we will be able to."

"Yes."

We kept running. I felt good that Kevin and I had had this conversation. Then I laughed to myself when I realized that, as usual, I had done almost all the talking.

On Christmas morning—day fifty-four of the expedition—we ran into Agadez, the geographic center of our journey. The city was a labyrinth of one-story sand-brick houses, dominated by the wood-spiked minaret of the grand mosque. I was shocked by how the population had swelled since I'd been here during the scouting trip. Mohamed said the water crisis had hit this area harder than anywhere else. Nomads, forced off the land, had come here out of desperation.

A year ago, Agadez felt light and cheerful. Now it seemed more like a bloated corpse on the verge of splitting open. Everywhere, hollow-eyed Tuaregs in filthy, ragged robes were watching over small herds of emaciated animals.

My exhaustion and ailments were self-inflicted; these people were suffering because they had no choice. I wanted to tell them that I was doing this for them, that I would help bring them water—that I was not just running for myself. But maybe that was a lie. I felt certain that even if I made it across the desert and raised millions of dollars, many of these people would be dead by the time H20 Africa dug its first well.

In a simple Agadez hotel room, I stripped down and stepped into a hot shower—my first in seven weeks. It felt fantastic, but I couldn't get the misery I had just seen out of my head. I had no right to use water like this. I reached for the handle and yanked it sharply to the off position.

We went out to the airport to greet Lisa, Kathy, and Nicole. They were tired from thirty-six hours of travel, but happy to be here. I hugged Lisa hard, and she felt good in my arms. I hadn't realized how much I had missed her.

After the women got settled, Don asked us to gather in the hotel's stone courtyard.

"So, I just got off the phone with the UN," he said. "I wish it was better news. Although the Libyans have known we want to come in for nine months now, we still don't have an answer. They haven't said no, but they haven't said yes. I don't think they are inclined to give us an answer. There is really nothing in it for them to say yes or no."

He added, "We're making calls to everyone we know." He said that Omar Turbi, a prominent Libyan American businessman, was working on it. Matt Damon had even flown from the *Bourne* shoot in London to meet with the Libyan embassy in DC. So far, nothing had helped.

"What are our options?" I said.

"We could go north to Algeria and Tunisia and finish at the Mediterranean. Or we go east through Chad or the Sudan. But we wouldn't have the support of the UN. The Sudan has announced that any Americans without proper paperwork will be considered spies. That means that if we are caught, we could be imprisoned or executed.

"Hey, it might still happen," Don continued. "It's a thousand kilometers from here to the Libyan border. There is time. They might say yes. But you could run those thousand K and still get a no."

There was silence. I felt a dangerous shift of attitude, as if maybe people thought that we might just give up.

"Do you think it's too late to call this Running *Most* of the Sahara?" I said.

Everyone but Kevin laughed.

Later, sitting at a long table at a restaurant in a traditional mud-brick house, we continued the conversation.

"I think we should just attack all the options," Don said. "We can go after Chad and the Sudan."

"Chad shouldn't be hard, right?" I said.

"It's not hard to get permission. But it's not predictable there. And in the Sudan, we'd be going right into the middle of the problem."

"Darfur?" Ray said.

"Yeah, right into Darfur. And it's all mined—you would see unexploded ordnances just sticking out of the sand. It's bad."

"What do you want to do?" I said, looking at Kevin and Ray.

"Definitely not go to Chad, right?" Lisa said.

"I'd like to hear that, too," Kathy said.

"I'm not going to say no to that option," Ray said.

Kevin scowled. I could tell by his expression he would probably quit if we tried to go through Chad. He was right to be scared.

"But, I think right now, we just head for Libya and go for it like we're not stopping," Ray said.

That seemed like the best plan. Run toward Libya and hope for things to work out. I could live with being turned away, but I could not live with not trying.

We ran east out of Agadez full of uncertainty. The girls rode in the support vehicles and greeted us at every break. It was nice having Lisa there, offering encouragement, and knowing she was seeing the Sahara for the first time allowed me to see it anew. And Kathy's presence had Ray bubbling over with happiness. For Kevin, though, having Nicole there seemed to heighten his loneliness rather than ease it. She reminded him of home, of everything he was missing. I could tell from their body language and expressions they were having serious conversations. I got the feeling that whatever they were talking about was not good for the expedition.

After four days of running east, Kevin came to me. "I'm thinking of leaving early."

"You don't want to do that, Kevin."

"I have my concerns. I don't mind challenging the environment at all. But challenging people could be quite dangerous. We have come a long way. If we stop, no one will laugh."

I told him we would talk about it later, in front of the whole group—and in front of the cameras. I felt obligated to capture any drama on film. And I figured that by the time we got everyone together, Kevin would have come to his senses.

On day fifty-nine, after eighty-four marathons, we gathered in a tent and Kevin announced to the group he was planning to leave the expedition. He would go back to Taiwan the next day with Nicole. I couldn't believe it. Part of me thought, *Fine, if he doesn't want to be out here, then he shouldn't be out here.* Another part of me wanted to scream at him that he had committed to doing this thing and he was going to continue. But I knew that yelling at Kevin would just make things worse.

Ray and I talked alone later after Kevin's announcement. We agreed we had to do everything we could to convince him to stay.

"We can't just let him quit," I said, "because I know how he will feel about that later."

"We're a team," Ray said. "We have to finish this together."

The two of us went to find Kevin. He was leaning against one of the trucks talking quietly to Nicole. He wiped away tears when he saw us. I asked if we could talk to him, and he walked with us.

"You can't quit," I said.

"You fought back from the knees, you fought back from the sickness," Ray said. "You have to fight back from whatever this is."

"This is very difficult for me," he said. "I love you guys."

"Expeditions are difficult. There are no answers!" I said. "That's the whole thing. You always have to wait and see what happens next. That's why it's exciting. If you don't want excitement, then run a marathon, you know? You can get water at every station and take a shower and sleep at night. But that's not you, Kevin. That's not you. You can *do* this. You don't want to quit. We are going to finish, but we want it to be with you. We're a team."

"Absolutely," Ray said.

Kevin stared at the ground.

"Don't quit," I said. "Just run to Libya. Ten more days. Five hundred K. If you still want to quit, then you can quit. Will you stay? Until Libya?"

Finally, Kevin gave us a slight nod.

"Yes!" Ray said with a fist pump. "Thanks, Kev."

I put my arm around his shoulder and pulled him close to me. "Thank you."

- - - -

On New Year's Eve, we said good-bye to Lisa, Kathy, and Nicole. It was difficult to see them go, especially for Kevin, who had, for a time, convinced himself he would also be heading for the airport. When we knew the ball was dropping in New York City, we had a small celebration with some horns and confetti Lisa had left for us. It was a new year. We had to focus on what lay ahead.

The next few days dawned cold and clear. We were in open desert now on terrain marked only by ripples made by wind, camel tracks, and the tire marks of our support vehicles. I felt obligated to stay upbeat, but at night, under the cold light of a million stars, I let uncertainty and fear seep in. My shin was killing me. Ray was also hobbled with leg pain and diarrhea. Kevin was distant and still emotionally raw. Though we forced ourselves to eat high-calorie food—cookies, Cheetos, Pringles, candy, peanut butter—we were all losing weight. Forty pounds so far for me, thirty for Ray, and twenty-five for Kevin. We had no fat reserves, nothing to tap into.

The worst of it was we didn't know where the hell we were going—other than vaguely east. What if this was all a colossal waste of time? At night, I allowed myself to fantasize about getting hurt, maybe breaking an ankle, something that would make it plain that I had no choice but to stop. It would be a graceful exit; no one would say I didn't try my hardest. I didn't want to quit, but it was impossible to be positive all the time. In the morning, I chased those doubts out of my mind. I was all systems go. I had to be.

"I don't know what's wrong with me," Ray said to me, as we labored across an expanse of windblown sand.

"Don't sweat it, dude."

"I'm just really doubting myself. I feel like I'm on the verge of wanting to quit."

"Don't worry about it. It's all going to work out."

"I'm scared today," he said.

"I know. I get it."

We ran in silence for several minutes.

"That fear, Ray? I don't think it's from this, you know?" I said. "The fear we have today is based in the fear we've had our whole lives, and that's exactly what brought us to this desert."

"Yeah," Ray said.

"Yes," Kevin said. I didn't know he'd been listening.

"It's why we're here," I said. "We're feeding that fear, you know? We're trying to feed the monster."

"It's just a hard day for me," Ray said.

"Look, we're only about thirty K from turning north," I said. "Hell, we could turn now, but I want to see Fachi."

"I want to see it, too," Ray said.

Fachi was an oasis town, an important stop for camel caravans over the centuries. Mohamed had told us it was a special place, but nothing prepared us for our first glimpse of it. It rose like a dream out of the arid moonscape—a movie set of feathery date palms and ruined fortress walls set against high sand hills. On the outskirts of the town, we passed checkerboards of salt pits. Hundreds of molded cones of salt leaned against a low wall waiting to be loaded onto camels.

Dark-skinned women, with a single gold ring in one nostril, squatted in bright printed dresses at the shallow salt pools. Donkeys grazed near low green shrubs. I reached down and brushed my hand against a bush and smelled the fragrant leaves of thyme. Men filled buckets at a well. There was water here. There was life.

As we ran, children appeared—five, then ten, twenty, fifty, a hundred—coming out of the shadowed alleys between the low mud-brick houses. The girls had close-cropped hair and colorful ankle-length dresses; the boys were in T-shirts and dusty pants. They fell into step with us, laughing and shouting.

"Bonjour, bonjour!" we said.

I felt someone grab my hand and looked down at a little boy, barefoot, scrawny, maybe ten years old, wearing a faded Chicago Bulls shirt. He beamed up at me. One of his eyes was bloodshot and oozing. He shouted something in Arabic as he ran.

"Good job, man." I smiled back at him. "Good job."

The boy laughed as he kept in step with me. More kids joined us, whooping and hollering. Dogs trailed along, barking and racing back and forth along the edge of the group. I started to play with the kids, getting them to mirror my moves. I lifted my knees in an exaggerated march and they all did the same. I went up on my toes and they mimicked my catlike prance. When I lengthened my gait into a comic slow-motion stride, they followed my lead. Kevin and Ray played along when they saw what was happening. Through it all, the little boy never let go of my hand, never stopped smiling. He squeezed my fingers. I squeezed back.

The kids sang and clapped and we bounced along with them. I felt myself being transported through this town as if on a magic carpet, borne up by these beautiful, smiling kids. Their joy was my joy. All the worries about whether we would get permission to go through Libya fell away. I forgot about the pain in my leg and the fear and the doubt. I could see in Kevin's and Ray's faces that they felt it, too.

There would be no quitting, no exits—graceful or otherwise. We'd come this far. We would go on. If Libya wouldn't let us in, then we'd turn north for Algeria or south for Chad. We'd keep trying until no one was left to turn us away.

The children dropped off from our group as we neared the far edge of town. The boy hung on to my hand for a bit longer, then I felt him slip away. When I looked back for him, he was gone. Ray, Kevin, and I fell into step together. Ray put out of his hand and we bumped fists.

"That was amazing," Ray said.

My eyes welled up as we passed the last of the settlement's low walls. Just that quickly, Fachi was behind us, but I felt changed by the experience. This feeling was why I wanted to do this run. Ahead was the great emptiness, the high pale dunes of the Ténéré—and beyond them, the Libyan border.

That night, the crew set up my tent for me, but I decided to sleep outside. The moon was full and so bright that I awoke a few times, thinking someone was shining a light into my eyes. At two thirty in the morning, I woke up again—to some kind of freight train howling. It was the wind. I sat up and found myself covered in sand. Forty feet to my right were the tents where Ray and Kevin were sleeping. It took me a few seconds to realize that my tent was missing. I put my hand up to shield my eyes from the blowing sand. In the distance, I could see a black dot bouncing along in the moonlight, probably a half mile away. My tent. I stood up and considered giving chase, but as I watched, the tent danced up the side of a massive dune, then launched itself into the air and disappeared. I laughed and wished the tent a happy journey. I hoped that someone who needed shelter would find it. I got back in my sleeping bag. I loved sleeping outside, and now I wouldn't have to make a choice anymore.

In the morning, the wind was still cranking. We figured it was blowing forty miles per hour—and we had to run directly into it. Because I was the largest and I was feeling the best, at least for the moment, I ran in front with Ray and Kevin tucked into my slipstream. To make things even more challenging, we had turned north and were no longer running parallel to the dunes. Instead, we had to go up and over the hills, like a surfer trying to paddle out to the break. We wore goggles and covered as much skin as we could, but the sand still found its way into our mouths and noses and ears.

Normally, we followed the tracks of our support vehicles when they had gone ahead of us, but in the blowing sand, their tracks were almost instantly obliterated. We had a handheld GPS with us, but even with that, if we were off by just half a kilometer, we risked missing the truck. One afternoon, we spent two hours trying to find our team—and the film crew that had been shadowing us came forward to tell us their satellite phones had gone dead and that they were lost, too. When we finally spotted the truck in the distance, we shouted with relief.

Later that evening, Don pulled me aside. I was grinning at him because I thought he wanted to apologize for getting so far ahead of us in the sandstorm.

"I may have to leave early," he said. "I've got some commitments."

I was stunned. "Leave?"

"Yeah, I've got an assignment. I have to be in Alaska."

I was shocked he would even consider leaving the expedition. But I didn't have the energy to have that conversation at that moment. I walked away. I told myself he wasn't serious. He would find a way to postpone whatever was creating the conflict.

- - - -

In midmorning on January 10, Ray, Kevin, and I spotted Don and the camera crew waiting for us up ahead. It was unusual to see them out here at this time of day. We weren't scheduled for a break for a few hours. My stomach flipped. Was it my kids or my mother? Maybe LivePlanet had pulled the plug. It took ten long minutes to reach Don.

"Gentlemen, I have news!" Don said with a big grin. "Libya! We're in!"

Omar Turbi had done it. He'd gotten the Libyan government to allow us to enter the country. We all cheered and hugged.

"All they ask is that we stop at a few places as tourists—but that's fine. We are in," Don said.

"Kevin, you understand?" I said playfully. "Now you have to keep going."

- - - -

My elation over being allowed into Libya faded quickly when Don, over lunch, said again that he would probably leave the expedition early. The whole crew was sitting there—and we were being filmed.

"I can't believe you are telling me that you don't want to stay to the end."

"I didn't say that. I said I had other commitments in February. I might go early. It might be February second or February ninth."

160

"If we haven't earned your respect after sixty-five days . . ."

"It's not about earning respect."

"This is nothing more than a job for you! I thought your commit-ment to this project was different than that. It's your absolute right to live your life the way you want to live it."

"Thank you," Don said sarcastically

"But I need you to go because if you don't want to be here, then I don't want you here."

"I didn't say I don't want to be here."

"You cannot commit now to staying to the end."

"When is the end?" Don raised his voice. "When is the end?"

"The end is when we get to Cairo!" I shouted.

When we started to run again, I was fuming. I went out ahead of Ray and Kevin, not caring about the wind or the sand or the lousy footing. I wanted to get away. I felt the pressure building inside me, the kind that fifteen years earlier, I would have known just how to relieve. I was angry and hurt. I felt as if I were being abandoned. It was such familiar territory.

The next day, during a break, I was approached by a camera oper-ator named Steve who had joined us in Agadez to work the Russian Arm, a special piece of equipment that allowed James to get shots from above. Steve had filmed the blowup between Don and me.

"That was rough yesterday," Steve said.

"Yeah." I didn't want to talk to this guy about what had happened. We had a rule—no conversation between the expedition team and the production crew.

"Don't lose your serenity, man."

I looked him in the eyes. *Serenity*—that AA buzzword. "Are you sober?"

"Yes, I am," he said. "For a lot of years now."

I felt some of the pressure ease as if a tourniquet had been loos-ened just enough to let the blood flow again. "Then you understand."

"I understand that right now, you are an untreated addict. You've gone almost three months without another drunk to talk to. No meet-ings in all that time. I'm surprised you haven't killed anyone yet."

I laughed. "No shit. I just feel like nobody wants to be out here. I would go to the ends of the earth for these guys."

"What other people do is not your responsibility. You can't control everything."

"It feels like my responsibility. The whole thing is my responsibility."

"Everybody is dealing with their own fears right now. Everybody has doubts and feels stressed. I'm stressed. But, maybe you should try being a little nicer to people, you know? You're sober, man! You're running across the fucking Sahara Desert! It's beautiful! You should be grateful to have this opportunity. You could be dead."

I knew he was right. I had so much to be thankful for. I was being too sensitive. I just wanted everyone to care as much as I did. We were all working hard and we were all exhausted.

I went looking for Don.

"I would like for you to stay and get us through Libya," I said when I found him near the truck. "No matter what I said yesterday. I was emotional. I appreciate what you've done, and if you need to go, I'll hug you and wish you well. And I'll hope you'll do the same to me. But I would love it if you would decide to stay."

- - - -

After all the phone calls and negotiations and hand-wringing, the Libyan border was laughably unremarkable. We walked past some coils of barbed wire, then between two metal oil drums with tattered solid-green Libyan flags flying on wooden sticks. No guards, no fences, no passport control.

"That's it?" I said to Mohamed.

He shrugged his shoulders and we all laughed. We would have our documents checked later in a town up ahead, where we would also be joined by Omar Turbi and our escorts—six truckloads of armed soldiers.

After months in the Sahara, I had long ago stopped feeling like a tourist. But this was Libya—and I felt like a wide-eyed child. Everything was a curiosity. We passed through prosperous-looking towns with shiny new gas stations and shops with well-stocked shelves. The local people exuded a confidence we hadn't seen in the other countries—a confidence that came from knowing they had access to water, food, electricity, education, and transportation. But those things came at the price of freedom.

The terrain was different, too. Beyond the rocky volcanic plains were flat-topped buttes and red-rock spires that reminded me of the American West. We wanted to run out across the open terrain, but our escorts insisted we keep to the paved highway. They said it was for our safety, but I suspected it was more for their own comfort. That meant we almost never were taking the shortest distance between point A and point B. One day we ran eighty kilometers but only gained twenty-six kilometers toward our goal.

Every day, we got a little weaker, a little more frustrated. Even our voices were going. Most of the crew were sick, including Doc, who had to teach Don how to hook him up to an IV. Ray's leg was so painful that we suspected it could be a stress fracture, but there was no way to find out. Ray was terrified that he was going to have to stop.

- - - -

It took twenty-eight days to get across Libya. Most days we ate pasta and Tuareg pizza, staples in the country, thanks to its occupation by Italy in the first part of the twentieth century. In the last town before the Egyptian border, we were given a big send-off: horns honked, people cheered, and kids slapped our hands. Our security guys hugged us good-bye.

The excitement of reaching Egypt was muted by the knowledge that this was where Don Webster would leave us. I was deeply disappointed that he had chosen to go. I thought not finishing what he had started was a big mistake—something that he would forever regret. Still, we embraced each other before he climbed into the truck.

"Get there, guys!" Don said.

We also said good-bye to Doc and Chuck Dale, who were going to Cairo to get medical supplies—and to meet up with Chuck's wife. They said they would be back in a few days.

There was no time off for Kevin, Ray, and me. Now that we were in Egypt, I decided that we needed to ditch our usual goal of fifty miles a day and go farther. We would run for as long as we could every day. We were all ready for this to be done. It made sense to push ourselves to our max. But I also had another motive. I wanted us to suffer. We had all been weak and we had all been strong, and now I wanted us to all be empty. That was the only sure way to let in something new.

Most days, we got in close to sixty miles. Midway across Egypt, Nicole and a large contingent of Taiwanese friends and supporters showed up to cheer Kevin on. His spirits soared. Whether he genuinely felt better or was just determined to look strong in front of his friends, Kevin was back to being a running superstar.

Kathy also rejoined the expedition, and Ray bubbled over with happiness. Chuck and Doc finally returned from Cairo after nine days away. I was pissed they had been gone for so long at a crucial time during the expedition. Ray and Kevin and I were out here falling apart, and no one was here to patch us up. I was cold to them when they came back, but Ray hugged them like lost puppies.

I didn't understand how they could leave us like that. They thought I was being a jerk, but my feelings were hurt. From the start, I had asked for their trust and loyalty. I had told them this would be the hardest thing they had ever done. I had asked them to leave their egos at home and give all they had to help this expedition be successful. They had done almost everything I asked for until the very end. I wanted to forgive them and to ask for their forgiveness if they thought I had been too hard on them. But I didn't have that in me.

On day 108, I woke up in serious pain. A blister, deep under a callous on the bottom of my foot, had grown to baseball size. I knew I was close to the end and that these final days could teach me the most about endurance and about life. But personal growth was the last thing on my mind. All I could think about was stopping.

Lisa's arrival the next day didn't so much give me a surge of energy as give me someone I didn't have to be strong for. I could be broken and hurt and scared. I had spent nearly four months trying not to show weakness or fear. But now I needed to be propped up. I needed someone to tell me I wasn't a bad person. I needed someone who believed that my words and actions came from a place of compassion and love. Lisa reminded me that none of this would have been possible without my commitment and determination. She told me that she was proud of me and that she loved me—and gave me strength to go on.

On day 110, we got up at 3:00 a.m. so that we could reach the Pyramids of Giza before they opened to the public—something Don's friend Zahi Hawass had arranged for us. We had only a two-hour window for the production guys to film. I tried to block out the pain in my foot as we ran in heavy fog toward the landmarks. I could see the cameramen set up, waiting for this crucial shot. Then the sun broke through the fog and the triangular silhouettes emerged. It was one of the most beautiful things I had ever seen. Ray, Kevin, and I joined hands and laughed and ran to the Pyramid's base. I had imagined this moment so many times, and now it was here. I touched the rocks and felt powerful and powerless at the same time. We lingered there, not wanting to let this moment go.

We decided to run the last 160 kilometers to the Red Sea without stopping. We had no reason to hold back now, nothing to save ourselves for. We made our way into the chaotic heart of Cairo, running along the shoulder of a busy highway. Buses spewed dark exhaust; cars and motorbikes darted around one another in a mad, unchoreographed dance. It felt more dangerous than anything else we had done so far. Darkness fell, headlights came on, and still we ran. The blister on my foot was growing larger and more painful with every step. I tried to focus only on forward movement. We stopped to eat and lie down for an hour or so, then we dragged ourselves off the pavement and went again.

James had told me long ago that the final scene of the film had to be shot in daylight. We had to pick up the pace to make that happen. But I couldn't go any faster. After 110 days of exhorting Kevin and

Ray to move, I had slowed to a walk. I couldn't believe this was happening. We would never make it to the sea in daylight at this rate. It was going to be my fault that we had to spend another night on the road. I couldn't do that to everyone. We needed to be done, whatever it took, whatever pain it caused.

The three of us walked all night. At about 10:00 a.m., on what would be our final day if we could get to the sea by sundown, Ray and Kevin said they wanted to take a break.

"Why don't I keep going?" I said. "I'll make it a goal to just get as far down the road as I can. Then you can run and catch up."

"Okay," Ray said. "That sounds good."

I limped away, whimpering with every footfall. Then, a little while after I left them, the blister exploded, gushing pus and blood into my shoe. The relief was wonderful and immediate. I was a new man. I took a few tentative steps and found I could manage a shuffling run. It was slow, maybe a fourteen-minute-mile pace, but it was faster than a walk. If I kept it up, maybe we could finish today, after all.

I passed the Taiwanese contingent and yelled to them to let Ray and Kevin know that if they didn't catch up with me soon, I would wait for them down the road. They clapped and nodded, but I wasn't sure if they understood my English. I continued to run, slowly, listening for Ray and Kevin to come up behind me any minute.

A couple of hours passed with no sign of them. I thought maybe they had fallen asleep. Finally, they were at my side.

We silently fell into rhythm.

"Smell it?" I said.

It was the sea. Ten miles, then nine, then eight, then four and three. And then we could see the calm silver water in the distance.

"Can you believe we did it?" I said.

"I'm surprised as shit," Ray said. "We ran all this way."

"What's next?" Kevin said.

"The Amazon?" I said.

"No," Ray said. "That's for crazy people."

With one mile to go, Lisa, Kathy, Nicole, and the entire crew joined us, and we walked to the shore. We had run seventy-five hundred kilometers—178 marathons—in 111 days without taking a single day off.

I had pictured this moment a million times. I imagined running full bore into the water and diving under the surface and coming up to shout and splash each other. Instead, Ray, Kevin, and I walked quietly to the water and dipped our hands in it. Then we embraced each other. Of course I was happy. We had done it. But I was also sad. I didn't want it to be over.

- - - -

On September 9, 2007, I joined Ray, Kevin, Matt Damon, Ben Affleck, and James Moll for the premiere of *Running the Sahara* at the Toronto Film Festival. In the darkened theater, I fought back tears. I loved the film—until I saw the end. James had used the footage of my going ahead of Ray and Kevin during those last miles to manufacture drama. He had gotten Ray and Kevin to say on camera that they were worried how far I was ahead of them and to wonder out loud if I might actually finish without them. I was stunned they could even entertain that idea. We were comrades; we were brothers.

If I had wanted to finish first, I would have encouraged them both to quit during the times they'd doubted they could go on. Or I would have just run away from them, since for most of the run, I was stronger than Kevin or Ray. I pushed the pace and went ahead on that final day to give us a chance to finish during daylight.

When I asked him later about how he put together those final scenes, James told me that he needed conflict to make the film more compelling—and that I was the best candidate to provide it. He was a storyteller and he had told a good story. There was no place for hurt feelings.

Despite my qualms with how I was portrayed in the final scenes, I knew it was a good film and I knew I had been part of something important. I spent the next year marketing it around the country—I'd run with a local club, give a talk about the expedition and the need for clean water, then screen the film. Thanks mostly to the audiences who saw *Running the Sahara* and felt moved to help, H2O Africa raised $6 million. If, after seeing the movie, a few people thought I was an ass (including my father, who told me he hated the film and the way I was portrayed in it), I could live with that.

CHAPTER 10

Failure is the condiment that gives success its flavor.
—TRUMAN CAPOTE

After I recovered from the Sahara run, I started thinking of what to do next. I decided that I wanted to see my own country—all of it—in that same intimate way.

I would not be the first person to run coast-to-coast across America. Athletes had been making the journey since the 1920s, when runners competed for prize money. Recently, it had become a way to raise awareness and money for a cause. I definitely wanted to connect my transcontinental run with a charity—but I also wanted to try to do it faster than it had ever been done. The record was set in 1980 by Frank Giannino, who ran from San Francisco to New York City in forty-six days, eight hours, and thirty-six minutes, averaging nearly sixty-seven miles a day. Giannino had done it at the age of twenty-eight; I was pushing forty-five. The odds were not on my side, but just because it seemed almost impossible didn't mean I shouldn't try.

My friend and teammate Marshall Ulrich—one of the most accomplished endurance athletes in the world—was also contemplating a cross-country run. He was facing even longer odds. Not only was he past his running prime at age fifty-eight, he also had no idea how to finance the attempt. He contacted me about partnering with him, and we decided to do the run together—not as rivals, but as compatriots spurring each other on.

My plan was to use the same model I had used for the Sahara—

find a film production company, bring in sponsors and investors, run across a giant landmass, then market the film about the adventure. After *Running the Sahara*, I received many invitations to do speaking gigs. I hoped that after another successful expedition, even more doors would open.

I spent most of the next year making calls, giving presentations, negotiating deals, calculating budgets, and planning the complex logistics for the cross-country run. It had been hard enough to line up financing with Matt Damon on board; without his star power, it was even more difficult. I finally found a production company that was interested in making a documentary about the run—and they shared my vision that the film could be about much more than running. We also wanted to explore how Americans were feeling about their country in the turbulent fall of 2008. As we traveled through their small towns and big cities, we would ask them their views on the wars we were fighting, the floundering economy, the housing-market crash, and the impending presidential election, which would take place about a week after we arrived, if all went well, in New York City. Then we would weave their stories into our own.

I lined up investors and sponsors, including Super 8 Motels, where we would stay as we moved east. I teamed up with United Way's Live United campaign for youth fitness. I also asked *News-2-You*, a newspaper for special-needs students that had covered my Sahara adventure, for help in coordinating visits to schools along the route. I assembled a great crew, led by Chuck Dale, who was, amazingly, willing to follow me slowly across yet another continent. And while I was doing all of this planning, I was also logging about a hundred miles of training a week. Oh, and I had gone through a breakup.

After we got back from the Sahara, it felt as if Lisa and I had reached some kind of natural stopping point. We decided that it made sense to take a break. But we both knew it was the end. Lisa had shown me that I was capable of love and I was grateful for that, but we were spending too much time arguing about what direction we should go next. I wanted to move ahead to the next race, the next big adventure, but I could feel that she was ready to go exploring on her own. I had opened her eyes to the bigger world outside North Carolina, and Lisa wanted to keep traveling—but not with me. We agreed that we were better off apart, but that didn't mean it wasn't stressful.

- - - -

"It looks like MRSA to me." I was lying on a bed in a San Francisco Super 8 Motel room, surrounded by camera equipment, food, and gear. Dr. Paul Langevin, the Running America team physician, was examining the painful lump on my butt.

"What's that?" I asked.

"Methicillin-resistant *Staphylococcus aureus*—a staph infection that's highly resistant to antibiotics. Tough to treat. Where'd you pick this up? You haven't been in any hot tubs or saunas lately, have you?"

"Both," I said, suddenly feeling guilty. I'd recently been invited to a spa to do a speaking gig. "But they were at a really fancy spa."

"Most people, if they are exposed to it, can fight it off. But if you're run-down . . ."

"Okay, but it's no big deal, right?"

"It can be. MRSA can be deadly."

"Can you give me something for it?"

"If I put you on a heavy course of antibiotics, there's no way you'll be able to run seventy miles a day. And they probably won't help, anyway. We'll watch it. Just try to keep your stress level low."

I looked at him and laughed. I was about to run eighteen hours a day—about five hundred miles a week—for the next month and a half. I had investors and sponsors who were expecting a return on their dollars, a film crew ready to document my every move—and a website that was about to go live with a tracking system that would let the world know where I was night and day.

Plus, I was executive-producing the film, and my budget was already screwed; it had been prepared based on gas being about $2.50 a gallon; now gas was up around $4—and we had two big RVs and several support cars to fuel for three-thousand-plus miles.

I'd also just found out that the one big job I had delegated—making a detailed turn-by-turn map of our route—hadn't been done. We could take any roads we wanted, but a record cross-country run would only be official if the runner logged at least 3,103 miles, as Frank Giannino had. That meant that the night before we were to begin, we had only a vague notion of where we were going. I was going to have to get on the computer and study some maps and figure it out quickly. No wonder MRSA was having a party in my bloodstream.

Despite all of this, at 5:00 a.m. on September 13, 2008, Running America began as scheduled on the steps of San Francisco's City Hall. Marshall and I smiled for the cameras and took off together on the hilly city streets, toward the waterfront. The smell of eucalyptus and salt air near the Golden Gate Bridge instantly brought me back to my days at the Presidio Adventure Racing Academy, where all of this happy madness had started. We ran through Sausalito, then back across San Francisco Bay on the Richmond–San Rafael Bridge and headed into the Napa Valley. Marshall moved out ahead of me and disappeared from view.

Every footfall sent a shock wave of pain from my infected butt cheek through my body. Still, I covered almost 140 miles in the first two days. On day three, at 4:30 a.m. I was back on the road, taking inventory as I ran the first few miles. The report was not encouraging: besides several new MRSA eruptions on my legs, I had sore hips, knees, and ankles, and a painful blister on the ball of my foot. Plus, I had a bad cold—my first in years. I had expected to struggle at the beginning. I knew from the Sahara that you had to be patient. Allow your body to break down, and then, after a few days, you could start building it back up. But this felt very different.

Highway 88 began its relentless climb toward Carson Pass at 8,650 feet. At about 5,000 feet, I caught up with Marshall, who had stopped for lunch. While we took our break, we heard the news on the radio that Lehman Brothers had filed for bankruptcy—sending the New York Stock Exchange plummeting. The landslide of mortgage defaults and foreclosures had brought them down. It was a small comfort to know that I was not alone in having to deal with foreclosures. But there was no time to dwell on that. I had to keep moving.

Marshall lived at altitude in Colorado and was an outstanding mountain runner. I was a sea-level guy. He moved easily past me, and though I fought to keep him in sight, before long he disappeared around a switchback and I was alone. I had a terrible altitude headache, my body hurt, and the road just kept going up. It was one of the worst running days I had ever had. I finally crested the pass near Kirkwood at about 7:00 p.m.

Now we were headed into Nevada on Highway 50, which, according to the road signs, was THE LONELIEST ROAD IN AMERICA. Not exactly a morale booster. The road rolled straight across desolate sagebrush scrublands and over a series of mountain ranges. The late-summer heat made the MRSA sores worse, which caused me to change my gait, which led to new blisters, which led to more gait changes, which brought on Achilles problems and severe bruising on the bottoms of my feet. Dr. Paul and I talked again about trying antibiotics, but he told me it was pointless to take them if I didn't also stop punishing my body. I was getting four or five hours of sleep a night; I couldn't afford more if I wanted to stay on a record pace.

By day six, Marshall was fifty miles ahead of me. I heard, though, that he had foot problems of his own. If he was gutting it out, then so would I. I told my crew that I wanted to keep going all night. I knew closing the gap on Marshall would reinvigorate me—and help ease some of the doubt I was feeling. I pushed through that night and the next, sometimes running, sometimes walking, as I tried to soften the blow of each painful step. I moved as if in a trance, pulled forward by the blinking red lights of my crew's RV a mile or so ahead.

Just after midnight on September 20, I realized it was my forty-sixth birthday. It was hard to believe it had been ten years since I'd celebrated with a cupcake in the fogged-in highlands of Ecuador. I wondered where I would be when I turned fifty-six. Would I ever stop moving? Would there come a time when I finished a race or an expedition and said, "Okay, well, that's done. I'm satisfied."

I had slowed to a walk. Clouds moved across the face of the nearly full moon, and I heard the high, wavering cry of coyotes.

They seemed to be all around me in the dark. I concentrated on the broken yellow paint lines in the center of the highway, trying to keep myself on a straight course. Then I noticed something strange up ahead. A woman with wild hair stood by the side of the road. I couldn't believe it: my mother. I'd talked to her earlier that day on the phone and she hadn't mentioned coming out here. She must have decided to surprise me for my birthday.

"Mom!" I called to her. I tried to walk faster, but the road was being pulled backward under my feet, like a moving carpet. I couldn't make any headway. "Mom!" She didn't seem to hear me. I lurched forward. When I finally got to the place where she had been standing, I saw only a tall bush. Wow. I was losing it. Spooked and delirious with fatigue, I limped on for another hour or so. Then I told my crew I had to stop for the night.

Austin, Eureka, Ely: I dragged myself across Nevada. Some of my maladies improved, but a new and worrisome injury had developed on the front of my right ankle, which was now red and swollen and hot to the touch. Chuck did what he could to treat it, but it grew more painful every day. I was embarrassed by my struggles and by my inability to just suck it up and work through it. In my daily blogs on our website, I apologized for the slow pace. People commented with such kindness. They said I inspired them, that I was their hero, that they knew I could do it. Their confidence in me was both uplifting and crushing. I didn't deserve their praise. They didn't know that I felt only fear—fear that every day would be filled with pain, fear that I was letting everyone down, fear that Marshall was getting out of reach, and fear that I would have to stop. I questioned my heart, my ability—and my sanity.

One day during a break, one of the film-crew guys came up to me when I was sitting with an ice pack on my ankle in a lawn chair wondering how I was going to make myself get back out on the road.

"Sucks, huh?"

"Yeah," I said.

"Let me ask you something."

"What?"

"Do you consider yourself a compassionate person?"

I looked up at him. "Yeah. I try to be."

"Do you feel any compassion at all for yourself?"

I knew the answer was no. I asked more of myself than I would ever ask of anyone else. I didn't want to hear my own bullshit excuses, not ever. I hated myself for even entertaining the idea of stopping.

"I don't want to feel sorry for myself," I said. "I asked for this."

"Dude, you really need to cut yourself some slack."

- - - -

Somehow, I made it to the Utah State line and my mood lifted, as it always did when borders were crossed. In the mountains, the air was cool and dry and the aspen leaves had turned yellow. Some friends came out to run with me, and with their encouragement I got in sixty miles a day for the next several days. I'd gone about 760 miles. We were almost a quarter of the way there. If I could keep this up, let my body heal a bit more, then I could ramp up to seventy-plus miles a day for the last few weeks. I could still get the record.

But as we moved farther into Utah, the ankle injury became excruciating. I'd never dealt with such pain. Even more troubling, the toes on my right foot had gone numb. Dr. Paul said that was a sign of nerve damage and warned me that I could be permanently hobbled if I kept running. I couldn't believe it had come to this. I was used to dealing with pain, but was I willing to risk an injury that could permanently end my running career?

On October 2, the twentieth day of the run, just outside of Provo, Utah, my crew gathered at a picnic table next to the RV. I sat in a folding chair facing them. I knew what was coming. I had been to more than a few interventions in my life.

"For your long-term well-being, this has to be the end," Dr. Paul said. "Today."

"I've never quit anything," I said.

"I know," Chuck said. "But I've never seen it like this for you."

"I'm getting e-mails every day from kids, saying, 'Are you still running, Charlie? Are you still running?' And I write back and say, 'Yes, I am.' And then I hear from their teacher how much those little words mean to them. How am I going to tell them I quit?"

"At some point, Charlie," Dr. Paul said, "there is a limit."

I looked at him and the glum faces of my crew.

"I'm sorry," I said, fighting tears. "I tried hard."

I knew then that Running America was over for me. All that planning, all that training, all that time spent away from my family—for what? What was the purpose? Maybe my father was right. It *was* pointless—all of this.

Ever since leaving San Francisco, I'd been blogging and tweeting about overcoming the odds, triumphing over adversity, toughing it out through pain. *Any lesson worth learning comes only as a result of weathering the storm*, I had written. Now I had to ask myself, Did I only believe these things to be true for other people?

I stared at the ground.

Then I had an idea. "Hey."

"Yeah?" Dr. Paul said.

"Can I ride a bike?"

He thought about it for a moment. "It might hurt like hell, but it probably won't do any more damage."

I commandeered a mountain bike from one of the cameramen and began to pedal. I told myself that all was not lost. Marshall was still out there running. We were still making a good film. I was still going to cross the country on my own power.

I caught up to Marshall and his crew, which included his wife, Heather, in a few days. He was exhausted, battling his own injuries and his own fears. He said he was worried about having to continue alone, without me spurring him on. He had told me long ago that, no matter what, you should never take yourself off the course; that had always stuck with me. I'm not sure he understood this decision to stop had been forced on me. Did he doubt my commitment?

Over the next several days, tensions built between the two of us. I was frustrated by my situation and worried about our strained budget. We had lost some crew members—and those we still had were exhausted and felt unappreciated. One afternoon during a break with my crew, I was told that Heather had demanded someone get her and Marshall chicken burritos in the middle of the night and had also insisted a crew member hand-wash Marshall's dirty underwear. They seem like little things now, but I was frayed—and I snapped. I pedaled after Marshall, amped up for a fight.

"Hey, your wife needs to back the fuck off," I said when I caught him. "She's running the crew into the ground."

"Don't talk about my wife that way. You're just pissed because you can't run anymore."

"You're right about that. I am pissed."

"You thought you were going to be the star, and you didn't care if I finished or not."

"That's bullshit! I busted my ass for more than a year to give us the chance at setting this record. You hardly lifted a finger to help."

"Look who's still running and look who is on a bike."

"Fuck you, Marshall." I pedaled away, boiling over with rage.

"Fuck you, Charlie!" Marshall hollered after me.

Later, I tried to patch things up. I was still executive producer of the film, and I needed Marshall to make it across the country. I shouldn't have confronted him while he was running. More than that, we had been friends for a long time. I didn't want it to end like that. But Marshall stayed angry.

Stung by the blowout, I searched for something positive to focus on as I pedaled across Colorado. One good thing about not running eighteen hours a day: I was better able to plan the timing of my visits to the schools that had been following my progress since day one. I focused on getting to Sidney, Iowa, and the Sidney Elementary School. I e-mailed Shannon Wehling, a teacher I had been corresponding with, to tell her I was hurt, but I was still coming.

As I pedaled closer to the Iowa border, though, I felt increasingly anxious. Did I really want to talk to these kids as the guy who quit? Maybe I should spare them the confusion and disappointment and just ride straight through town without stopping.

The day that I arrived in Sidney was chilly and rainy. My ankle was still tender, but I was able to run into town. I was surprised to spot Shannon and a group of her students standing under umbrellas on the side of the road, about a mile out of town. They were cheering and wearing bright green T-shirts that said RUN CHARLIE RUN! The kids crowded around and hugged me, then we all jogged toward their school. The downtown streets were lined with more people in the same bright shirts, and they were chanting my name. Some kids were holding banners that said WE BELIEVE IN YOU. I was overwhelmed.

In the school assembly hall, the kids peppered me with questions. They asked me if my foot hurt and if I missed my kids. They asked me what I ate—and, of course, where I went to the bathroom. I talked about the importance of being healthy, eating well, and getting exercise. I told them to go after their dreams, to never give up, to have courage, to know that if you wanted something badly enough and worked hard at it, it would come to you. Even as I heard the words come out of my mouth, though, I felt like a fraud. I had given up. The thing I wanted had not come to me.

That day, Sidney Elementary was launching a new Walking to Wellness program, timed to coincide with my visit. The goal was for the kids collectively to run or walk 3,103 miles to mirror my journey. After the assembly, we all went outside to run the inaugural mile together. Before we got going, a little boy tugged on my hand.

"Yes?" I said.

"Will you come back through here when you try again?"

"Yeah, will you? Will you?" several of the kids said.

I saw their shining faces looking up at me expectantly. There was no judgment, no disappointment—only acceptance, and love. We started to run around the playground. The kids were shrieking with delight. I remembered running like that myself as a kid—running for the pure joy of it, for the way it made me feel free.

I had set out to break a record, to go down in history, to leave my mark. But on that wet October afternoon surrounded by these kids, none of that mattered. It was one of the best days of my life.

- - - -

On November 5, just outside New York City, after more than a month and nearly 2,300 miles of pedaling, I ditched the bike and ran across the George Washington Bridge. My ankle was still sore, but much improved. Marshall would run up the steps of City Hall later that day. He'd made it all the way. A monumental accomplishment. But he had not beaten Frank Giannino's time. The record stood.

CHAPTER 11

No one is so brave that he is not disturbed by something
unexpected.

—JULIUS CAESAR

I scanned the crowd for Brett and Kevin and spotted them across the
room. They looked confident and comfortable in their polo shirts
and khakis with just enough of an unkempt style to still be cool.
I smiled as I watched them mingling. They were doing their own
thing, unaware of my surveillance, and I liked that. It was May 19,
2010, and a packed theater had greeted me in Greensboro for the
world premiere of the *Running America* documentary. Even though
I'd fallen short of my goal for the expedition, I was proud of the
movie. It was beautifully shot and told a compelling story. As the
screening wrapped up and I was surrounded by family, friends, and
a sea of smiling strangers, I was as happy as I could ever remember.

- - - -

The next afternoon, six armed IRS agents stormed out of a coffee shop
and grabbed me just as I was about to enter my apartment building.

My first thought was that this must be a case of mistaken identity.
Or maybe a murderer was living in my building and these guys were
trying to protect me. Before I could think of other plausible explana-
tions, I was spun around and handcuffed. I was under arrest. As I was
hustled across the parking lot, I felt a kind of surreal vertigo. Everything was spinning. I fought to keep my footing. *This isn't happening.*

This is just a twisted dream. Wake up, Charlie! It's time for a trail run around Lake Brandt.

But I didn't wake up. As I was shoved into a silver unmarked car, I looked hard at one of the agents who had grabbed me. He looked familiar. *Damn, where have I seen him before?* Then I remembered. Special Agent Robert Nordlander. He had shown up at my apartment building more than a year ago, asking me questions about my investments and my income. I'd answered them honestly—I had nothing to hide—and he'd left. Though I was bewildered and a little shaken by his visit, I had all but forgotten about it.

They booked me at the county courthouse. I called my friend and attorney Chris Justice, and he said he'd come down as soon as he could. I waited for him in a locked interrogation room.

"They sent a SWAT team?" Chris said as soon as he came through the door. His face was red.

"Yeah."

"That's absurd. Outrageous!"

He said those tactics were usually reserved for dangerous criminals. I was no Al Capone; I was a middle-aged, middle-class guy who lived in a modest apartment and drove a ten-year-old car in the suburbs of North Carolina. I'm sure Chris said some things to reassure me and promised he'd get to the bottom of it, but all I heard was "Charlie, they shouldn't have done this to you. But I have to tell you, man—this is really bad."

I asked Chris to call my dad and tell him what had happened.

After Chris left, I was taken to a crowded cell where men were lying on every flat surface—including the floor. Some were snoring, some were staring at the flyspecked ceiling, and a few were crying in that viscous, blubbering way only drunks can cry. *No problem,* I said to myself. *I have slept in plenty of uncomfortable spots before and maybe with people even more screwed up than these guys. I will think of this as the world's worst frat party. I'll get through this night and straighten this mess out tomorrow.*

Around 5:00 a.m., a guard called out, "Engle!" My hands were cuffed, my ankles shackled, and I was taken across the street to the federal building to wait for what I was told was an early-morning arraignment. I was placed alone in a holding cell with a steel toilet and one long, hard metal bench. *Remain calm. Breathe,* I told myself. *You can handle this.*

A guard waddled in and handed me a stack of official-looking paperwork. I began to sort through the papers, hoping to understand why I was here. At the top of the first page were words that I never expected to see: *UNITED STATES of AMERICA v. Charles R. Engle.* I was holding a fifteen-count federal indictment against me. I read and reread the indictment with equal parts dread and fascination. Most of it was nearly indecipherable, filled with legalese. Finally, I figured out that the US government had arrested me for allegedly overstating my income on a home-loan application—and for that I could be sentenced to thirty years in prison. My stomach rolled.

Trying to make some sense of this unimaginable situation, I thought back to that day when Special Agent Nordlander had buzzed the intercom to my apartment from downstairs, identifying himself as a Greensboro police officer and asking to be let in. I assumed there must have been a break-in at the building or a fire-code violation, so I pushed the button to unlock the ground-floor entrance and waited for him to reach my third-floor apartment.

I opened my door, expecting to see a cop in uniform. Instead I was met by a short, round man in a plaid sport coat and tie. Another man, a head taller and three times as wide, stood behind him. Nordlander said they were with the IRS Criminal Division. They flashed wallet badges at me in such sync I thought they must have practiced it. As Nordlander returned his badge to his waistband, he revealed a holstered gun and looked at me to be sure I saw it.

I was puzzled by Nordlander's identification of himself as an IRS agent and not the Greensboro police officer he claimed to be from the downstairs intercom. I guessed his assumption was that I might not welcome the IRS into the building. He may have been right. Having been raised largely in the South, I was inclined toward politeness, even with IRS agents who had fibbed their way into my apartment. I offered the men a place to sit, which they accepted, and something to drink, which they declined.

Agent Nordlander wanted to ask me some questions about the mortgages I'd taken out four years earlier on my properties in Cape Charles, Virginia. I couldn't imagine what could be interesting about those old loans but I answered every question. He also asked me about my income and assets and debt, about the hail-repair business, about *Extreme Makeover: Home Edition*, about losing my savings on a bathroom-remodeling business, and, finally, about running.

My answers seemed to frustrate him. "Why would a bank loan *you* money?"

I found it an odd question and told him he would have to ask the banks.

Then he pulled a piece of paper out of a folder with a flourish. He said it was a loan application and pointed to the document. "Is this your signature?"

I looked at the paper. I saw my name, but it was definitely not my handwriting. "No."

"Did you initial this here and here and here?" Nordlander pointed with a stubby finger.

"No." Those were my initials, *CE*, but I had not put them there.

Nordlander asked a few more questions. Then he and his side-kick sat in awkward silence. I was anxious for Laurel and Hardy to leave. Finally, they stood up and headed toward the door.

"Can I just . . . ? Why are you asking me these things?"

"I saw that movie about you running across the Sahara Desert," Nordlander answered, "and I got to wondering how a guy like you could afford to do something like that. I decided to open an investigation into you."

I was rattled enough by their visit to call Chris Justice as soon as they left.

"IRS agents?" he said. "You didn't talk to them, did you?"

I admitted that I had spoken with them at length. "I have nothing to hide."

I could feel him shaking his head over the phone. "The Feds don't knock on your door unless they have already decided that you are guilty of something. Do not talk to them again without me."

Chris's words left me on edge for a while, but as time passed, I forgot about Nordlander. I figured my answers had satisfied him. Now, with this indictment in my hand, I knew they had not.

Hours went by. I paced. I sat and stared. I paced again. Finally, a little before 3:00 p.m., a guard appeared and said it was time to go. Chris had arranged for Scott Coulter, his law partner, to represent me, and Scott was waiting for me in the courtroom.

"Nice suit." He grinned and gestured at my red prison jumpsuit.

"Thanks." I knew he was trying to put me at ease.

The charges were read and a date was set for my next court appearance, which was to be in Norfolk, Virginia. Then the lawyer for the Feds asked the judge to keep me in custody. I should be considered a flight risk because of my vast travel experience, he said. Thankfully, the judge didn't agree and released me on a $15,000 bond.

I had not slept or eaten in thirty hours. I was filthy from sitting on the floor of the county jail. I thought of the dirty dishes I'd left sitting in my sink. I couldn't wait to wash them. Normally, I was not big on household chores. Now, the thought of doing something normal, cleaning up a manageable mess, comforted me.

After shedding my jumpsuit and signing some papers, my jailer walked me to an elevator that went to an underground garage. When the elevator doors opened, there stood Special Agent Nordlander next to his car.

"How was your evening?" he said with a smirk, feigning Southern manners.

"Lovely."

I asked Nordlander how I was supposed to retrieve my property. As if by magic, he held up a plastic bag that contained my cell phone and few other things that were in my pockets when I was arrested. He handed me the already-opened bag, and I reached in for my phone while he watched me intently. When I arrived, the phone had been fully charged and I had turned it off before they took it from me.

Now it was dead. Shit. How was I going to get home if I couldn't call someone to come get me?

"Need a ride?" Nordlander asked.

I lived about ten miles from the courthouse. I looked at Nordlander's car parked conveniently right in front of me. His partner was standing next to the open driver's-side door, looking at me over the roof of the car.

I hesitated. I just wanted to get home. "Okay, sure."

"Turn around, I need to cuff you again," said Nordlander.

I protested, but he put the cuffs on and shoved me into the backseat. Then he leaned in close, reaching over me to fasten my seat belt. His aftershave was overpowering, and his holstered gun was inches from my face. He went around the car and slid in beside me.

We pulled out of the garage and headed toward my apartment.

After about five minutes of silence, Nordlander leaned over to me. "You want me to give you some unsolicited advice?"

I hesitated. Then, with an edge of sarcasm, I said, "Sure."

"We have you on tape. You should go to the US attorney and make a deal."

I didn't know what Nordlander was talking about, but I was too exhausted to give it more thought. I got home, took a shower, and called my kids. They were upset, but I assured them that there was no need to worry. Then I called my mother. She was becoming increasingly forgetful and confused, so I explained to her in the most simple terms what had happened. I told her it was all a wild misunderstanding and it would be sorted out soon. Finally, I called my dad.

"Charlie! I just talked to Chris Justice," he said. "This is absolute horseshit!"

"I really don't understand what's happening."

"I've been selling real estate for fifteen years. What the banks were doing during the mid-2000s—if you had a pulse, you could get a loan! What someone earned had almost *nothing* to do with it."

"So, you think it will be okay?"

"Absolutely. Just keep your head on straight. We're going after these bastards. Send me everything you have and try not to worry too much."

"Thanks, Dad. I love you."

"I love you, too, Charlie."

Early the next morning I reported, as ordered, to the office of Karen Franks in the Greensboro Federal Building. She was to be my pretrial probation officer, whatever that was. Ms. Franks treated me with kindness, even though one of her jobs was to make sure that my new ankle monitor fit. I asked if she had any colors other than black. She gave me a courtesy laugh. I think she'd heard that one before.

I was allowed to travel only within the Middle District of North Carolina. I couldn't leave home before 8:00 a.m. and had to be back by 7:00 p.m. If I wanted to go anywhere else, I needed permission. Without the ability to travel, I had no way to earn money. Paying my rent and providing for my kids required work outside my ankle monitor's home range.

News of my arrest seemed to be everywhere: in the newspaper delivered to my front door, on television, and on running blogs that I regularly read—the same outlets that only days before had been touting my accomplishments. Their reports of my "downfall" seemed to have a certain glee. Many simply reprinted the government's press releases about my "mortgage fraud scheme," and my guilt became the de facto truth. Not a single reporter bothered to contact me.

I realized that people who had decided I was a jerk after seeing *Running the Sahara* were quick to believe that I was guilty of a crime. Online, I saw comments like "See, I told you he was an asshole" and "He stole millions from his water charity." "He burned his properties down for insurance money." "Career criminal!" "Con man!" A few people even suggested that I stole money to finance the run across the Sahara—as if Matt Damon had needed me to spot him cash.

I always believed I didn't care what others thought about me. I was wrong about that. I was devastated. But I knew it was pointless to defend myself. It would just add fuel to the fire.

On the plus side, I also had many supporters. Friends offered to help with my boys. Others spoke to the media on my behalf and wrote letters to the local newspaper attesting to my character. Some brought me casseroles and pies. Over and over I heard, "Charlie, I'm so sorry," as if I had been diagnosed with a terminal disease. I didn't want people to be sorry. I hated the sadness and worry in their eyes. I found myself comforting them, telling them everything would be all right.

I had to appear before a judge in Norfolk to determine my trial date. At the brief hearing, I was told my modest income qualified me to have a public defender if I wanted one. I said I did. Then I was told to see the "pretrial probation supervisor." I greeted a woman seated behind a desk. I asked her if I was in the right place. She didn't look up. I waited. She picked up a piece of paper and without inflection began reading a long list of what I could do and could not do.

Then she finally made eye contact. "Don't screw up or I *will* put you in a jail cell until your trial."

I nodded.

"Down the hall." She pointed. "Piss test."

I wasn't worried about what the urine sample would show. My problem was the actual peeing, which had to be done with an officer hovering over my shoulder, close enough to hold my penis if he chose to. Thankfully, he did not. Since my arrest, I had gotten little sleep, and I hadn't been eating or drinking enough. I was stressed and so dehydrated that I couldn't get any pee to come out. It was already past 3:00 p.m., and I was anxious to get started on the long drive back to Greensboro, so I drank about a gallon of water while I sat in the waiting area, hoping this would speed things along.

After two more attempts, I still couldn't go. If I didn't pee by 5:00 p.m., I would have to come back in the morning to try again. I stood over the toilet with my eyes closed, trying to ignore the officer behind me humming an Elton John song. I had the water running in the sink, willing tiny drops of urine into the cup below. Each time I pushed, I would get a little more, but I just couldn't quite let it go. If I pushed any harder, I was sure I would shit my pants. The officer behind me made small talk, trying to help me through the ordeal.

One final push unleashed a furious fart that parted the poor guy's hair, but released enough pee to get the job done. I turned around and apologetically handed the officer a thimbleful of my warm urine.

My pee was "clean" and I left the courthouse a few minutes after 5:00 p.m., exhausted but well hydrated. A $50 parking ticket was tucked under the windshield wiper of my car. With the combination of rush-hour traffic and my stopping to pee every twenty minutes, the drive home took more than seven hours.

The damage the arrest did to my life was swift and sweeping. Sponsors dropped me without discussion. I was uninvited from several speaking engagements that I had been counting on to pay the bills. Most painful of all, I was kicked off several nonprofit boards, including that of H2O Africa, the clean-water charity I helped found. I wasn't just removed; I was purged, erased—as if I had never existed.

A few months earlier, I had started seeing Norma Bastidas, an accomplished runner and mountaineer and a no-nonsense woman devoted to her two young sons. At the moment of my arrest, she was halfway up Mount McKinley. Even if I could have contacted her, I wouldn't have. I had climbed that mountain and knew that it required complete focus. I'd tell her once she finished. We had gotten serious quickly, but I guessed that this would be the end of us. I was right.

- - - -

Walter Dalton, the public defender assigned to my case, was about my age, slender with graying hair and a thick mustache. Right off, he told me that he was a runner. This seemed like a good omen. My excitement was short-lived. Dalton spent the next twenty minutes sighing and rubbing his brow and telling me about his overwhelming caseload. He was spread too thin, he said, to devote much time to my case—and he knew little about real estate. He had only defended one case relating to mortgage fraud.

"And how did it go?" I asked.

"Oh. He pled guilty. Pretty straightforward."

I tried to stay upbeat. I hoped that once Dalton understood the facts of my case, he would see the likelihood of getting a win. I was pumped when he suggested that we go to his office to review the "discovery" materials. During discovery, the prosecution was required by law to turn over all the information gathered during their investigation, even if it was not favorable to their case.

I walked into Dalton's office expecting to see a large box of paperwork that we'd soon have strewn on every surface. Instead, he handed me a CD.

"That's it?"

Dalton nodded. "There are hundreds of files on that disc. You've got your work cut out for you."

I would have preferred to hear, *We have our work cut out for us.* Either way, I just wanted to get started. "Could you give me an idea of what's on it? What am I looking for?"

"No idea. Haven't had a chance to look it over. . . . Oh, one thing was mentioned in the note attached from the prosecutor. Besides documents, there are about three hours of audio files on the disc."

He had my full attention now. Ever since Nordlander's baffling statement about having me on tape, I had scoured my memory, trying to think what conversation could have been recorded. "We're listening to the audio now," Dalton told me. I was thrown by his use of the word *we.* Just then, a young woman in her midtwenties stepped into the office.

He introduced her as his intern and said that she would be helping us out for a few weeks. She said she had listened to the first two hours of the recording and had so far found nothing of significance. She pulled up a chair for me and booted up a computer.

I watched in amazement as file after file dotted the home screen. "Are these all to do with my case?"

She raised her eyebrows and looked at me. "You haven't seen anything yet."

She was right. Every file folder had within it dozens of documents. I had just been handed a giant haystack. I had to assume some needles were to be found, but I had no idea where to begin.

The intern put headphones on and went back to listening to the audiotapes. Time melted away as I navigated my way through the hundreds of pages of documents. Some were related to mortgages; others were filled with jargon that was so confounding that I couldn't categorize them.

"Oh! I think I found what we are looking for!" Dalton's intern said loudly. She took off the headphones. "Do you remember having lunch with a female undercover IRS agent?"

I looked at her blankly. That seemed like something I would remember.

"Her name was Ellen Burrows. Does that ring a bell?"

I thought hard for a moment, then recalled meeting a woman named Ellen outside my apartment building about a year ago. She was attractive and fit and told me that she was moving into my building. She asked me a few questions about the neighborhood and about me, and she told me she was an avid runner. Then she invited me to lunch.

"Sure!" I had said, flattered and pleased that I had made such a great first impression.

We had lunch once and I never saw her again. I had chalked it up to a mutual "nice, but nothing special" feeling.

"It's just a few sentences." The intern handed me the headphones. "Sorry. You almost got out of there alive."

I was embarrassed that the intern had just listened to what I'd thought was a private conversation. In more than two hours of talking to a pretty woman over lunch, who knows what stupid things I might have said. I hit play. Then I rewound and listened again, certain that I must be missing something. I took the headphones off and turned to the intern. "Is that it?"

She nodded yes.

"There's nothing there. How could the prosecution possibly use that against me? Do you hear a confession in that?"

The intern shrugged and searched the air for a response, but found nothing. "You should probably talk to Mr. Dalton about that."

Ellen Burrows had told me that she was in the business of helping people with their investments. I remembered she had steered our conversation in that direction. That wasn't one of my usual go-to topics, but she seemed fascinated by what I was saying, so I went with it. The alleged evidence was a thirty-second clip of my talking to her about real estate. In one run-on sentence, I told her I'd had a couple of "liar loans," and that a mortgage broker had listed my income as $400,000 even though he knew it wasn't true. It was a casual remark—I didn't explain that I'd only learned about *liar loans*—lender slang for loans that required little or no documentation—recently, when I watched a *60 Minutes* investigative report by Scott Pelley. After I watched the show, I had been curious enough about my own loans to dig out of a drawer the envelope containing the closing paperwork for one of mine where I'd tossed it in 2006— unopened—when it came in the mail. My broker had filled out the application for me over the phone, and I hadn't paid much attention to the details. Sure enough, I seemed to have gotten the kind of loan Pelley had described.

I sat frozen as I realized this was what the prosecution was calling a confession. This wasn't evidence of anything other than my misguided attempt to impress a woman who seemed oddly turned on by mortgage talk. I didn't confess to a crime. If anything, I had accused John Hellman, my mortgage broker, of lying about my income without my knowledge. And anyway, how could I confess to something I didn't even know existed at the time I took out the loans back in 2005 and 2006?

Invigorated by the flimsiness of Nordlander's so-called evidence, I spent several more hours looking at files: internal IRS memos, MOIs (memorandum of interview,) bank statements, mortgage paperwork, and tax returns. I was shocked to see an inventory of my trash. Really? Nordlander had been diving in my dumpster? Suddenly I felt queasy. I had seen and heard enough for one day.

I met with Dalton a few more times. I was dismayed to realize that he was developing my "defense" on the assumption that I would plead guilty. He may have believed that I was innocent, but his strategy was built around avoiding the worst possible outcome, which would be my being found guilty after going to trial. He said if that happened, I would receive a longer prison sentence than if I just pleaded guilty now.

Dalton was relieved and excited when Assistant US Attorney Joseph Kosky and Agent Nordlander came to him with a plea deal. I could plead guilty to any of the fifteen charges against me. Take my pick! Dalton sketched out the charges on a dry-erase board, then explained the weight of each one and crossed out the ones I should avoid.

Dalton's Pleading Guilty 101 lesson was clear and thorough, but he was wasting his energy. Under no circumstances was I going to plead guilty. I felt a little bad for him. This was the most animated I had seen him since this all started. I studied the board for a few moments to at least appear to be considering his counsel. Then I said, "Why don't we just try telling the truth and see what happens."

Dalton looked at me as if I had two heads. "If you go to trial and take the stand in your defense, you will almost certainly be charged with obstruction of justice."

"What?"

"If you take the stand to defend yourself and you are found guilty, the court will assume that you lied, therefore that you have obstructed justice. And that could add two years to your sentence."

"Are you telling me that in America, if I go to trial and defend myself because I contend I am innocent, I might have two years added to my sentence if I'm found guilty?"

Dalton nodded.

I left his office confused and scared. I felt that I was being funneled into some kind of choke point in the federal justice system, like cattle herded into the killing chute.

My father now had his own copy of the discovery disc, and he was spending hours reading, printing, and organizing documents. We talked on the phone several times every day, excitedly sharing tidbits that we felt sure would turn the tide. We knew Dalton wasn't doing any digging of his own; it was up to us. We decided that I should request permission to go to California for a week so that we could work on this side by side. If we could get the facts in order for

Dalton, we could walk him through it. I sought permission to travel and got it.

Dad met me at the airport, hugged me, and started right in. "What a crock of shit this is. These brokers really stuck it to you," he said, as we walked to his car.

"I know."

"They used the banks' nonexistent lending guidelines and the government's lack of oversight to screw borrowers by saddling them with predatory loans destined to fail—but they didn't care because they weren't lending their own money! The bankers got rich and you lost your ass!"

"Exactly."

"And now they want to put you in prison? This is total bullshit! Those crooked bastards." He climbed into the driver's seat and looked at me. "So, how was your flight?"

I laughed. Dad's bulldog approach to things had sometimes caused problems between us, but at this moment I loved him for it. For the first time in my life, my dad and I were a team. It felt good. I was just sorry it had taken this to unite us.

My dad's office was a sea of documents laid out on tables and the floor.

We felt we could prove beyond doubt that my home loan was handled per the status quo of those years. Brokers inflated the incomes of borrowers without their permission, often forged their signatures, and for that they were rewarded with big commissions. My loans were no different from the ones millions of other Americans took out at the time. I didn't ask for a certain type of loan. That's not how it worked. John Hellman put me into a no-doc or stated-income loan, which type, only years later, came to be known colloquially as liar loans. If I was guilty of anything, it was of trusting the professionals.

Most of the treasures I excavated while sorting through the documents were generated by Special Agent Nordlander. Page after page revealed new information about the tactics he had used to investigate me. He had spent more than seven hundred hours investigating me and my past tax returns—yet internal IRS documents showed no sign of unreported income. That did not deter Nordlander.

Eventually he used the Patriot Act to express nonspecific and unsubstantiated concerns to his superiors regarding money laundering. This allowed him and his IRS cohorts to search through my garbage, sort through my mail, and keep me and even some of my friends under surveillance.

For whatever reason, he seemed to have started with "Charlie Engle is guilty of . . . something" and worked backward. I didn't understand it. What could I possibly have done to put myself in this guy's crosshairs? The grand jury, I read in the transcripts, had wondered the same thing. One juror had asked Nordlander how he became so interested in a runner with no criminal background.

To this, Nordlander replied, "I mean, there's no way a guy could be going to the Gobi Desert, running here, going here, doing all these things in the last couple years, with no income."

The grand juror had followed up, "I'm still having a hard time understanding why you picked on Mr. Engle here. Is there something else going on with him that you were following him for? It seems like we are missing something. Do you do this for other people?"

"Well, ummm, sometimes it's just a—really—it could be as simple as a nice Ferrari. If I pull his information, it looks like he makes five hundred thousand dollars a year, it looks good. No problem. Doesn't look good, I look into him more."

- - - -

One afternoon, Dad looked up from his desk wide-eyed. "You know what? There is no FDIC-insured lender involved in your loans! Your lenders, except for Shore Bank in Cape Charles, were what they call pretender lenders. They just do the loan origination and then bundle it and sell it off. Your one loan with Shore was a full-documentation loan and you paid it off in full. The others were not FDIC insured."

"So did Nordlander not understand that or did he know it and ignore it?"

"Shouldn't matter. As soon as the Feds saw there was not a federally insured bank loan in the mix, they should have dropped the case. The federal government had no standing to bring charges. But they already had seven hundred hours invested."

I returned to Greensboro fired up, certain we had what we needed to convince a jury that these charges were bogus. I arranged a meeting with Chris Justice. I wanted to show him what we had found—and I wanted to hear him tell me we could win.

"Check this out." I pointed at some handwriting on a loan document. In what looked like black Sharpie, the words "NO INCOME NEEDED, THANKS!" had been circled. "Hellman never even asked for my income!"

"Okay, I see it," Chris said.

"And look. This document shows where the underwriter calculates that the income required is thirty-two thousand five hundred dollars per month, and magically that's the figure that appears on my loan application with the forged initials. The underwriter works in the same place as Hellman. It looks like they were in this deal together."

"Yeah, maybe. But you got the closing paperwork in the mail and you signed it—including the loan application with the false figures. I know the loan was already approved by then, but still, you signed it."

"I signed where the red sticky notes were! I didn't read the closing package. Does anybody ever read it?"

Chris shrugged. "Some do, not many—but that doesn't matter. You signed it."

"I didn't know I was signing something that was full of lies! I just signed where the notary told me to sign—like I have always done."

Chris placed a hand on my shoulder. "Charlie, I get it. Really, I do. This situation sucks. I can see that you've worked hard and you are right about pretty much everything. You're getting screwed. But you need to know something. When a person is indicted by the Feds in America, he has a ninety-nine percent chance of being convicted whether he goes to trial or takes a plea deal. I'm sorry, Charlie, but you *are* going to prison."

I brushed his hand away. "That's a fucked-up thing to say."

"That's just the way it works. You can't beat them. Nobody can."

I wanted to punch him. I grabbed all of my perfectly organized documents and stormed out. I got in my car and drove to Country Park. I had already run ten miles earlier in the day, and I still had running clothes in my car. It was nearly dusk, but still hot, and the parking lot was empty. I changed into my shorts and T-shirt, then took off too fast down the wooded trail. I ran for a few miles at a blistering pace, wanting to get quickly to the purge, the feeling of relief that I so desperately needed. I knew every inch of these paths. I knew where the roots had pushed up through the earth and where the camber wanted to send me off the trail.

Finally, when I couldn't push any longer, I slowed my pace. It was dark now and I felt the tall oak trees envelop me. I heard the rasp of cicadas and the trill of tree frogs. I was drenched with sweat. When I reached the parking lot, I stopped and looked up at the sky. The light breeze felt cool on my damp skin. *At least I have this*, I thought. *I have running. They can't take this from me.*

- - - -

After much discussion about Dalton's attitude regarding my case, my father and I decided that I needed to find another attorney. Dad offered to put up some money toward getting an attorney from the private sector. He wasn't a wealthy man, so this was no small thing. I could never have asked him for help, but I was grateful that he offered.

Attorney Paul Sun, a partner of one of my dad's childhood friends, agreed to work on a sliding scale. This was great news. I had only one reservation: he'd gone to Duke Law School. As a die-hard Tar Heel, I had to set aside my genetic predisposition against anybody who went to Duke University. Paul agreed to ignore the Carolina T-shirts I wore almost daily. I promised that if he could make this mess go away, I would commit to wearing a Duke basketball shirt during the upcoming hoops season.

Paul, whose office was in Raleigh, was about my age and an avid cyclist. He struck me as quiet and understated for a lawyer. I hoped he would be assertive when it counted. He had little experience with real estate law. But I thought if my dad and I could sort out the details of my case, Paul could do the same.

My trial started on September 28, 2010. The prosecutor called me a liar a hundred times and ranted about my *lifestyle* as if I lived in a penthouse on the Riviera. The thirty-second tape recording was played over and over. I waited anxiously for my attorney to present my case. But each day, I grew more worried about his approach. He seemed more concerned about not offending the judge than using the parts of our defense that I thought packed the most punch. He didn't ask Nordlander about his grand jury testimony. He didn't even press John Hellman, my mortgage broker, who the prosecutor brought out and had already pled to his crimes and had not yet been sentenced. Plainly, he anticipated his own sentence would be reduced if he pointed a finger at me.

I had one moment of hope during a strategy meeting with Paul. I told him about Nordlander's offering me a ride after my arraignment. Paul was livid. He said handcuffing me and tossing me into the car after my release was considered false imprisonment, and the interrogation that followed was illegal since my attorney wasn't present. Paul brought up this matter with the court, and though the judge seemed upset with Nordlander, nothing came of it.

Six long days of confusing testimony about mortgages and loans and bank regulations seemed to put everyone—even the judge— into a stupor. Several members of the jury nodded off, then woke up with a start, only to look deeply disappointed that they were still sitting in this airless courtroom, having to listen to more ramblings about loans and faxes and notaries. By the time the trial wrapped up, I was pretty sure Chris Justice had it right. I was screwed. And in fairness to Paul, I realize there was probably nothing he could have done about it.

Late in the afternoon of October 8, 2010, with my family sitting behind me, I was found guilty of twelve counts of bank fraud, wire fraud, and mail fraud. Ironically, I was found not guilty of providing false information on a loan application. My first reaction was relief: knowing was better than not knowing. But then I turned and saw that my mother was crying. It broke my heart. I knew I would find a way to get through this ordeal, but I wasn't sure that she would.

The judge allowed me to go back to Greensboro to wait out the ninety days until my January 10 sentencing.

I cleared out of my apartment, put my life into a storage unit, and moved in with my friend Chip Pitts. I spent as much time as possible with Brett and Kevin. I hugged them incessantly, trying to store up a surplus of love. I visited my mom often, always trying to keep our conversation simple and light, though it inevitably turned to the subject of prison. She seemed to be disappearing before my eyes. If I was sent to prison, I didn't think I would ever see her again as a free man.

To add to the misery, Brett was stopped for drinking and driving on campus at UNC Greensboro. His blood alcohol level was below the legal limit, but he was underage so the university suspended him. He was floundering and I was sick with worry about how he would deal with my absence.

In those weeks after the verdict, my need to run became maniacal. It was like my early days of sobriety when I felt I might die if I didn't run. Nothing else relieved the pressure. I went out day after day, pounding out miles with ferocity, the ankle monitor rubbing me raw. Then one day I started down a trail and was in so much pain that I couldn't take another step. I had first noticed a twinge in my right knee after falling at the Barkley Marathons in Tennessee a few weeks before my arrest. The pain had gotten worse, but I had run through it—until it was, at last, unignorable. With dread, I went to the doctor. He said I had a torn meniscus that would have to be surgically repaired before I went to prison. It required a more complicated and riskier procedure than I'd had with other knee surgeries. Tiny holes would be drilled in my knee, injuring it further to make it work harder to heal itself. My doctor said it only worked about half the time.

Something shifted in me, like the barrel of a lock being slid open. I found myself thinking about booze and drugs. I hadn't had "using" dreams in years, but now they came to me almost nightly. I often woke up sweating or in tears, certain that I had relapsed. I knew how to make this pain inside go away. A few drinks, a little blow. It would be so easy to let that relief wash through me. I understood that if I got caught, my situation would get much worse, but I couldn't turn off the craving.

I had the surgery to repair my torn meniscus. Afterward, my friend Liz picked me up to drive me home. After my previous surgeries, I had used only ibuprofen and some natural anti-inflammatories. I knew I couldn't risk taking narcotics; I might like them too much. But this time, when Liz asked if we should go by the drugstore to fill the prescription I'd been given for painkillers, I said yes.

We got to Chip's house and she put the bottle of pills on the kitchen counter. Then she got me set up on the sofa with food and drinks and pillows. Chip was out of town and wouldn't be back for a few days, so Liz promised to come back later to check on me. I fell asleep immediately, and when I woke up, I had an urgent need to pee. I grabbed my crutches and stood up too quickly, nearly passing out from the pain.

It was much worse than I remembered from other surgeries. I hobbled toward the bathroom and noticed the bottle of pain pills in the kitchen. I had a hazy memory of stopping at the drugstore. After I peed, I went over to the counter and picked up the pills. "*Oxy-co-done*," I sounded out. Oxy-anything sounded like something I might like. I had never been a pill user, but I had plenty of friends who were. It said right on the bottle, "Do Not Drink Alcohol While Taking This Medication." Alcohol!

I thought I remembered seeing some beer in the fridge. I went to the refrigerator and peered in. There in the door were a couple of bottles of beer, brands I was unfamiliar with. I took one out and set it on the counter next to the pills. Sierra Nevada Pale Ale—that sounded refreshing. I sat down at the kitchen table and stared at the beer and the pills. I stood up and grabbed the beer again. It was wonderfully cold. I liked the way it felt in my hand. Then I examined the pill label: "1–2 pills every four hours as needed." It was a big bottle.

I left the pills and beer on the counter and hobbled back to the sofa. The pain in my knee was unfathomable. Why couldn't I be a normal person and take a couple of pain pills to help me rest after having surgery? What was the big deal?

Just do it, I thought. *It's* medicine. *It's not a relapse.*

I went back to the kitchen and shook out one pill, then another. I put the pills next to the beer. The beer had a screw top. Had beer always had screw tops? I couldn't remember. I grabbed the top and turned it. Stuck. I tried again and still couldn't open it. I pulled out a drawer and found a bottle opener and wedged it under the lid. *Pssst.* That sweet sound I had heard so many thousands of times. The bright piney smell of the beer rose to my nose. Fantastic. I wanted it.

I had memorized dozens of catchy AA slogans, but at that moment I couldn't come up with a single reason not to take these pills and drink this beer. If things got out of hand, I reasoned, I could just use prison as my rehab and nobody would ever know. I had decided.

I had to plan, make sure no one would interrupt me. Was Liz coming back? Maybe I should wait until she checked on me. Or I could call her now and tell her I was fine, she didn't need to return. My kids might stop by in the morning, so I should text them to say I was feeling sick and they shouldn't come. I picked up the phone to call Liz, but before I started dialing, it rang in my hand. I saw that it was my mother's number. I clicked the ignore button. It rang again. Maybe she was in trouble. I answered.

"Hi, Mom."

No response.

"Mom? Are you there? Hello?" I said louder.

"Hello?" I heard her say. "Is somebody there? Hello?"

"Hi, Mom. It's Charlie. You called me. Is everything okay?"

"I called you? I don't think so. But since I have you on the phone, I have a question for you."

I waited. Silence.

"What did you want to ask, Mom?"

"*Damn*, I can't remember." She let out a long, deep sigh.

"Was it about the dogs? Or maybe your medicine?"

"I'm not sure. Oh, wait. I'm glad you called. Do you know where the coffee filters are?"

She had asked me this before. "Look in the cabinet just above the coffeemaker. I think that's where you keep them."

"I looked there already and they aren't there."

I thought for a second. "Have you looked in the freezer, where you keep your extra coffee?" Several things, including her phone, had ended up in the freezer lately.

"Oh, there they are! How did you know that?" She didn't wait for an answer. "Okay, thanks for calling. I love, love, love you. Talk to you later."

I kept the phone to my ear. I heard some bumping and banging. I realized she hadn't hung up; she had just set the phone down. I heard cabinet doors open and close. I heard water running and the dogs barking. She walked out of the room, then came back in singing an old Lucinda Williams song that we both loved. I heard her pick up the phone again. I could picture her standing there, puzzled by the apparent call in progress. Then I heard her breathing, listening. I said nothing. She hung up.

I looked at the pills in my hand. No. I couldn't do this to my mother. I couldn't do it to myself. Not now. I picked up the bottle of oxycodone, opened it, and returned the two pills. Then I walked over to the sink, put the beer up to my nose, and sniffed. It didn't smell *that* great. I poured it out.

Shaken, I went back to the couch, stretched out, and closed my eyes. I was so tired. *Tomorrow*, I thought, as I was drifting off to sleep. *I give myself permission to drink and use drugs if that's what I feel I need to do. To let go, to say, "Fuck it," take the plunge. I submit to the intense relief of these words. I will feel the alcohol flow into my body and the drugs course through my blood. I give myself permission . . . to get wasted . . . TOMORROW. Not today. If I wake up tomorrow and still want to use, then I can.*

When I woke up the next morning, I knew. My arrest and conviction had already taken so much from me. I would not let it take my sobriety.

I announced to family and friends that I was going to throw a party the weekend before my sentencing. The shindig would be on

Saturday night, with a ten-mile fun run on Sunday morning. About 150 people showed up. I had painted RIP onto palm-size rocks and gave them to everybody that came to the run. I told them the letters stood not for "rest in peace" but for "running in place"—which I figured I would be doing a lot of, once my knee healed, in prison. Most people laughed. I felt my strength returning.

On the Sunday night before my sentencing, I went to an AA meeting for the first time since my arrest. AA required absolute honesty, and even though I had done nothing wrong, I worried that people would view me as an impostor, someone who pretended to be clean while living some shady, illegal existence. In my heart, I knew that AA was not about judgment, but I couldn't shake the feeling that even after eighteen years sober, I was no longer welcome.

I sat in the back of the room and listened to people talk about gratitude and fear and acceptance. I felt they were speaking directly to me. Their words helped me remember how much I still had to live for. I decided to not be scared, to simply accept whatever came next. I could not control what happened, but I could control how I dealt with it.

The next morning, I drove to Norfolk, Virginia. The courtroom was filled to capacity. Runners, recovering addicts, family, old buddies, former girlfriends, and strangers had come from all over the country to give their support. Pam, my boys, my mother, my dad, and my stepfather were all in the front row.

Nordlander and Kosky picked up right where they left off, arguing for a stiff sentence. Eventually it was my turn to speak. My voice quavered as I read from a statement I'd written asking the judge to please send me home, to give me a chance to serve out my sentence by helping others in my community. I choked up when I spoke about my mother and my kids. I could hear sobs behind me.

The judge acknowledged receiving 120 letters from people attesting to my good character—the most he'd ever gotten for a single case. I felt a spark of hope.

Then he cleared his throat and sentenced me to twenty-one months in a federal prison.

CHAPTER 12

Anger is an acid that can do more harm to the vessel in
which it is stored than to anything on which it is poured.
—MARK TWAIN

On Valentine's Day, Brett and Kevin, my friends Chip and Liz, and
I left Greensboro to make the three-hour drive to Beckley federal
prison in Beaver, West Virginia. For most of the ride, we managed
to pretend we were off on a fun road trip. We filled the time telling
tasteless jokes, quoting lines from movies, and singing off-key to the
radio. But then, at about 4:30 p.m., we rounded a turn and saw the
prison gates, and I felt the full weight of my impending incarceration.

High barbed-wire fences and sentry towers ringed swaths of manicured grass. It looked like every A&E prison show I had ever watched;
I would have been fascinated if I were just visiting. But the anguish on
Brett's and Kevin's faces was crushing. I hadn't been sure if bringing
them was the right thing to do, but they had wanted to come. I thought
not seeing it might be worse for them—that their imaginations would
make it even more awful than it was. I was proud of my sons for being
here with me, even though I knew they were scared. I was scared, too.

We parked and got out of the car. The sun was bright but a strong
wind made it feel much colder than the fifty degrees reported on
the radio. I took off my sunglasses, emptied my pockets, and handed
everything over to Brett. In my hand I held three $2 bills given to
me as change at a grocery store a few days earlier. When the cashier
handed them over, she shrugged and smiled, acknowledging the

oddness of it. I handed one to Brett and one to Kevin, then tucked one into my own wallet, which Brett was holding.

"Keep those in your wallets," I said. "Think of me when you see them."

Brett and Kevin looked at me solemnly and nodded.

"Or at least don't spend them unless it's an emergency," I said with a laugh.

We lingered outside a moment longer. In the months since my sentencing, we had said little to each other. Nothing ever seemed right. Now, in these final moments, I felt every thought I'd had fighting for its turn. I was desperate to take away their pain, to assure them that all would be okay, but we were in uncharted waters. I had no idea how to make this better.

I hugged Kevin and then Brett one last time. I could see them struggling not to cry as I turned to walk to the front door of the prison.

I gave my name to a guard at a desk and told him I was a "self-surrender." He said they were expecting me a couple of hours earlier and that I would miss dinner. I wasn't hungry.

Next I was led to a storage room and told to remove my clothes and put them in a box on the floor. They would be shipped back home. My welcome-to-prison strip search included lots of lifting and holding, followed by some squatting and coughing. I was issued too-big gray sweatpants, slip-on orange rubber flip-flops, a white T-shirt, and underwear that appeared to be clean but not new. Then I was put in a temporary holding cell, and the door to my old life slammed shut.

I was grateful nobody else was in that cell with me because I was a mess. I sat down on a bench, but my knees shook so violently that I had to jump to my feet and pace around the cell. I had been preparing myself for this moment for months, but saying good-bye to my kids had done me in. I felt on the verge of breaking down. I couldn't do this. I had to get out of here.

Then I got angry with myself. *Don't be a pussy*, I told myself. *Suck it up. Deal with it.* I had a long history of rising to the occasion when things got tough. I needed to do that now.

After I waited an hour or so, a different guard came to collect me. I had a lot of questions but I thought it was best to keep my mouth shut and see what happened next. The guard walked me out the front doors and pointed at a small, dented white pickup truck parked at the curb. Was I supposed to get in the back? I wanted to tell him to speak, but he just motioned for me to go. I opened the truck door and slid into the seat. The guard closed my door, turned, and walked away without having ever spoken a word.

The driver of the truck was a white guy, thick through the waist, maybe sixty years old, with a bushy gray mustache and a strange pageboy haircut. Out of habit, I looked for my seat belt. There wasn't one.

"Parham." He stared straight ahead.

I looked at him blankly. Then I realized that Parham was his name. Normally, I was a first-name guy. "Engle."

Parham seemed nice enough. If all the guards were this friendly, maybe this wouldn't be so bad. He put the truck in gear and pulled away from the curb. I felt oddly excited, stepping into the unknown. We drove about a mile and pulled up in front of a one-level brick building that looked like the entrance to a strip mall. Parham pointed to the front doors.

"Go inside and tell the CO who you are."

"Ummm, C-O?"

"Correctional officer . . . guard . . . guy with the badge."

"Oh, okay. Thanks."

Once inside, I approached a counter with a Plexiglas divider. I assumed the man behind it was the CO.

"Yeah?" he growled without looking up.

"I was told to report here."

"Who told you that?"

"The guard, I mean . . . CO who drove me over here from the main building."

He looked up and gave me the once-over. "Who the hell are you?"

"Engle . . . with an *E*. I'm a self-surrender."

He looked down and flipped through a stack of papers, running his finger over a list of names.

"If you don't have a reservation for me, I can just come back later."

Nothing. Tough crowd.

"Sit down over there. Wait. Just so you know, that was an inmate that drove you over here. Not a CO. You should probably learn the difference. Oh, and you are going to miss dinner because you were late. So I don't want to hear you bitching later."

I turned and took a seat and waited and said the Serenity Prayer to myself:

God, grant me serenity to accept the things I cannot change, courage to change the things I can, and the wisdom to know the difference.

I had said it thousands of times in nineteen years of sobriety, but it had never had more meaning than at that moment.

A glass door to my right opened, and a short, stout black man in his fifties walked over with a big grin on his face. He was wearing dark green pants over black, steel-toed boots and a dark green long-sleeved shirt with a white T under it. The shirt had a name and number on it. I realized then that the driver who had delivered me here had been dressed the same way.

"Are you Engle?"

"Yes . . . with an *E*."

"You're late. But don't worry, I saved you a plate. I'm Pick-n-Roll, but you can call me Pick."

I stood to shake his hand. He offered me his fist and I bumped it firmly. "I never met anyone named Pick-n-Roll. You play basketball?"

He stared at me, not unkindly, and seemed to be assessing me. "You ever been down before?"

"Ummm . . ."

"Have you ever been in prison before?"

"No, first time."

"What's your bid?"

"Ummm . . ."

"How much time did you get?"

208

"Oh! Twenty-one months."

"That's not even enough time to unpack your things. Follow me."

As we walked through an open courtyard, he pointed at doors. "Medical . . . laundry . . . barber . . . commissary." Then we entered a cafeteria. It was deserted, except for one black guy mopping and another wiping tables.

The inmate mopping looked up with a scowl and yelled, "We closed. Get the hell out!"

I stopped in my tracks. Pick and the man busted out laughing and pointed at me.

"Oh, Lord, you should have seen your face." Pick wiped his eyes. "Come on, Engle with an *E*, sit down over here and I'll get you a plate from the back."

I wasn't really hungry but I felt obligated to eat. My new friend watched me force down mushy green beans, white rice, and a piece of dry corn bread. I tried to look as if I were almost enjoying it.

"Tastes like shit, don't it? You gonna eat that chicken?"

I shook my head, and Pick looked around, then pulled a plastic bag out of his pocket as if he were going to do a magic trick. He reached over, plucked the chicken from my tray, dropped it into the bag, and tucked it into an interior pocket in his jacket.

We went back to the laundry and I was issued some sheets, a pillow, and a pillowcase. Then we walked up a long sidewalk to Evergreen, my housing unit and home for the next year and a half. Evergreen. I wondered who had come up with that name for this place. The walls were gray and the air had a smell that was hard to identify; it was nutty and sweet and cheesy and fishy, with undertones of body odor. The front door opened to a common area that separated the two sides of the housing unit. Straight ahead were two TV rooms that could accommodate about twenty-five guys each. In between them was a big table that held three microwave ovens that would be the source of some of the direst arguments I saw in prison.

Pick explained how the commissary and phone system worked, and finally he led me to my cell. "Welcome to the bubble."

I could see why he called it that. From the hallway a big plate-glass window looked into the room, creating a fishbowl effect for the inmates inside. We walked in, and two guys on bottom bunks looked up at me. I nodded nonchalantly, but they looked away and went back to talking. Another inmate was snoring on a top bunk. The room had four gray metal bunk beds set on surprisingly shiny linoleum floors. Next to each bunk was a locker and a corkboard covered with photos of kids and dogs and nearly naked women torn from magazines. The only natural light came from two tiny windows, high on the outer cinder-block wall.

I had been assigned a top bunk. Pick told me the bottom bunks were for guys with health problems or seniority. "If you want to stay around six or eight more years, I can probably get you a bottom bunk." He elbowed my ribs.

He pointed to my locker. "Don't put anything valuable in it until you buy a lock. Make your bed every morning or else everyone in the bubble gets punished. And be sure you're here for count time."

I wasn't sure what that was, but I was so overwhelmed with information, I was afraid to ask.

"Oh, and one more thing. When you meet with CO Whacker, don't have your hands in your pockets. He don't like that and he'll send you to the hole. Some inmate whipped his ass years ago, and he's afraid somebody might shank him." Pick smiled as if he had just delivered good news, smacked me on the shoulder, and walked out of the cell.

Then I heard heavy footsteps coming from behind me, and when I turned, I was face to chest with a light-skinned black man who had to be seven feet tall. He looked down at me and asked if I was the new guy. I said yes.

He extended his massive hand. "Shorty."

I should have guessed.

Shorty said he'd been there only a few days and was still learning the ropes himself. He told me a few more helpful things, such as what time breakfast started, the best time to take a shower, and what jobs I should try to get. "Oh—and do not have your hands in your pockets when you meet with Whacker."

Shorty asked me if I had been out to the "yard" yet. I said no. He motioned to follow him. It was comforting to be walking next to him. I felt as if I had a bodyguard. He greeted some inmates with head nods and fist bumps. Some he passed in silence, and when we were out of their earshot, he leaned in close and said, "You don't want to know that motherfucker."

We walked out to a basketball court and stopped to watch a heated game. I looked up at him, and before I could ask, Shorty said, "Yeah, I used to play, but I hurt my knee a long time ago."

Beyond the basketball courts loomed a snow-covered expanse, illuminated by lights on tall poles. I noticed a wide shoveled path that extended in an oddly shaped loop around the rec area. "Is that a track?"

"Yeah."

"Any idea how long it is?"

"Shit, I don't know, man. Do I look like a runner to you?"

I could see one old white guy with a beard and long gray hair jogging on the track.

When he got close, Shorty yelled, "Yo, Frank, how long is this track?"

"Quarter mile!" he yelled over his shoulder, and kept going.

"Do a lot of guys here run?" I asked Shorty.

"Only Frank, maybe a couple more. Lots of 'em walk though."

We turned back toward the housing unit.

"What are you in for, man?" Shorty asked.

I was tempted to say something cool, such as armed robbery. I mean, mortgage fraud? What was I going to do, get a prison tattoo of a fountain pen?

"I was charged with overstating my income on a mortgage application."

Shorty gave me a blank look. "Mmmm . . . mmm . . . mm. Who did you piss off?"

I laughed and we kept walking.

He pointed at another door. "That there is the library."

I had expected to spend a lot of time reading and had asked

friends and family to send me books—but it hadn't occurred to me that I'd have a library to use. I asked Shorty if he minded going in. He said he needed to head back to the bubble. I almost asked him if he had a date, just to be funny, but I stopped myself. On the outside, I liked making people laugh. In here, I needed to learn what was amusing and what wasn't.

I resisted the urge to tuck in behind Shorty and follow him. I thanked him for showing me around and said I would see him later. He told me not to be late for the 10:00 p.m. count. I said I wouldn't be, even though I still didn't know what *count* meant. Whatever it was, I figured I had until ten to find out.

I hadn't realized how noisy the prison was until I stepped into the wonderful quiet of the library. Several inmates were reading newspapers and books. They all looked up at me, then went back to what they were doing. I browsed some shelves and saw plenty of familiar authors: Hemingway, Steinbeck, Stephen King, Paulo Coelho. One section held law books, which I gathered could be used for research. I picked up *The Grapes of Wrath*, one of my favorites. Now I needed to figure out how to check it out. I asked an older man seated behind a desk what to do.

"This is prison, you ain't gotta do nothing. Just take the book. Ain't like you going anywhere with it," he said matter-of-factly.

A trim, middle-aged white man with light brown hair pulled back in a neat ponytail stood up and walked over to me. He had the *New York Times* in his hand. "You may have this when I'm done, if you'd like. It's a few days old."

"Thank you."

"You're welcome. I'm Howell Woltz." He was the first inmate to introduce himself by his full name.

"Charlie Engle." It was the first time I'd said my given name in prison.

"Welcome to Camp Cupcake. What brings you to this fine establishment?"

I felt at ease enough to risk a joke. "Mix-up with the travel agent. You know how it goes."

A couple of long beats passed, then Howell started to laugh. Once he started, the others joined in. I felt comforted by their reaction. Howell told me he had been in investment banking in the outside world. I wasn't surprised. He had a sophistication about him that suggested yachts and good Scotch. Howell introduced me to some of the other guys in the library. There was Doc, a physician "and genuine drug kingpin," Howell said; and Phil, a financial adviser "who had the great misfortune of being sentenced right after Mr. Madoff."

At about 9:00 p.m., Howell, Phil, and Doc stood up to leave.

"Care to join us?" Howell asked. "We are going for our nightly stroll."

"Sure. Do I have to get permission from someone to go out?"

"No, no. Come along."

I felt as if I had been granted membership into a gang of prison nerds. We headed out to the track, past a few disinterested guards. The sky was clear and full of stars. We started walking.

"That's Orion." Doc pointed up. "And Gemini. See the twins?"

We did a couple of laps, then Phil asked me what I had been convicted of. I had been warned before coming to Beckley that I should be careful who I talked to, but I couldn't help myself: I took a deep breath and launched into my story. It lasted most of the next six laps.

A loud voice came over the intercom telling us that the recreation area was closed and it was time to return to the housing unit. I followed along.

When we reached Evergreen, Howell looked at me. "Are you all right?"

I was touched by his concern. He had already been here for more than five years and had seen plenty of guys come and go. I think he sensed that I was strong and cool on the outside, but maybe things weren't so calm in my head.

I hesitated, not wanting to show any weakness. "I don't really know."

"Listen, it's up to you how you pass your time here. You can sit around in a funk if you want. You'll have plenty of company. Or you can keep an open mind about this experience. I don't know who you pissed off to get sent to this place, but it's up to you what to make of it. I have a feeling you'll be fine."

"Thanks." I turned toward the door.

"Oh—and, Chuck?" I smiled and turned back. Nobody had ever before called me Chuck. "Remember this. The COs aren't your friends, and neither are most of these guys. Don't talk about yourself or your family too much. Don't get into arguments, but don't take any shit either. And don't talk to anybody else about your case. If what you say is true, you need to be cautious. If you aren't, some snitch will tell the US attorney that you admitted to killing somebody. Keep your head down."

I was the only one in the bubble. I climbed up to my bunk and picked up my book. A few minutes later, the loudspeaker blared. "*Count time!* This is a stand-up count. Do not screw up my count."

Guys scrambled into the cell and stood still, as if they were waiting for something. I waited, too. Then, just outside the door, I heard someone bang on the wall and yell, "Count time!" A heavyset white guard with a crew cut stepped in and pointed, one at a time to each of us, counting silently with his lips. He left the room and everyone relaxed. A minute later, a giant black CO came in. He did his counting by nodding his head at each of us. I almost nodded in return, but I realized this was not a greeting.

After he left, Shorty walked over to me. "Don't mess with that guard. He's the real deal."

The lights went out and I climbed into my bunk, still wearing my sweats and T-shirt. I pulled the wool blanket over me. Little reading lights blinked on in the other bunks. I closed my eyes. I was wiped out. The day had been so busy that I had managed to shove aside the reality of where I was. But now, I felt a dark panic overtake me. I was in a federal prison on top of a frigid, windblown mountain in West Virginia. It was fucking Valentine's Day. I would be here for Memorial Day and the Fourth of July and Halloween and Thanksgiving and Christmas and next Valentine's Day and next Memorial Day.

- - - -

In the morning, I was issued my prison "greens"—two pairs of long green pants, two long-sleeved green shirts, and two short-sleeved green shirts. I was also given a green winter coat—a bulky thing with lots of pockets. Every piece of clothing had a glued-on patch with my name and inmate, or "register," number—26402-057. The first five numbers identified me as the 26,402nd man incarcerated in federal prison from my district, 057, in North Carolina. Those last three numbers also meant that other inmates could identify me as being from Greensboro, which wasn't necessarily a good thing. I couldn't imagine wanting to see any of these guys on the outside.

Over the next few days, I did all I could to blend in, learn the rules, and avoid anything that seemed even remotely like trouble. I felt like a kid who had been dropped off at the world's worst summer camp. I was homesick and heartsick. I was also anxious to let my family and friends know that I was doing okay. We had all watched too many prison shows and movies. At the least, I wanted them to know I hadn't been shanked.

Before I could make phone calls, I had to have money in my PAC, or inmate account. I couldn't arrange for that until I met with my counselor, Johnny "Don't Keep Your Hands in Your Pockets When You Talk to Me" Whacker. Whacker would also approve my official list of visitors—and I was eager to get that squared away. His days off had coincided with my arrival at Beckley.

When he returned, I was told I could see him. He stood when I entered his office and looked me up and down. He had a crew cut, tiny eyes, and one of those unexplainable round bellies that protrude from a skinny frame.

"What do you have there, Engle?" I handed him my list of visitor names. He sat down, cocked his head slightly to one side, picked up a cup on his desk, and spit tobacco juice into it. Then he grinned at me as he reached back and shoved my visitors' list into a shredder on a low table behind his desk.

"You don't need no visitors, Engle. Don't nobody want to see your ass anyway."

I was furious, but I knew I had to keep my anger in check.

Whacker stared at me while his tongue worked its way behind the wad of tobacco tucked into his lower lip. He popped the brown mass out into the cup.

"What's your religion?" he asked, pen in hand.

"None." I hadn't been to church in years, and I didn't want to declare myself to be a part of anything until I understood what I was committing to.

"Do you mean you ain't sure what kind of Christian you are? Or do you belong to one of those fake religions like Buddha or Islam or some other shit that makes you wear a rag on your head?"

I said nothing.

He spit again. "Okay, asshole, but you can't never change your answer, so don't come back in here at Easter and tell me you're a goddamn Jew just so the kitchen has to give you those lousy crackers. Now get the fuck out of my office."

After I had closed the door behind me, I said, under my breath, "That went well."

- - - -

A basketball tournament was scheduled on my first Saturday. I wished I could play, but I couldn't risk it only weeks after my knee surgery. I went out to the courts to watch. When I got there, a big guy shouted, "Anybody else want to sign up for the three-point contest?"

Without thinking, I walked over to him. He was at least six feet five, 250 pounds, with a shaved head and biceps the size of my thighs. "You want in?"

"Sure, why not?"

He handed me a clipboard and told me to add my name and my inmate number. Discreetly, I pulled a slip of paper from my pocket because I hadn't memorized the number yet. The sign-up sheet contained several dozen names. This was going to take a while. I considered backing out, but the big dude was standing over me. I signed my name to both the three-point list and free-throw list.

He took the clipboard back and stuck out his hand. "James, but they call me Mo in here."

I shook his hand. Before I could say my name, he turned and yelled, "Another white boy signed up. That makes five of them."

The yard had two courts, so while the contest started on one, I went to the other to practice. I hadn't shot a basketball in years. Mo called out names, and one by one, each contestant stepped up to shoot. A lot of the players were good, but the baskets were old-fashioned with unforgiving double rims. Most guys missed the first few shots—and each time Mo would heckle them. A few actually missed all ten shots and were razzed off the court. Maybe entering had been a bad decision. Maybe I should just head back to the unit.

"Engle!" Mo called. Too late. Mo threw me the ball. "You got to beat seven to win."

I dribbled the ball a few times to get a feel for it, then launched my first shot. It banged hard against the back rim and bounced all the way into my hands again.

"Oh for one," Mo said.

I shot the ball again and it hit the front rim, bounced high, and dropped through.

"Lucky bounce. One for two."

My next shot slipped cleanly through, hitting only net and making a nice *pop*. I hit my next shot and the four after that. I felt the crowd ramping up, paying attention. A clump of white guys cheered for every basket I made.

"Seven for eight," Mo yelled. "All you need is one more."

I felt good and nervous at the same time. I launched the next shot and it barely nicked the front of the rim. Some of the inmates hooted.

"Seven for nine. Lot a pressure for the new guy!"

Without waiting, I threw up my final shot—a high-arching ball. I knew it was going in as soon as I let it go. The ball went through the net cleanly, and the crowd let out an *"Ohhhhhh."* I had gotten lost in the moment. Suddenly, I realized that I had attracted a lot of attention—exactly what Howell had told me not to do.

Mo walked over with my winnings: four packets of Gatorade. As he handed them to me, he clamped one of his giant hands on my shoulder. "You're a pretty good shooter, Engle, for an old white dude. Then he leaned in close, squeezed my shoulder a little harder. "Some friendly advice. If I were you, I would make sure I didn't win the free-throw contest."

I nodded. When it was my turn at the free-throw line, I missed seven out of ten. I looked over at Mo, and he winked.

- - - -

When I finally had money in my PAC—and managed to find an available phone in the busy hallway—I called my kids. I was afraid I would cry when I heard their voices. I told myself to keep it together, not make it worse for them. I did everything I could to keep the conversation light. I even made a few inappropriate prison jokes. My allotted fifteen minutes passed quickly. I reminded them we would get through this together. When I hung up, I felt empty and desperate to talk to someone else. I had to wait an hour to use the phone again, and when I was allowed to, I called my mother.

She answered after a few rings but was confused by the recording that greeted her, asking if she wanted to talk to an inmate at Beckley federal prison. I was afraid she would hang up, but she hit the right button and said a quavering "Hello?"

"Hi, Momma."

I had called my mother *Momma* for the first twelve years of my life. After that, it was mostly *Mom*. But when I heard her voice, I felt like that little boy again.

"Hi, Momma. It's Charlie."

I told her I was fine, that she shouldn't worry about me. She told me a story about her cat and talked about how much she wished she could focus on writing but her mind wasn't working right. Then she launched again into the story about her cat. I didn't have the heart to stop her. She sounded so far away, so uncertain, so lost. My throat tightened. She was slipping away. I wasn't sure there would be anything left by the time I got out.

Besides three hundred minutes of monthly phone time, we had limited access to an e-mail system. We were charged by the minute.

I exchanged daily e-mails with my father, who was still in full battle mode with my case. He was combing through the trial transcript and other documents. He kept me up-to-date on the national news; every day, he said, came more astonishing revelations about the collapse of the housing market. Banks were being hit with record fines—but not with criminal charges, something we both found outrageous. My father's doggedness made me smile. I'd known he had a deep streak of cynicism when it came to the government. But now this was personal. Big government had come after his son. It felt good to know he was on my side. For all our differences, I knew he loved me—and he was determined to not let these assholes win.

- - - -

My knee was feeling a little better, and I was anxious to run again. Before I could even attempt my first running steps, though, I had another problem to solve. I didn't have running shoes—only the poorly fitting steel-toed boots I had been issued with my standard greens. I could order shoes from the commissary, but I had to wait for money to be put into my account. The purchase would also have to be approved by Whacker, and based on my first encounter with him, I didn't think he would rush to sign the approval form. I suspected if he knew how important running was to me, he might never allow me to buy shoes.

I decided to see if I could make a deal for somebody's old shoes. On the outside, I would never consider wearing castoffs. Running shoes wore out in specific ways based on how their owner ran. Wearing used ones could lead to injuries. Plus, anything you didn't buy through the commissary was against the rules. If I was caught, I would get a *shot*— be written up for an infraction—and risk being sent to the *hole*, solitary confinement. Still, in the short time I'd been here, I'd witnessed a robust free market. Guys traded each other daily for watches, boots, artwork, and food. I was desperate for shoes. I'd take my chances.

One day, a huge black guy, maybe four hundred pounds, massive arms, approached me in the long lunch line. "You the dude looking for kicks?"

I glanced around to see if any guards were within earshot. "Yeah."

"Cost you some mack."

"No problem."

I didn't actually have any packs of mackerel or tuna or stamps or anything that was viewed as currency at Beckley because I hadn't yet been allowed to shop in the commissary. But I wanted shoes. We'd have to work out a deal.

A few days later, the guy showed up outside my cell with black Nikes under his arm. He slid them over to me. "Check 'em out."

The ratty-looking shoes had holes in the sides and worn-down soles. I pulled the tongue up to check the size, and when I did, I got a whiff of them. They were size twelve.

"Yeah," I said, trying to hide my excitement. "Okay. All right."

I promised him a dozen packs of tuna and a jar of peanut butter, even though I had been told owing an inmate anything could get you in serious trouble. I'd deal with that later. The shoes were mine. When he was gone, I took off my heavy boots, laced on the Nikes, and bounced, as best I could on my sore knee, around my cell. Yeah, these would work. Now I just needed my knee to heal.

- - - -

After I made two more attempts, Whacker finally approved my visitors' list. Thinking maybe he had decided to be reasonable, I went back to him with another request: I wanted a job in the recreation department. Inmates were not required to have jobs, but I wanted to stay busy and make a few dollars to spend at the commissary. I got the head of recreation to sign my request form—a *cop out* in prison lingo—and went to see Whacker.

"Do I give this cop out to you?"

"Why the hell would I want that?" Whacker glared at me.

"I was told that rec needed people and I would like to work there. Mr. Wahl signed off on it."

"I don't give a shit what he signed. It's not your fuckin' choice. I'll assign you a job tomorrow."

The following Monday, I was assigned to recycling. My job was to sort through the garbage from both my camp and the medium-security facility next door. Most of it was routine crap, but some days I discovered little surprises: hypodermic needles, soda cans cut in half and used to hold ink for prison tattoos, and the occasional blood-soaked piece of clothing. It was disgusting. I earned $5.25 per week, just enough to buy a jar of peanut butter only six months past the expiration date and some crackers to go with it.

I continued walking with Howell and the guys around the track every night before count time. In his former life, Howell had been an investment banker managing a big portfolio for some powerful people. He told me he had been asked by an unethical prosecutor to give false testimony about one of his former clients. He refused to lie, which made him the target for the same prosecutor. He lost his legal battle and was sentenced to eighty-four months. Because of what had happened to him and so many other people he'd encountered in the federal prison system, Howell had become an advocate—and pro bono jailhouse lawyer—for inmates who needed help filing grievances or appeals.

Howell wanted to help me, too, and I gratefully accepted. I gave him every document I had relating to my case, including the grand jury testimony and the trial transcript. After reading it all, he told me that mine was one of the worst cases he had ever seen. He encouraged me to keep fighting.

Without running—and with no AA meetings to attend—my anxiety level was skyrocketing. I knew I had to try to run, no matter how sore my knee was. One evening after dinner, I put on my black Nikes for the first time and walked out to the yard. A few guys were exercising, and as usual the smokers were out in force. Smoking was against the rules, but this stopped no one from lighting up in a wooded area near the track.

I walked four laps and then started to move a little faster. I leaned into each step, trying to prepare myself for my first running strides since my surgery. I picked a starting mark and pushed off with my good leg. When I landed on my bad leg, it buckled and I went sprawling to the ground. I scrambled back to my feet as quickly as I could and started to walk again, trying to act as if nothing had happened.

When I came around to the smokers, nobody said a word. *Good,* I thought, *they didn't see me fall on my ass.* Then I made eye contact with one of them.

"Nice one," he said with a smirk. I said thanks and kept walking. As I got past the group, they all busted out laughing. I turned around and gave them a little wave, and they went back to their cigarettes. This was worse than high school.

I was depressed and worried after my running experiment—but I could do nothing to speed my recovery. I couldn't see a physical therapist or take fish oil or glucosamine—things I would have turned to in my normal life. In prison, the prescription for every ailment was "vitamin I"—ibuprofen, the duct tape of prison medicine—which had never worked well for me. All I could do was ice my knee and wait and hope.

One day, I was on my bunk, and Rowdy, one my cellmates, walked in. His jacket was bulging with things he had stolen from the kitchen: tubs of cottage cheese, fresh tomatoes, bags of broccoli. I was a vegetarian and I was in a serious nutritional deficit: not one fresh vegetable had crossed my plate in the cafeteria since my arrival. Maybe it was being stolen before it could be served.

Rowdy intimidated me, not physically, but because of his comfort with this place. I was still learning, and Rowdy had a PhD in the economics of prison. I asked him how I might be able to acquire tomatoes and broccoli.

He looked at me as if assessing whether I was worth his time and effort. "Let me lay it out for you. Every prison has its own economy. In some places, it's tuna or mackerel packs. In the old days, it was cigarettes. At Beckley, it's mostly stamps. So if you want this tomato, it'll cost you four stamps. Broccoli, five stamps. This tub of cottage cheese, which I don't see how anybody eats, will run you a full book—twenty stamps."

"So where do I get stamps?"

"You ain't shopped at the commissary yet?"

"No, Whacker is holding me up."

"I hate that motherfucker and he hates me back—because I beat him at this game. You can get stamps two ways. You can buy two full books at the commissary every week for full price, like nine dollars apiece, just like on the outside. Or you can get them from me for six dollars a book. I give you the stamps, and when it's your turn to shop at the commissary, you get me six dollars' worth of shit that I want. Once you have stamps, you can buy vegetables or porn or drugs or damn near anything you want. On the streets I had to work for my customers, but in here, I got over four hundred guys want what I got."

"You worried about getting caught?"

"I been caught a few times but it don't matter. This is my life. I ain't got nobody on the outside, so this is the only way I can get something for myself. Believe me when I tell you, everybody got they hustle in here. You may not think so, but you gonna find your hustle, too."

- - - -

After a few weeks in the bubble, I was moved into a two-man cell in what was called the Trailer Park section of the prison, populated mostly by white guys who had been meth dealers and addicts. Meth heads usually made their own drugs, but they were bad businessmen—because they liked their product too much. The other side of the housing unit was known as the Hood and was occupied mostly by black guys who had been crack dealers, but not addicts. The Trailer Park talk was all about NASCAR and fishing and hunting and pussy. The Hood was all about basketball, hip-hop, Jesus Christ—and pussy. At least there was some common ground.

My new roommate was Whitey, a meth head whose brother was on death row in Georgia for murder. Whitey was trying to get his own sentence reduced by testifying against some guys on the outside that he used to do drugs with. I knew I had to be careful around him; I certainly wouldn't be talking to him about my case.

I continued to have daily e-mail exchanges with my father. He'd contacted Joe Nocera, a business columnist for the *New York Times*. Nocera had written an op-ed saying that no one had gone to prison for the financial crisis. Dad contacted him to say he was wrong about that; Dad's son was incarcerated. He hoped Nocera might mention me in an article. On March 25, I got an e-mail from Dad saying that in that day's *Times*, Nocera had devoted his entire column to me—and that he'd come down heavily on our side.

I went to the library to see if the *New York Times* was in yet. Howell was there reading it.

He looked up at me and grinned. "Chuck! This is your ticket out of here!" He brought the paper over to me. On the front page of the business section was "In Prison for Taking a Liar Loan." I sat down and devoured it:

Mr. Engle's is a tale worth telling for a number of reasons, not the least of which is its punch line. Was Mr. Engle convicted of running a crooked subprime company? Was he a mortgage broker who trafficked in predatory loans? A Wall Street huckster who sold toxic assets?

No, Charlie Engle wasn't a seller of bad mortgages. He was a borrower. And the "mortgage fraud" for which he was prosecuted was something that literally millions of Americans did during the subprime bubble. . . .

I kept reading, my excitement growing with each paragraph.

. . . The Engle case raises questions not just about the government's priorities, but about something even more basic: did he even commit the crimes he is accused of?

. . . The more I looked into it, the more I came to believe that the case against him was seriously weak. No tax charges were ever brought, even though that was Mr. Nordlander's original rationale. Money laundering, the suspicion of which was needed to justify the undercover sting, was a nonissue as well. As for that "confession" to Ms. Burrows, take a closer look. It really isn't a confession at all. Mr. Engle is confessing to his mortgage broker's sins, not his own.

"Holy shit," I said. "This is fantastic!"

"This changes everything for you!" Howell said. "We need to file an appeal right away. By God, your old man pulled off an amazing feat here. The *New York Times*!"

I headed straight for the phones to call my father.

"Dad, you did it! I can't believe it! You think there's a chance I could get out of here?"

"I'm certain of it. Nocera embarrassed the Feds. I can't imagine why they would keep you locked up after that article."

"Yeah, but they aren't going to just let me go."

"Fuck them. They ought to. Those dickheads ought to just open the doors and let you walk out of there today."

"Okay, Dad. Be careful what you say on here. I'm not out yet." I knew the call was being monitored.

"I hope they are listening, those assholes!"

I hung up. I was ecstatic—and ready to start packing my bags.

Joe Nocera's story brought a slew of interview requests: reporters from the *CBS Evening News*, *Dateline NBC*, PBS, ESPN, *Sports Illustrated*, and *Men's Journal* all asked to come to Beckley to talk to me. Media requests were processed by Assistant Warden Mullins, a large black woman with a perfectly coiffed weave. For each interview request, I was required to sign a separate approval form, so I made many trips to her office. I would fill out the paperwork and she would give me her practiced bureaucrat's smile and say, "I'll see what I can do." I assured her I simply wanted to talk to them about my own case—not about life in Beckley.

Nocera's article had mentioned my run across the Sahara, and word started getting around the prison that I was a well-known runner on the outside. One day, an inmate named Anthony stopped by my cell and asked if he could borrow my copy of the *Times*. He wanted to read the article about me. I'd seen him around; he was a workout fiend who spent hours doing push-ups, pull-ups, and crunches—and he had the body to show for it. I handed him the newspaper. A few hours later, he returned with it.

"The Feds really stuck it to you, Running Man." He shook his head. From that day on, whenever he saw me, he'd say, "Yo, what's up, Running Man?" Eventually other inmates started calling me that, too.

Nocera's column also mentioned my blog, *Running in Place*, which I had started writing before I reported to Beckley. I'd been able to keep it up from prison thanks to my friend Chip, who posted entries I e-mailed to him. Writing it was cathartic—and entertaining. In mid-March, I had posted one I called "Beckley Prison 101"— meant to be an amusing primer to life behind bars. I talked about the crummy food and the endless paperwork and confounding rules and my ass-busting counselor (though I didn't reveal his name). Mostly, I wrote about how I had decided to view being in prison as a challenge, and how I was adapting to my new routine—and learning "to keep the flames low without allowing my fire to be extinguished."

Suddenly, scores of online comments appeared on my blog— mostly from people who had read Nocera's piece and were offering their support.

Several days after the article appeared, I left the cafeteria and noticed the warden standing near the exit. I had seen him around but had never spoken with him.

I was surprised to see him hurrying toward me. "Engle, you screwed up."

"I don't know what you mean, Warden."

"You said you wouldn't talk about the prison in interviews. But you did. Ms. Mullins showed me this morning."

"Sir, I don't know what you are referring to, but I have not spoken to any media outlet about this place. I want to talk about my case, not Beckley."

The warden poked me hard in the chest with his finger. "You . . . are . . . a . . . liar." Then he threw several sheets of paper in my face. "I can guarantee you there won't be any cameras allowed in my prison," he snarled.

He turned and walked away. I was dumbfounded. I picked up the pages he had flung at me. It was a copy of my "Beckley Prison 101" post. All I could think was that he thought a journalist had written it after interviewing me. But these were my own words. Shortly after the encounter, I heard my name called over the intercom; it was Mullins.

I went to her office and she closed the door behind her, something she had never done in all my previous visits. She walked around her desk and sat down, but did not ask me to sit.

"You know you really riled up the warden. He is not a happy man."

"I got that impression. But he's talking about a blog, not an article. I wrote it myself."

"Well, you shouldn't have done that. But, you did me a favor. This makes it easier for me to turn the media away."

"That's not fair!" I said a little louder than I probably should have. "They only want to talk to me about my case."

"That may be true, but it doesn't matter anymore."

"Just because I am in prison doesn't mean that I lose my right to free speech."

"You are right. But if you keep talking about Beckley, somebody might just decide to use a lock in a sock on you."

"Is that a threat?"

"You take it however you want to. Now you go on back to your unit and have yourself a nice day."

I went straight to the library to find Howell. I asked him to walk with me.

Once we reached the relative privacy of the track, I told him what had just happened. When I got to the part about the "lock in a sock," he stopped in his tracks.

"What the hell does that even mean?" I asked.

He told me that it was common practice for an inmate to drop a combination lock into a tube sock and use it as a weapon, usually while his target was asleep. It was used to break bones—and spirits.

Howell and I met every night at the library to work on my appeal. We combed through paperwork; I answered his questions. My situation was complicated, he said, primarily because I had not filed a direct appeal. After sentencing, my lawyer had explained that if we challenged the judge's ruling, the government might appeal the sentence and I could end up serving a lot more time. Given how hard the government had come after me to this point, I didn't feel I could take that chance. Now, there was no legal basis to appeal any of the issues argued during my trial. Instead, we had to come up with an appeal strategy based on newly discovered information—if we could find any.

Dad was on the job researching real estate fraud and illegal foreclosures from around the country—hoping he might stumble upon something that could help. One afternoon just before dinner I checked my in-box and found an e-mail from my father. The subject line was "JACKPOT." I hurriedly opened it.

> You are not going to believe this but I found out last night that Jim Alberts, the property developer who sold you the condo in Cape Charles, was convicted of conspiring with Hellman on several properties. They used straw buyers and falsified loan documents and every other illegal thing you can think of—including forgeries and falsely inflated appraisals. And your loan officer who worked with Hellman, Michael Schmuff, was also convicted in the conspiracy. The judge in his case asked him if "all of the business they did was fraudulent" and he admitted that it was. They suppressed evidence. That's a violation of your rights under the Brady Rule. If Hellman, Alberts and Schmuff did the crime, then you couldn't have been guilty. But, Charlie, the real point is that we had the right to put those assholes on the stand at your trial.

I was stunned. We had always suspected others were involved because we found internal memos buried in the discovery materials that pointed to a "conspiracy involving several others." I hurried to catch up with Howell in the dinner line so I could tell him what Dad had discovered.

"Those crooked bastards," Howell said.

- - - -

The warmer temperatures and longer days of April fanned my desire to get back to running. But my knee was still painful. I was going crazy—waiting to be able to run, waiting to hear if something was going to change in my case. One afternoon, I decided that no matter how much it hurt, I was going to run. I would do what I'd often advised others to do when they asked me about beginning a running program: just get started. I set my sights on running one lap. I walked several laps as a warm-up, and by the time I finished the fourth one, I was walking as fast as I could.

I leaned forward and tried to roll smoothly into a run. Instead, I did a strange hop-hitch-slide thing, like a newborn colt trying to take his first steps. I felt as if I had forgotten how to run. One awkward stride rolled clunkily into the next. After about a dozen steps, I pulled up to take a quick inventory. I think I actually looked behind me to see if any parts had fallen off. Nothing there. I took a deep breath and started up again. This time I made it about one hundred yards. The pain was manageable. It wasn't pretty, but I was running.

I finished my lap and then walked once around the track. I had achieved my goal. The prudent thing would have been to stop for the day. But, of course, I didn't. I ran another lap and then another and kept going until I had completed a mile. My knee felt sore but not injured.

I went to the track every day after that. Even though I still limped, I felt stronger with every outing. I upped my distance and my pace, and my mood improved dramatically. Every athlete who ever had an injury knows what it's like to have it taken away for a while—and knows what it's like to get it back. It felt like a resurrection.

- - - -

After three months at Camp Cupcake, the bewildering newness of it had worn off. Day by day, I'd gotten more adept at getting what I wanted and staying away from anything that looked like trouble.

In the chow hall, I'd learned how to negotiate deals with my meat-loving fellow inmates, who eagerly traded their vegetables and fruit for my burgers and chicken. I'd gotten wise to the practice of bringing a big plastic bag to every meal—you had to be ready if some treasure appeared. When sweet potatoes were served, I'd fill my bag, take them back to my unit. Then I'd scoop out their insides, put the mush into a plastic container that I'd bought at commissary, and sweeten them with brown sugar I'd scored from Rowdy for five stamps. I never once saw anything served in the cafeteria that I thought might contain brown sugar—but somehow Rowdy always had a supply.

I had also mastered the nuances of Beckley bathroom etiquette. There were only eight toilets for more than two hundred men. When you went into a stall to take care of business, you were expected to do a courtesy flush, that is, to flush immediately after pooping to minimize the stink. Once you did that, it was fine to linger in the stall—wiping, reading, whatever. But if you neglected to flush right away, you would be shouted down. The showers, too, demanded a certain protocol. With only ten showers, men were often lined up waiting for a turn. If you went more than five minutes, you'd hear about it. Even keeping it that short, the water was rarely warmer than tepid.

I had also learned the proper way to walk down the corridors. Under no circumstances were you to idly gaze into the cell you were passing. However natural it might have been to glance around, prison was no place for people watching. I became adept at looking only at the floor directly in front of me as I moved through the unit.

One thing I would never get accustomed to, though, was the noise. An unceasing din of jabbering, sneezing, shouting, coughing, laughing, nose blowing, farting, arguing, throat clearing, singing, and burping—punctuated with jarring loudspeaker announcements and sudden high-pitched screams—came from all directions at all times of day and night. To never be free of it was torture. Several well-meaning friends sent me books about meditation, and every exercise started with "First, find a quiet spot to sit, where you can relax." I had to laugh. There was no such place.

On Saturday, May 14, I "celebrated" my official three-month anniversary in prison with an early-morning fourteen-mile run on the track. I needed to burn off nervous energy: I had a weekend full

230

of visitors lined up. My mother was coming that afternoon for her first visit, and Pam and Kevin, who had already been here once, were coming on Sunday. As much as I wanted and needed to see the people I loved, visits were stressful. I tried not to think too much about the outside world; it was the only way to get through the day. Visitors disturbed the manageable orderliness of my routine — and more than that, when they headed for the exit and I headed back to my cell, I was forced to confront once more the reality of my situation. They go. I stay.

My mother could no longer drive, so she enlisted a close friend to bring her to Beckley. When my name was called for visitation, I nearly sprinted to the inmate entrance. After a quick frisk by the CO on duty, I stepped into the room and spotted Mom and her friend, Kimberly, sitting in two chairs. Mom beamed as I walked forward with my arms reaching out to her. I hugged her and felt her tininess. She squeezed me hard. When I had talked to her on the phone, it had been hard to gauge how she was doing. She often rambled or sounded confused. I knew in that instant that whatever Alzheimer's had taken, the essence of my mother was still alive.

We were allowed to hug visitors twice, once upon their arrival and once when they were leaving. Other than that, there could be no contact. I so badly wanted to reach out and hold my mother's hand as I sat across from her. We talked about her animals, and she asked me about the food and if I was sleeping well and how my knee was feeling. I told her I was doing okay.

"I think about Attica a lot," she said. "Do you remember that? Being there?"

"I remember those cinnamon rolls you used to bring me from the bakery downstairs."

She and Kimberly stayed until visiting hours ended at 3:00 p.m. When they left, I went back to my cell and buried my face in my pillow. Crying is not advisable in prison, but the tears would not stop. I gave in to them for several minutes, then fell into a fitful sleep that lasted until the screech of the loudspeaker announcing the 4:00 p.m. count.

On Sunday morning, I went for another long run and then waited anxiously for Pam and Kevin to arrive. The visitation room was already loud with friends, families, and girlfriends—many of whom had likely been making the trip to Beckley for years. Kevin seemed taller, and his hair had grown in the six weeks since his last visit. Though he was technically a junior, he had already earned his diploma through a school for gifted students called the Early College at Guilford and was now taking college courses at Guilford College. I had discovered the school when they had invited me to speak there about *Running the Sahara*.

Unfortunately, Brett was not doing so well. Things had been difficult for him since UNC Greensboro had suspended him for a year, a penalty that seemed incredibly harsh to me for a first offense. Pam told me he was "floundering."

"What do you mean?" I said.

"I think he's doing heroin," she said quietly. "Shooting up."

"No way! Not Brett. He's afraid of needles."

"I think he is." She looked stricken. "Coke, too."

I felt as if I might implode from grief. I had brought this on; I should have been out there helping him fight it.

"Maybe we could get him into a treatment center," I said.

Pam teared up. Of course, with me in prison, there was no way to pay for that.

"I'm so sorry," I said. "For not being there."

"You have nothing to apologize for," Pam said. "Nordlander did this to you."

"It's not your fault," Kevin said.

I felt him shaking when I hugged him good-bye. "I love you, Dad. I'm sorry for what you are going through."

I held him a few seconds longer. "I love you, too."

I don't think I had ever said good-bye to either Brett or Kevin without saying I love you. Maybe saying it so much diluted the impact of those words, but at that moment they had great power.

I walked back to my housing unit. I could still feel Kevin's hug, and it dawned on me that maybe the toughest part about being in prison was the absence of physical contact. The deprivation of touch coupled with the complete lack of positive reinforcement of any kind turned already damaged men into emotionless shells. I knew one guy, Dwight, who had been down for nearly ten years and had never had a visitor. Imprisoned when he was nineteen, he had now gone almost a decade without a touch from a loving human being. That would have been a death sentence for me.

- - - -

Not long after my visits from Mom, Pam, and Kevin, something amazing happened at Beckley federal prison. Correctional Officer Johnny Whacker disappeared. Nobody knew why, though there were plenty of rumors. One was that was he caught having sex with a married female CO. Another was that the stack of complaints and lawsuits filed by inmates against Whacker could no longer be ignored, even by the Bureau of Prisons. Most likely, though, he was promoted and shipped to a new prison, where he would have a fresh crop of inmates to torment.

My new counselor, Mr. Painter, was a fifteen-year veteran in the system, and from the moment we met, I could tell he would be the opposite of Whacker. He was pleasant and polite when I went to see him to request a change of cell. I had become friends with a twenty-three-year-old inmate named Cody, who worked out like a maniac in the yard every day. We had arrived at Beckley on the same day, though he had already served nearly a year in a county jail. Cody had nine years to go on his sentence for conspiracy to sell marijuana, though he swore he had only been a customer. His cellie was being discharged, and he asked me if I wanted to take over the empty bunk.

Painter approved my request on the spot, so I decided to push my luck and ask him if I might also be able to move to a job in the rec department. He said it was fine with him. I moved in with Cody the next day and started my job—cleaning the pool-table room, and teaching classes such as "Weight Loss and Obesity," "Dealing with Diabetes," and my favorite, "Overcoming Addiction." In a prison filled with drug offenders, I didn't know how much of an impact I could have. I hoped I could reach a couple of guys and show them that they had options in life other than drinking and drugging, that a sober life was possible and had benefits. But in truth, I needed to talk about sobriety and the 12 steps and to tell my story to others because it kept me sober and sane. It was the closest I got to an AA meeting.

Now that I was running again, I yearned for a goal, something to keep me motivated and help me stop obsessing about Brett and my mother and my case—all the things that were agonizingly out of my control. But Beckley had no races on the rec schedule, no training groups to join. In fact, any kind of organized exercise was technically prohibited. I suppose the worry was that in case of trouble, the guards would rather deal with fat and out-of-shape inmates.

As the days got warmer and longer, I found myself daydreaming about Badwater. In years past, in late May I would be maxing out my training for that race—going for runs of twenty-five or thirty-five miles in the Greensboro heat wearing five layers of clothing, to simulate Death Valley. It seemed as if every running magazine I was sent had a story about Badwater; I lay on my bunk reading and fuming, picturing my friends happily pounding out miles in preparation. It killed me to think I would be in this dump when they were on the starting line at Badwater Basin. I ached for it, that beautiful struggle, that incandescent pain.

One afternoon after reading yet another article about Badwater in *Runner's World* magazine, I went out to the track feeling pissed off and sorry for myself. My mother was deteriorating, my son was off the rails, and though Howell was working as fast as he could, my appeal wouldn't be ready to file for weeks. I stretched and started to run.

The smokers were out, as usual, and the basketball courts were full. Inmates were playing horseshoes and bocce, and sitting in the bleachers staring straight ahead. I heard the wind rattling the tops of trees when I rounded the far corner by the woods, and then on the straightaway the sun hit my face. I had been reading *The Star Rover* by Jack London, about a prisoner serving a life sentence who took fantastic journeys to other lives and other places simply by imagining them. I liked this idea of inner mobility—that no matter what fences you were behind, no matter how limited your movement, you could travel anywhere freely in your mind.

The sun was warm and I allowed myself to pretend it was a Death Valley sun, that I was breathing Death Valley air. Then I was on Badwater Road. I saw the white salt pan near Furnace Creek and the arrowweed clumps at the Devil's Cornfield; I saw the old wooden wagon in front of the Stovepipe Wells General Store; I saw the red-rock gash of Rainbow Canyon and the old gas station in Keller. I saw the strange, potato-shaped boulders of the Alabama Hills and the gray-stone teeth of Mount Whitney.

Maybe if we rushed with my appeal, I'd be out of here by mid-July. Maybe I could get special permission to be a last-minute Badwater entrant. I pictured myself surprising everyone—Ulrich, Reed, Smith-Batchen, Gingerich, Lopez, Farinazzo—as I walked casually up to the start.

I stopped running. *Shit! You're an idiot, Engle.* I wasn't getting out in time to run Badwater. I was going to miss it this year and maybe next year, too. That was a fact.

I had an idea.

What if I ran Badwater here on this gravel track? I did the math; I'd have to do 540 laps to match Badwater's 135-mile course. It would require about twenty-four total hours of running over two days. Even with stopping for head counts, I thought I could do it. Unless there was fog; when fog enveloped Beckley, the guards got twitchy, as if we might all just walk out into the murk and disappear. Fog counts were more frequent; movement was restricted. But if I got lucky with the weather, and if I could keep the snitches from reporting me, and if my knee held up, I was absolutely going to run Badwater this year. I'd be twenty-three hundred miles from the actual start on July 13, but I'd be toeing a line of my own.

CHAPTER 13

... what is there in a storm that moves me so? Why
am I so much better and stronger and more certain of
life when a storm is passing? I do not know, and still, I
love a storm more, far more, than anything. ...

—KHALIL GIBRAN

I told no one about my plan. This was for me. To keep my sanity, I
would do the insane; it had always worked before. Deciding to run
Badwater sparked a feeling of purpose in me that I had not felt since
I arrived at Beckley. I had been in survival mode. But now I knew I
had to do more than simply get through this. Fair or unfair, I would
probably be in federal prison for at least another year. There was no
point in wasting time wishing for a different outcome.

I signed up for classes in everything from blood-borne pathogens
to parenting. I read classic novels—A *Farewell to Arms*, *Travels with
Charley*—and then took tests to get credit for the reading. I piled up
dozens of academic certificates of recognition, which I had been
told might help me get an early release date. I dedicated two hours
every day to writing in my journal. I even joined Toastmasters and
told stories to a packed house about my adventures. The more things
I signed up for and the busier I was, the better I felt.

I reached out to Ray Zahab, my Sahara teammate, who had stood
by me since my arrest, and asked him to send me some workout
plans. We had no weights to use, so I had been relying on pull-ups
and push-ups. Now I needed more. Right away, Ray sent me detailed

running programs to build endurance and body-weight exercises that would help build muscle.

My change in attitude and my commitment to getting stronger and faster did not go unnoticed. Guys started sidling up to me in the yard or in the chow line to ask for advice about running, exercise, and diet.

"How many miles you do today, Running Man?" they'd ask, and I'd tell them ten or twenty or thirty.

Their eyes would get big. "Damn," they'd say. "How do I get started?"

They saw me doing it; they wanted to do it, too. Within a few weeks, I was working out with half a dozen guys every day. Sometimes I ran with them, sometimes I gave them a plan and waited for them to come tell me excitedly about the eight-minute mile they had just run or how far they had gone over the weekend. We used rocks and horseshoes for weights, did dips on the picnic tables and pull-ups under the bleachers.

I also fielded lots of questions about diet and weight loss. Being a vegetarian in prison was like being a whore in church. Everybody looked at you funny, casting some judgment, but they all wanted to ask you questions in private. I didn't try to push guys toward vegetarianism—but I did get some of them to stop eating biscuits and gravy for breakfast every morning.

Not everyone who came out to exercise with me stuck with it. Some wanted results but didn't want to do the work. Some couldn't keep to the schedule and drifted away. Some probably decided I was just too batshit crazy. But the handful of men who stayed were committed, and they understood the importance of working together.

Butterbean was one of the regulars. A friendly guy, he loved basketball, had a teenage son, and weighed 310 pounds when I met him. Adam was a six-foot-five-inch, red-faced, heavy-breathing giant who weighed 437 pounds when he asked me if I could help him. With some encouragement, he started walking. Every day, he clocked five miles—more than I wanted him to do, but once he got momentum, there was no stopping him.

Dave was the only Jew in Beckley, and I joked with him that I let him in the group only because he could get matzo in the commissary, the key ingredient to a good prison-block pizza. Short, balding, with an impressive potbelly, Dave was chronically late and complained daily about how difficult the workouts were.

One day I'd had enough: "Go the hell away with your bad attitude. We don't need you here bitching and moaning."

He was shocked, but knew that I meant it. Later, I took him aside and told him he was welcome to rejoin the workout group if he kept his mouth shut and actually did the exercises. To my great surprise, he showed up the next day and never missed another session.

Block called himself our token black guy. I had noticed him standing nearby while I worked out one day. Since I had never seen him before, I assumed he was a transfer from another prison or maybe from the in-house drug program. He was obviously in great shape.

"You want to join us?" I asked.

"Sure."

That was it. No small talk, no questions. Block was in.

Our ragtag group got together almost every day. We pushed each other and got stronger—and the guys who needed to lose weight started melting away pounds. And week after week, I ramped up my own mileage and speed. I also started doing yoga, something that had helped me avoid injuries in the past. One afternoon, I decided to risk the smokers' ridicule, and I walked out onto the softball field inside the track. I took off my shoes and socks and started my yoga routine. I started with a standing breathing exercise. From there I went into half-moon, then the eagle pose. It felt good to be stretching and balancing. I made it all the way to triangle pose before I heard Shorty's deep voice behind me.

"You look like a damn pretzel." He laughed. "You better be careful or you're gonna get stuck like that."

"Why don't you come on out here and try it?"

"I'm almost seven feet tall. You look silly, but I would look downright stupid."

When I finished with my routine, I put on my socks and shoes and headed for the unit for 4:00 p.m. count. That evening, three guys came up at different times to ask me if I would let them know next time I was doing yoga. They wanted to try it. I didn't expect that. Beckley was full of surprises.

- - - -

One day in mid-June, a major shakedown occurred at the camp. That meant that everyone had to vacate the housing unit. The rumor in the yard was that guards had been tipped off about some cell phones. Phones were strictly prohibited, and anyone caught with one got a year added to his sentence. The shakedown was followed immediately by a lockdown; we were stuck inside the unit until further notice. The timing was lousy. I had a fifteen-mile, hard-tempo run planned for that afternoon. Now I couldn't do it. I paced back and forth in my cell, did some push-ups and sit-ups, and hoped the yard would open again soon.

We were allowed to go to dinner but had to report back to our cells immediately after. The compound, we were informed, would not open again for two days. As I walked back to Evergreen, I remembered a letter I had received from my friend Justin not long after my arrival at Beckley. He was a strong runner and triathlete, but he was also a numbers nerd. He had calculated for me how long a person had to run in place to cover the equivalent of a mile. He called it a SWAG—Scientific Wild-Assed Guess—but he felt it was pretty accurate. I looked through my old letters and found his detailed report.

If I did 674 steps, lifting each foot six inches off the ground, for eight minutes, Justin had written, I would have done a virtual mile. I asked Cody if it would bother him if I ran in place in the cell for a while. He laughed and said no, but that he would go find someone less weird to talk to. I spent the next two hours running in place next to my bunk. By the time I was done, a shallow pool of sweat had collected on the linoleum floor. By Justin's calculations, I had run more than fifteen miles, going absolutely nowhere. It was one of the hardest workouts I had ever done.

I couldn't sleep—not for the usual reasons, the noise and the uncomfortable mattress. I was anxious because in the morning I would run Badwater. How many times had I lain in bed like this watching the clock on the night before a big race? It was a familiar, welcome feeling—one I never expected to have in prison.

My watch alarm went off. Race day. After 5:00 a.m. count, I made myself three peanut-butter-and-jelly sandwiches—one for breakfast and two to take out to the track with me. I packed them into a mesh bag, along with granola bars, almonds, graham crackers, and two of the packets of Gatorade I had won in the three-point shooting contest. I had been acquiring these items and squirreling them away in the weeks before the run. I filled a small, leaky watercooler I had bought from another inmate for two stamps. I didn't have any moisture-wicking shirts or compression socks, but I did have some awesome cutoff gray sweatpants with a drawstring, a nice white sleeveless undershirt, and a pair of dingy white socks—all cotton. In my vintage Nikes, I looked as if I'd just stepped out of a seventies catalog. All I needed was a terry-cloth sweatband around my head.

I packed an extra pair of socks and a hat, then slathered my body with sunscreen and Vaseline, both acquired in trades. Now I just had to wait for my unit to be called to breakfast. Finally, the call came over the loudspeaker. The guys in my unit pushed their way outside. The crowd went left toward the cafeteria, and I veered right toward the recreation area. A few guys called out to me that I was going the wrong direction. I just smiled and waved.

It was already warm—nothing like Death Valley, but I thought it would probably reach a respectable ninety degrees by midafternoon. I walked to the far end of the track, as far away from the buildings as possible, and set my stuff down at the base of a tall light pole. Then I gathered a handful of small rocks to use as a makeshift abacus. After every fourth lap, I would move a rock into a new pile. I set out my drinks and my food: my aid station was in order.

I studied the track. After the flat section where I was standing, the path dropped about ten feet over a stretch of forty yards and curved to the right. Then it leveled out between the bocce court and the horse-shoe pit. Those areas would get busy later in the day, but they were empty now. The next curve took me between the basketball courts and the building that housed the library and the recreation office. The track turned again at the far end of the courts, then skirted the woods, where the postbreakfast smokers would soon be.

My plan was to get in as many miles as I could before the end of the day. I'd change direction every five miles. At some point during the morning, I'd have to hustle into the rec department to do my job. And I would have to make sure I was in my cell for the 4:00 p.m. count. Other than that, all I had to do was run. I looked at my watch: 6:15 a.m. There would be no starting gun, no cheering, no words of encouragement. I was off.

For maybe the first time since my arrest, I felt free.

I covered ten miles in about ninety minutes, probably a little faster than I should have gone out, but I couldn't help myself. By 11:00 a.m., I had logged thirty miles. I was feeling good physically, but I was anxious about my job. If I didn't get it done soon, I was afraid that the CO in charge of rec might come out and ask me what the hell I was doing. If he did, then my day—and my Badwater—could be over.

I threw my greens on over my sweaty running clothes and changed into my boots. I walked inside the indoor recreation area and casually went about cleaning the pool table. I walked by the CO's office and saw him through the small window in the closed door. He looked up and gave me the slightest nod, which was all that I needed. I was in the clear. I had been seen and acknowledged. As soon as the door clicked behind me, I hurried back to the track, stripped down to my running clothes, changed my shoes, and grabbed a sandwich. Just like at Badwater, I would eat on the run.

As it closed in on 1:00 p.m., I thought about what was happening at the real Badwater. The starts were done in three waves, 6:00 a.m., 8:00 a.m., and 10:00 a.m. I had always been given the third start time. As I ran, I envisioned the racers lining up; I knew their pulse rates were jacked, their mouths were dry. At one o'clock sharp, 10:00 a.m. in California, the gun went off in my head. For some reason, I started to cry. I wasn't sure if I was sad or angry, but for a few minutes I felt pathetic. I slowed to a jog. Who was I kidding? I was in prison running around in a circle like a zoo animal.

I stopped to take a drink and compose myself. I removed my $6 commissary sunglasses and wiped my face and my eyes.

Don't be such a fucking pussy, I said to myself. *Nobody gives a shit if you do this or not. But you will know the truth, and that's all that matters.*

I walked a little and then started to run, mentally tucking myself into the middle of the pack in Death Valley. Fifteen minutes later, I hit the forty-mile mark. When I came around the first corner at the basketball courts, I noticed Whitey, my old cellmate, standing by the side of the track with his arms crossed. This was not good.

I slowed to a stop. "Hey, man."

"Hey. What the hell ya doin'?"

"Walk with me." He fell into step next to me. "I'm just going to run all day."

"All day? Why?"

"I want to see how many miles I can do."

"You're fucked-up."

I snorted.

"Really fucked-up."

"You may be right. Keep it quiet, though, will you, man?"

I knew Whitey liked to gossip. I knew the odds were slim that he wouldn't run and tell the first dozen people he saw what I was doing. We walked in silence around the far end of the track.

"You need anything?" Whitey finally said.

I was shocked. I had learned that in prison any act of kindness came with strings attached—anything from doing an inmate's laundry to doing an inmate, with his pants down around his ankles in a bathroom stall. I had managed to avoid—and was committed to avoiding—both of those fates.

"Yeah. Actually, I could really go for a Coke. Would you get me a Coke? With ice?" I only drank sodas during races, and I had been thinking for the last two hours about how good an ice-cold Coke would taste.

"Yeah. I can do that. No problem."

Whitey headed to the housing unit. Fifteen minutes later, I saw him coming back with a can of Coke in one hand and a plastic cup filled with ice in the other. I couldn't believe he had done it.

The first cold swallow was wonderful. "Ahhhh." I let out a satisfied belch. "Fantastic. Thanks."

"Okay. Cool." He turned and started to walk way. Then he looked back at me. "Good luck, man."

I felt strong and reenergized. I realized I felt something else: I felt happy. I didn't think that could happen here. But at this moment on this day, I was perfectly happy. I was doing what I loved, even if I was doing it behind prison walls. At about three thirty, I knew my time outside was getting short. I'd have to head in for count soon. In three more laps, I would have completed fifty-four miles.

"The compound is closed, return to your housing units . . . *now*." Beckley announcements always had an aggressive edge, but this one felt threatening.

Screw them. I was going to finish my fifty-four miles. I picked up the pace and peeled off the last lap as the recreation area emptied. Then I gathered my stuff and hurried to my unit. I got to my cell and pulled on my greens. It was exactly 4:00 p.m. I tucked in my shirt just before the guard yelled, "*Count time.*" Sweat streamed down my face. I couldn't leave the housing unit again until dinner was called at 5:00 p.m. I hated waiting, but I tried to use my downtime wisely, just as I would during a race. I ate a honey bun and another sandwich, then got comfortable in my bunk and elevated my feet.

At 5:05 p.m., Evergreen was called to dinner. Once again, everyone went left and I went right. I got situated and started to run again. My body was feeling good and my mind was running free. I had four hours left; I thought I might get in a total of eighty miles. I was in that rare zone that every runner knows, the one where it feels effortless and easy. I had been running for enough years to be grateful for this feeling—and to know that it could disappear in an instant. I said a prayer out loud, giving thanks to my higher power for giving me a body that could endure and asking for the strength to continue, and to do my best. I also acknowledged the runners doing the official Badwater in Death Valley because I knew the pain they were in at that moment. I asked that I be allowed to suffer like that in order to learn more about myself.

At about 7:00 p.m., a couple of other runners came out to the track.

One of them trotted up next to me and stayed at my pace. I knew him as Stick. "I hear you are running a hundred miles today. Is that true?"

"Where did you hear that bullshit?"

He laughed. "Everybody knows."

Now I knew that Whitey must have spread the word. Stick ran with me until about 8:00 p.m. Butterbean and Cody were both out walking on the track. Every time I passed them, they razzed me:

"Pick your knees up, Engle."

"My mama runs faster than that—and she's got one leg!"

The rec yard was filled with inmates. On a nice evening, plenty of guys were always outside, sitting in the bleachers or playing hoops. But this seemed different. I heard someone say, "Go, Running Man," as I ran past the basketball courts. As I went by the smokers, I was shocked to hear, "Good job, Engle." I kept moving.

At eight thirty, I heard an inmate whistle, a signal used to tell everyone within earshot that danger was coming. In this case, danger was a CO riding on a John Deere four-wheeler out to the track—probably hoping to catch smokers or looking for anything out of place. I knew this CO. He was a decent guy. He pulled up next to me and motored along at my pace. I was trying to be nonchalant, pretending that I was just out for an evening jog.

"Is it true you ran a hundred miles today, Engle?"

"Where'd you hear that? No, I did not run a hundred miles."

"Figured that was bullshit. Nobody can run that far."

That hit a nerve. I couldn't stop myself from saying, "I only ran eighty miles today." I should have kept quiet but my ego got the best of me.

"That's the craziest shit I ever heard." He motored away from me. I didn't know what he was going to do with this information.

The compound closed for the night at nine thirty. I had run eighty-one miles—324 loops around this misshapen track. I was exhausted and starving, and now I was worried. I hated the feeling of not knowing if I would be allowed to continue. I was mad at myself for my big mouth. But beneath it all, I was deeply satisfied. And I also had a secret that made me feel better. As I stood in my cell waiting for the 10:00 p.m. count and lights-out, I smiled. If they wouldn't let me continue on the track tomorrow, I could finish my Badwater right here in this cell—running in place.

I showered, ate whatever I could scrounge up, and climbed into my bunk. I stared at the ceiling, exhausted but too jazzed to sleep. I knew this feeling well. I was scraped clean, made new, fully open. People asked me why I ran. I wish I could let them feel this way for just a few minutes; then they would know. I loved this feeling of being raw more than anything else. Even in prison; maybe especially in prison.

At 5:00 a.m., I got up and made my preparations for another day on the track. Breakfast was called, and I veered off to the yard. I heard a couple of guys say, "Good luck, man."

I felt old and creaky as I started up again. My body hurt. I was sunburned and had some chafing in my crotch and under my arms. I needed to distract myself. I had a small radio with me, which picked up both kinds of popular West Virginia music, country *and* western. I opted for NPR instead. I tuned in to *Fresh Air*. I started to feel better as my body loosened up. The radio weather forecast called for afternoon thunderstorms. That could be a problem. If they were really bad, the compound would be closed and I would have to go inside. But for now, I was running well.

At about 11:00 a.m., I went in to the rec department to do my job. The CO was not in his office, so I quickly cleaned the pool table and headed back outside. When I got back to the track, I saw the rec CO standing next to my pile of stuff near the base of the light pole.

"You know you're not supposed to leave things out here unattended," he said when I got close to him.

I nodded. There was a long pause. I was afraid that my Badwater was over.

"I hear you're running some long distance?"

"That's right."

He looked me in the eyes. "Well, get on with it."

Midafternoon, I had to use the bathroom, and when I finished, a rush of men pushed their way into the unit. "Storm's coming!" Whitey shouted when he saw me.

I shoved past the crowd and made my way outside. It was only raining lightly, but a platoon of dark clouds was rolling in from the west, and the afternoon light had taken on a strange green pallor. I heard distant thunder. By the time I reached the track, the rain was coming down hard.

It was two forty-five and I was running in a kind of panic, desperate to get finished. The rain had flooded the low spots in the track, and I splashed through the pools. Staccato lightning bursts illuminated the yard and the basketball courts and the woods along the track. I was alone; even the smokers were gone. I could not remember the last time I had been by myself.

When I got to the light pole, I peeled off my wet shirt, which was most definitely not allowed, and let the rain pound my bare skin. I dropped the shirt and ran. Lap after lap, I ran. I was not an inmate or a number. I was a skinny kid from North Carolina. I was a runner.

With two laps to go, the announcement came that the compound was being closed for weather. It was also nearly time for the 4:00 p.m. count. I struggled to go faster and willed myself to roll into a sprint. My legs were dead but I was going to finish. I was going to finish this thing even if it meant missing count and getting sent to the hole.

I passed the marker for the final time at 3:47 p.m. I had done it.

Thunder cracked and the rain came at me in sheets, but I didn't care. This past year had taken so much out of me, from me. Running my Beckley Badwater had replaced some of what had been lost.

- - - -

As summer rolled on, I continued to send Facebook and Twitter posts to Chip so he could put them on my accounts. Mullins pulled me aside several times and strongly suggested that I stop sending them. Some of my e-mails to Chip started to disappear from the secure e-mail system, so I resorted to mailing them to him instead. By law, the prison was not allowed to open outgoing mail, although Howell was certain they sometimes did it anyway. I wasn't really afraid of Ms. Mullins. No rule prohibited having my friend and website manager post things on my Facebook. I wasn't telling people how to smuggle in contraband or escape. I was talking about my running and my diet and the people I was hanging with and my family, all the same boring stuff everybody else posts on Facebook.

Sometimes I asked Chip to send me books, ones that had been reviewed on NPR or in *Vanity Fair*. He'd put the request on Facebook, and the books—*The Art of Fielding* or *So Much for That* or *Cutting for Stone, The Sense of an Ending, Three Day Road, Freedom, The Alchemist, King Leopold's Ghost*—would magically show up, sent by friends and strangers. Before long, I had so many books in my personal library that I could barely close my locker. I shared them with Cody and with my workout group and eventually with anyone who wanted to check one out from me. I only had one rule: return the book within a week.

- - - -

Meanwhile, my running group swelled to more than twenty guys. I didn't charge for coaching them: the satisfaction of watching their progress was payment enough—but they found ways to thank me. Thursday was Grapefruit Day. Everyone knew I loved grapefruit. I would sit at my table and guys would come by and put their half grapefruit on my tray. I felt like the Grapefruit Godfather.

In August, with Howell's help, I filed my appeal using a rule that allowed for judgments to be reversed in cases where there had been blunders, fraud, incompetence, or misrepresentation. Howell had done a brilliant job, spelling out the new evidence we had discovered and the things that had been hidden by the prosecution. The motion was filed in my judge's court in Norfolk. Unfortunately, he had recently retired, and the new judge, for whatever reason, declined to make a ruling.

My motion was sent back with the instruction that if I wanted to pursue the matter, I would need to recharacterize the filing as a writ of habeas corpus. To argue for this, we had to show that I was being held in prison illegally because I had been wrongfully convicted in violation of my constitutional rights. I didn't understand the legal jargon, but Howell did. This motion was met with the same swift dismissal. There was no ruling on its substance—only a rejection of the manner of the filing. Howell was incensed and swore he had followed the letter of the law, but we could do nothing.

I sent all of the materials we had put together to my dad, who was not ready to give up. He said he was going to hire another attorney. I was getting tired of riding this roller coaster, but I couldn't bring myself to say no. We talked on the phone every few days. While he raged at the justice system and Nordlander, I cringed, knowing my calls were being monitored. When I tried to get him to tone it down, he ramped up. He even told me he had hired a private investigator to dig into Nordlander's past.

"The guy ran for city council before he joined the IRS. You know what his platform was? Abolish the gay pride parade! He compared homosexuals to murderers, pedophiles, and rapists!"

I understood Dad desperately wanted to be heard. It was tough for him, but it was even tougher for me. I was the one getting the warnings from Mullins about my conversations; I was the one who would suffer the consequences.

In October, a producer from NBC contacted me and said that *Rock Center*, a news show, wanted to do an investigative story about my case. I told her that the warden would not allow any cameras or recording equipment into the prison.

I laughed when she asked me why. " 'Due to safety and security reasons, no cameras or recording equipment will be permitted . . . ,' "

I said. I had it memorized. I told her I'd been given no further explanation. She said she would ask again—and she said that they were committed to telling my story, either now or after I was released.

I called my mom to tell her about the latest developments. She didn't answer that day or for the next several days. I finally reached her friend Kimberly and found out that Mom had been hospitalized with pneumonia. Apparently, she had forgotten to close the doors to her house at night a couple of times and she nearly froze to death. I felt panicked. She should not have been living alone anymore. I wanted to be with her and comfort her—but I could do nothing.

- - - -

Fall turned into winter. I was still running hard, even with the temperatures dropping. In fact, the colder it was, the better I liked it because not so many guys were outside. My workout group stayed strong and committed and kept logging miles. I kept teaching classes, cleaning the pool table, trading for vegetables and fruit, giving speeches at Toastmasters, taking naps, and reading as many books as I could get my hands on.

Of course, I didn't want to be here. Loss of freedom was a terrible thing, but I took a strange comfort in the deprivation. No rent to pay, no food to cook, no grass to mow. I was sent to prison as punishment, but I would survive it, damaged in many ways but stronger in others. But so many others were caught in the blast. My family was being punished. The charities that I had raised millions for were being punished. The taxpayers footing the bill for this monumental waste of time were being punished.

Before I had arrived in West Virginia, I assumed that I would most need to fear the inmates, but in fact, the prison staff presented the most cause for concern. Some of them were fair and decent, but many of them seemed to view their job as an opportunity to make lives miserable.

One CO I knew only by his nickname, Johnny Cash, called me into his office when I was in the middle of a visit. This had never happened before so I was surprised to hear my name being called.

Cash was leaning back in his chair with his feet on his desk. He held up a pill bottle and said, "I found hydrocodone in your locker and I'm sending you to the hole."

I stood motionless. I had absolutely no clue what he was talking about, but I knew this was serious. "There must be some mistake. Why were you in my locker anyway?" This was maybe not the best question to ask, but I couldn't help myself.

"I'll go in your goddamn locker anytime I please. In case you hadn't noticed, you are an inmate. Now I want you to tell me about the narcotics I found."

I lifted my hands in an I-have-no-clue-what-you-are-talking-about motion.

He yelled, "Are you trying to hit me?"

I was speechless. CO Harvey, another guard who was there but had been silent until now, chuckled.

Johnny Cash tossed the bottle to me. "Here, take your stupid stomach pills back. But don't forget, I can set you up anytime I want. Now go enjoy the rest of your visit."

They had taken a bottle from my locker that contained two antacids and used it to screw with me. They were still laughing as I walked out.

- - - -

As the holidays approached, visits slowed down. People were busy with their lives. Many friends sent cards, but I could tell they didn't know what to say. I didn't blame them. Hallmark didn't have any *Have a lovely Thanksgiving in the hoosegow!* or *Enjoy your incarcerated Christmas!* cards.

My mother was back home but still recovering from her illness and couldn't travel. I did have a visit from Brett and Kevin just before Christmas. Kevin was still doing well, but Brett's downward spiral was continuing. I could tell that he was uncomfortable sitting in front of me, knowing that I knew what he was doing. But I didn't want to use my only time with him for a lecture, so we just ate crappy food from the vending machines and talked about Carolina basketball. We quoted way too many Austin Powers movies, with Brett saying to Kevin, "I knew you were crazy, but now I can see your nuts." We laughed so hard that the CO on duty told us to quiet down. Kevin leaned over to me and said, "What's he going to do . . . kick you out of prison?"

It was a good visit but I wanted more. I wanted to feel as if I were their dad, as if what I said mattered. I wanted to be a part of their lives—not just someone they joked around with. After they left, I recalled a conversation that I had with Chris Justice not long after I reported to Beckley. He had told me not to expect too much of my family and friends. He said that their early enthusiastic support would eventually fade. The letters and e-mails would slow down. The visits would become less frequent. But, he added, this was not necessarily a bad thing. It meant they were living their lives and not spending every day worrying about me.

"Don't make your family do your time with you," he had said.

I told myself it was selfish to want more. Brett and Kevin had to go on without me for a while longer. They were giving me what they could.

- - - -

Christmas arrived, and as a present to myself, I decided to run a marathon that day—and for the next eight days. Howell, Ashe, Bootsie, Eric, Patrick, David, Adam, and at least a dozen more guys joined me off and on. Mostly, I ran slow and steady, but on New Year's Day, I went after it to see if I could break three hours. I finished in 2:58.

In mid-January, my dad came to see me. He maxed out the visit by arriving at 9:00 a.m. and staying until 3:00 p.m. We talked about the case the entire time. Dad was still so angry. I thought I was, too, but when I searched inside myself, I simply did not find the same rage anymore. Staying angry made it difficult for me to sleep and impossible for me to think straight. I had to let it go to keep my sanity. Sobriety had taught me that bitterness was nothing more than self-inflicted poison. I had to survive prison on my terms. Acceptance did not equal agreement. Fists up wasn't the only way to fight.

With strong encouragement from my father, I filed a Rule 33

motion asking for a new trial. While my other filings covered a broad spectrum of issues, this filing was based primarily on Brady material. We contended that the prosecution knowingly withheld exculpatory information from me. The prosecution never disclosed that they were investigating other people who might have been directly involved in falsifying and forging my loan applications. To put it mildly, this was a serious violation of the rules of justice.

I had been in prison for about a year, with only six more months to serve. The thought of having to endure a new trial was akin to having my testicles twisted in a vise, not something I would normally volunteer for. I wanted justice; I wanted to see my conviction overturned—but I had seen what the justice system did to people who fought them. My sentence was nearly over. What if a new trial got me five years . . . or seven . . . or more? In so many ways, I just wanted to move the hell on with my life.

My workout group shrank and grew as some guys got out and others came in. Shorty was released in late March. He didn't even say good-bye. I started to see that everybody in Beckley would get out someday, but that Beckley—like prisons everywhere—would always be full. There was no correction, no rehabilitation, only humiliation and overcrowding and neglect—and, most likely, lasting damage.

- - - -

In mid-April, I was called into my case manager's office. John Carter was a retired Marine and a disciple of Johnny Whacker, so I avoided him. Usually he called me in to tell me I needed to complete some course or sign some paperwork. But on this day, he had some good news: he was issuing me my release date from Beckley.

On June 20, I would be headed to a halfway house in Greensboro, he said. I'd be given five hours to report to them, and I would be there for two months unless they released me to direct home detention. I thanked him and left his office. What I didn't tell him was that I was considering turning down the halfway house and serving my last two months at Beckley. I had a plan: I wanted to run the two hundred miles from Beaver, West Virginia, to Greensboro—back to my life.

One evening in late April, I called Brett's cell phone. I just wanted to hear his voice. He picked up the phone, and as soon as I said hello, he confessed he'd been doing hard drugs for six months—"mostly heroin."

My heart dropped. I felt nauseated. I didn't ask questions. I was afraid of what else he might admit—and I knew prison ears were listening. The line went silent for an unbearable instant.

"But, Dad, I'm going to rehab."

A family friend had found a ninety-day drug rehab for him in Baton Rouge, and my father had said he would pay for it. As Brett spoke, his voice gained strength. He had been at the bottom and now had a solution. I recognized the relief and optimism he was feeling. I was so grateful that my friends and family had stepped up to help him. I knew it would not be easy—but at least I was sure that for the next three months, Brett would be safe.

I had always known Brett and I are a lot alike. We both want desperately to please and to be loved. We are sensitive, and when things go wrong, especially when we disappoint the people we love most, chaos follows. Hurt feelings become a catalyst for destructive behavior.

It was so hard to pull back from that place, especially when you felt wounded, too. Much easier to say, "Screw it! I've already fucked up so much that I might as well get high and escape to a better place." After all of these years, I had learned that wasn't the answer, but Brett was young and vulnerable and didn't yet understand that what looked like a bunker was actually a bottomless pit.

"I'm proud of you, Brett." I tried not to let my voice crack. "I'm here for you."

The hollowness of that declaration killed me. I wanted to be *there* for him. If it would have helped my son, I would have walked out the door, crossed the yard, and bushwhacked off this mountain to be with him—and faced the consequences later.

But I had to stay rational. Brett's decision to go to rehab made it clear what I had to do. I would leave Beckley on June 20 and go to the halfway house in Greensboro. If I stayed in prison just so I could run home, some grand gesture for my own satisfaction, I'd never forgive myself if something happened to Brett or my mother in those two months when I could have been close to home.

I told Howell my plans. He understood. His own mother had passed away a few months earlier, and his request for a furlough to go to her funeral was denied. I watched him suffer through losing the most important person in his life and agonize over not being there with his family. I knew I couldn't risk that.

With my departure date less than eight weeks away, I suddenly had a long list of things to do. I told my workout group that I would soon be leaving. Before any of us got teary, I warned them that they better not slack off after I was gone.

I had answered ten to fifteen letters a day while I was in prison—and I had saved every one. Many of them were from people I had never met—sober people or those who were still trying to find sobriety. Some had written to me dozens of times since my arrival. Now, with my departure approaching, I wanted to make sure I answered every letter I had left to reply to—and let people know that I was getting out and that they could reach me by e-mail.

In the midst of my preparations to leave, I received a letter from Kimberly saying that Emory University wanted to archive my mother's life work: plays, articles, interviews, everything. I was elated that Mom would get the recognition she deserved, but saddened that she probably wouldn't comprehend what an honor that was. Kimberly said we would wait to box up Mom's writing until she moved into a care facility.

That same week, I also received a large envelope in the mail—the answer to my latest appeals. Based on Howell's assessment and my dad's confidence, I was optimistic that I would at least be granted a hearing in front of a judge allowing me to present the newly discovered evidence. I opened the envelope and scanned the letter. Not only was no hearing granted, but we were also chastised for even asking the court to consider such a thing. The judge felt that we had not proven our case and even implied that we were wasting the court's time.

It was time to let it go for now, to focus on the future. I was lucky to have a job offer from my old friend Steve Lackey, who owned

Endurance Magazine, in Durham, North Carolina. He had offered to hire me as a writer and to help develop some ideas he had for events. I also had a place to live, thanks once again to my amazing, loyal friend Chip Pitts, who had agreed to let me move back into his guest room, knowing that I had no idea when I'd move out.

On May 1, I was allowed to leave Beckley for an appointment in town. I had been bothered by groin pain for several weeks, and Doc thought I had a hernia. My request to see a doctor had finally been granted. I rode to the local hospital in a van, sealed off from the driver by a metal wall. I peered out the window and marveled at a world that I had not seen for fourteen months. I glimpsed a woman grabbing a towel out of her backseat before heading into a tanning salon, kids on playground swings, a dog riding with his head sticking out of the car window, a pretty woman with sunglasses in a convertible, her hair flying back. There were hotels, grocery stores, restaurants, gas stations, and people—people in normal clothes, doing normal things, coming and going, free to do as they pleased.

I was allowed to sit in the waiting room with no handcuffs. I had on my prison greens, but nobody seemed to notice. This was a prison town and West Virginia was a prison state, so the people who lived here were used to seeing this uniform. A nurse even offered me a cup of coffee and I eagerly accepted—after my prison escort nodded his approval. The coffee was weak but still fantastic—my first cup of non-instant in fourteen months. I considered asking if I could go to the hospital cafeteria for a bite to eat, but I didn't think they would accept stamps as payment.

The doctor confirmed that I did indeed have a hernia. He looked at his schedule and said he could work me in for surgery in October. I thanked him and told him I was headed home, but that I appreciated the diagnosis. He wished me luck, and in his voice I heard kindness and concern.

- - - -

On June 1, the *New York Times* ran a second column by Joe Nocera about my case. Once again, he told my story and expressed his disbelief that not a single top executive at any of the firms that nearly brought down the financial system had spent so much as a day in jail. "For whatever inexplicable reason, prosecutors really wanted to nail Charlie Engle. And they did," Nocera wrote. I was grateful that Nocera once again acknowledged my plight, but whereas his first article had given me hope, this one made me feel anxious. Despite all the evidence, I no longer had any hope that my conviction would be overturned.

On the same day, I spoke to Dad and he told me that a film crew from NBC's *Rock Center* planned to be in front of the prison waiting for me when I walked out. I hurried to end the call; I did not want the Beckley eavesdroppers to know anything about a camera crew. Dad and I continued the conversation through e-mail, using a kind of secret code. I told him to be careful and not to get me in trouble — or get himself arrested.

- - - -

My last few weeks at Beckley passed surprisingly quickly. I stayed busy reading, teaching addiction classes, working out with my group — preparing to say good-bye to my friends. I never expected to make real friends in prison. Unlike the closing of other chapters in my life — graduations or relocations — these good-byes felt final. I could not have contact with them again, even after they had been released. I suppose this rule was meant to prevent ex-cons from conspiring to commit new crimes, but the result was that many guys walked out of prison without a single person to talk to. It gave real poignancy to that last handshake. What could I do but say, "Good luck. Have a nice life"?

As anxious as I was to get out, I realized a small part of me was going to miss the simplicity of life in prison. Here there was only good and bad and worse. Nothing was hypothetical. I faced few decisions. When I first got to Beckley, I had heard guys talk about how much less complicated life was in prison than on the outside. Now I understood what they'd meant. Still, I had no desire to come back. I was ready to face complications.

As my release day approached, I felt my hunger—for all things—returning. I was hungry for love, starved for adventure, ravenous for freedom. I wanted to gorge on fresh tomatoes and sweet corn, devour art and movies, race through the woods.

In prison, my insides had been scraped out, the sludge of my ego washed away.

Who would I be when I left this place? I believed that I would be the absolute core of who I was supposed to be, and all the space around that core would be filled with love and truth and humility and simplicity and passion. I knew that eventually my ego would catch up and climb back aboard, but I didn't plan to let it drive.

CHAPTER 14

Throw roses into the abyss and say:
"Here is my thanks to the monster who
didn't succeed in swallowing me alive."
——FRIEDRICH NIETZSCHE

I walked out the prison doors and saw my dad. He greeted me with a hug and a Venti Starbucks triple-shot mocha with whipped cream. I wasn't sure what I was more excited about. I was allowed five hours for the four-hour drive to the halfway house in Greensboro. I wanted to stop and eat, but not until we had crossed into North Carolina. I had had enough of West Virginia. Since my clothes were stored at Chip's house, I had asked him to pack a bag for me and give it to Dad. I changed in the car, loving the feel of my own shorts and T-shirt.

A camera crew from *Rock Center* had been on the prison grounds, waiting to film me leaving Beckley, but officials got wind of it and sent them away. One of the crew called my dad's cell phone and asked to meet at a rest area to interview me there. Technically, I was on a "furlough" and prohibited from talking to any media. I had signed a form agreeing to that. While I had certainly bent a few rules at Beckley, I decided that it was best not to take chances now. I said no. Once my time in the halfway house was completed, I could do as many interviews as I wanted.

As we drove, Dad talked about filing one last appeal.

"No," I said. "No more attorneys. You can't spend any more money. Besides, there is no way any court is going to side with us.

Our best bet is just to tell the story and let the court of public opinion weigh in. Maybe I'll get a presidential pardon."

Dad laughed, but I knew he was disappointed that I didn't want to fight anymore.

The halfway house was an unremarkable two-story redbrick building that I had driven past dozens of times without knowing what it was. I stepped inside the front door with a small duffel bag and a backpack. Behind a glass partition, a light-skinned black man with a long ponytail greeted me with a casual smile. He said his name was Michael.

I asked him if I could step outside with Dad to say good-bye, but Michael said that once I came in, I couldn't go back out. He pointed us to a small room with a television. Dad and I sat together for a few minutes. I thanked him again for picking me up and for all he had done for me.

Dad told me he loved me, and I said I loved him, too. I hugged him one more time and he left. Even though my life had been ripped apart, the closeness I now felt with Dad almost made it worth it. I wondered if it would last. I knew he would never get over what he found to be an outrageous injustice. A veteran and a patriotic American, he felt betrayed. I hoped he would find a way to get past it someday.

Michael buzzed me through a locked door and took me back to an office. I was checked in, which meant more paperwork that I didn't read and an extensive search of my belongings. A woman came in and explained the rules to me: no smoking; no food allowed anywhere except the dining area; and absolutely no cell phones anywhere on the premises. The people running the Dismas Charities halfway house were contractors, not BOP. They were quite nice and didn't seem interested in making this a miserable experience. The same cannot be said about my new roommates, who ranged from murderers to rapists to all manner of violent criminals. In the federal system of postincarceration, people from all security levels are funneled into the same halfway houses. This was the true definition of a melting pot.

After a twenty-four-hour waiting period, I could leave the halfway house to go to the gym and to the public library down the street to use the computers or check out books. Most important, I could go to AA meetings. The Summit Club, where I had attended meetings for years, was right down the street. I spent the evening unpacking my few belongings and reading. I spoke briefly to a couple of my fellow residents, but I needed no more felon friends, so I planned to keep to myself. I hoped I wouldn't be there for long. Since I already had a job offer and a place to live, I was eligible for direct home detention.

I spent a fitful night in the loud dorm-style room with twenty other men, several of whom were talking on cell phones. I finally gave up on sleep and went downstairs to wait for breakfast. No plastic bag or any meat trading was needed because the food was tasty and plentiful. I ate pancakes and eggs and grits and cereal and muffins and fruit. The woman doing the cooking had been there for years and clearly took pride in feeding hungry men good Southern food.

After breakfast, I checked out and headed down the street to the Summit Club, as giddy as a kid going to an amusement park. The early-bird meeting started at 8:00 a.m., and when I walked in, I saw some people that I recognized. A few said hello to me. If any of them knew I had been in prison, they didn't let on. When the meeting started, I closed my eyes and listened. It was the first time I had heard someone else say the Serenity Prayer out loud since I went to Beckley. As the meeting progressed, I heard talk about gratitude and acceptance. It was just what I needed. I could feel myself shedding the heaviness of the past eighteen months.

Saturday brought a steady stream of friends. I received them with gratitude. I had asked so much of them while I was away. They had fed my kids and taken them on trips and helped in a hundred other ways. Later in the day, Pam and Kevin came to see me. Kevin was so at ease and confident. I marveled at how much he had matured. I relished the moment, sitting with the two of them, talking and laughing. They filled me in on Brett, who was still in Baton Rouge for another month. Pam said he was doing well, and she gave me the number where I could call him.

That night, after a couple of tries, I reached Brett. It was clearly a house phone and I couldn't hear him well because of all the background noise.

He yelled something and the noise died down. "Sorry about that. A few guys are graduating tomorrow and the place is a little crazy."

"No worries, buddy. I only get five minutes to talk now anyway."

"That's funny. Me, too."

"I guess we are both in halfway houses of a sort."

"Halfway to what? That's what I want to know." Brett laughed.

"Hopefully halfway to something better."

"Well, I think that's up to us."

"Who is this? What have you done with my son?"

When the phone went dead, we were both still laughing.

- - - -

I talked to Brett every few days. He always sounded so good. He was lifting weights every day and feeling healthy. He talked about one of his counselors there and how much he admired him. He said he might want to be an addiction counselor someday. I could tell Brett was fully immersed in recovery. I had gotten used to thinking of him as an addict, as if that were all he was. My love and energy as a father had gone into wanting him to stay alive. With each conversation, I remembered how much more there was to him. He was funny, kind, empathetic, and a great athlete. I had always been proud of him. It was a huge relief to allow these positive images back into my mind.

- - - -

I started my job at *Endurance Magazine* later that week. Their office was in Durham, about an hour's drive from the halfway house. Steve Lackey and I had been friends for years, and he'd visited me at Beckley a couple of times. He didn't need me at the magazine, but he offered to hire me at minimum wage if it would help me get out of the halfway house. We spent the first couple of days in Durham catching up and talking about possible stories I could write. I loved driving back and forth to work every day and going to AA meetings in the evening.

Two weeks after leaving Beckley, I was fitted with an ankle monitor and allowed to serve my last six weeks at Chip's in home detention. Chip had enough cable channels for me to spend the next year catching up on shows I'd missed. I especially liked *Dexter*, about a good-natured serial killer. We didn't get Showtime at Beckley.

Chip had planned a huge Fourth of July party with a nearly professional fireworks display. Dozens of friends showed up. I loved it because having so many people there took the pressure off me. The only awkward moment came when it was time for the pyrotechnics. At the end of Chip's road was a cul-de-sac where he always set off the fireworks. I started down the driveway with the others to watch the show, but realized that if I kept walking, I would be out of range for my ankle monitor.

I made an excuse to head back to the house and told them I would catch up. When everyone was gone, I went out on the front porch and watched the fireworks from there. I liked the solitude, listening to the cheers and the laughter and the booms from afar. The last Fourth of July, the best thing that had happened was that I got a tiny cup of nondairy, chocolate-flavored ice cream with a wooden spoon. *Yeah, I could live with this.*

- - - -

In the weeks after my release from Beckley, I tried to focus on what was right in front of me and what mattered most: my family and closest friends. I forbade myself to think about what had been lost, but that was like telling my lungs not to breathe. When negative thoughts broke through, I tried to deflect and redirect them. Though my future was uncertain, I believed that good, even great, things would come my way if I just kept doing the next right thing. Against my nature, I willed myself to be patient, to allow things to unfold on their own.

I applied for a furlough to go to Virginia to visit my mother. It was approved, but I was not allowed to stay overnight, so I had to do the round-trip—six hours each way—in one day. I arrived in Cape Charles early afternoon. My mother's sister, Laura, was staying with her for a few months while her own house was being renovated, and I was grateful. My mom greeted me with hugs and kisses. She seemed surprised to see me, even though I had told her a couple of times that I was coming. Laura told me that Mom didn't remember I had been in prison, so there was no need to bring it up. Maybe there was an upside to Alzheimer's, after all.

Brett left Baton Rouge on July 21 and came to see me at Chip's. When he walked up the driveway, I almost didn't recognize him. The skinny, beaten-up-looking kid who'd visited me at Beckley was now a clear-eyed young man who emanated energy and confidence. The sweet and kind person who was emerging from the wreckage of these past few years amazed me. My twenty-year sobriety anniversary was on July 23, so we celebrated by going to an AA meeting together.

In mid-August, I received yet another request for an interview from *Rock Center*. I followed the rules and told them they would have to contact the Bureau of Prisons for permission. As soon as NBC asked, I was ordered back to the halfway house, interrogated, and placed in lockdown. Prison officials, I had learned in the last year and a half, hated media coverage and would go to any lengths to stop it. On August 20, I signed my final release paperwork and walked out the door for the last time and into the arms of my boys. No more ankle monitors, no more curfew. I still had five years of probation to deal with and $262,500 in court-ordered restitution to the bank, but I would worry about that later. I had my kids, and that was more than enough for now.

We headed to breakfast at Tex & Shirley's, my kids' favorite place for all-you-can-eat pancakes. We talked about everything from prison to girls to sobriety. I told the boys I wanted to take them somewhere soon, maybe the beach. Kevin reminded me that he was starting his senior year in a few days, but maybe we could go on Labor Day weekend. As we sat there laughing and gorging ourselves on pancakes, I was astounded at how easy and natural this all felt. Everything seemed right with the world.

After breakfast, I headed back to Chip's. I realized that I had nothing that I had to do, and nobody to check in with. My time was my own, and that meant it was time to run.

I hadn't been for a trail run in nearly two years. I was actually nervous as I laced up my shoes and headed out the door. I felt unsteady as I jogged up the road to the entrance of the greenway, the paved path that ran through a section of Greensboro. After half a mile, I saw what I was looking for—the narrow trail that led to the nine-mile loop around Lake Brandt. My breathing settled. Instinct took over. I dodged low-hanging branches, rounded turns, leaped over rocks, skirted puddles. I was focused on everything and nothing.

A steady rain started to fall. I pulled my hood tightly around my head, which amplified the sound of my breaths. The trail had gotten slippery and I had to focus on every footfall. I could feel the water squishing between my toes, making a vacuum that sucked my slipping heel back into the footprint. Gasping, I rounded a bend at the top of a long climb. The ground leveled and my breathing calmed. As I ran, I inhaled the smell of wet leaves and North Carolina red clay. The sun broke through the clouds and the trees, giving me a tunnel of light to run through. It was perfection.

- - - -

That night, I got a phone call from my friend Mike Prstojevich. He wanted to know if I would be interested in coming to Northern California in September to be a speaker at a multiday event called the DO Lectures. I told him I couldn't afford the plane ticket. He said it was all-expenses paid and I only had to show up and tell a good story. I said yes.

I turned fifty the day after I arrived in Hopland, California. To celebrate, I went for a great run in the lush hilly vineyards around Campovida farm, which was hosting the conference. I spent the next three days being inspired by the other speakers, eating organic food from the garden, and soaking up the energy of the eclectic group of attendees. I was the next-to-last speaker on the final day. Like the others, I had been given twenty-five minutes to tell whatever story I wanted.

I hadn't prepared a speech, but when it was my turn, the words flowed out of me. I talked about my childhood and my mother and my kids. I described the depths of my addiction. I told them about my love for adventure and running, and about the deserts and jungles I had crossed. I explained why I thought suffering was the best teacher, and I encouraged them to find some suffering of their own. Twenty-two minutes into my talk, I told them I had just gotten out of prison. The room fell silent. Then I told them that I did not recommend prison as a path to enlightenment. They laughed. I closed by telling them that I believed that adaptation was the key to happiness. Anything could be overcome with the right attitude. I finished in twenty-four minutes and thirty-six seconds, without ever looking at my watch. I made no excuses and blamed no one. I knew then I was done with being angry. I was finished with being a victim.

The final speaker was Cheryl Strayed, the author of the bestseller *Wild: From Lost to Found on the Pacific Crest Trail*, the story of the death of her mother and her cathartic eleven-hundred-mile hike on the PCT. After she finished speaking, we shared the stage to answer questions. I mentioned I had heard Cheryl on NPR while I was at Beckley, and I had seen the glowing reviews in several magazines. Dad had eventually sent me her book, and I loved it. Of all the books that I loaned out when I was at Beckley, hers was the most popular. I gave away most of my books to other inmates, but *Wild* was one of the few I brought home with me. I couldn't believe I was standing there with her now.

A few days after I got back from California, Harry Smith and the *Rock Center* crew finally came to Greensboro. Before we got started, I rode with Harry over to the apartments where I was living when Nordlander arrested me. He wanted to see the dumpster my trash was pulled from. Once we got back to Chip's, the crew set up for the interview, which lasted four hours. The questions were tough but fair, and I answered them all. When the interview was over, Harry said that there had to be something we didn't know about Nordlander's motivation for coming after me.

"Or the guy's just a jerk," Harry said. "Who knows?"

In October, my friend and fellow ultrarunner Chris Roman invited me to run with him and Tony Portera, another ultra friend, along the Caminho da Fé (Path of Faith) in Brazil. The plan was to run a race called the Brazil 135, a sister event to Badwater. But we wouldn't just run the race; we would first run 135 miles to the *start* of the race and then join the rest of the field for the official event. Chris told me that Mario Lacerda, the race director, had offered to pay all expenses because he wanted to see me get back in the game.

The offer was generous, but I still needed to get my hernia fixed. Besides, I wasn't sure that I could run that kind of mileage. I would also have to get permission from my probation officer to leave the country. The prudent thing to do would have been to politely decline, but I had never been prudent. I said yes, I wanted to do it. I hung up the phone feeling sick but excited.

My probation officer shocked me by saying I could go to Brazil. My hernia surgery went well and I recovered quickly. The doctor told me to be careful about lifting anything heavy or exerting myself too much. I asked him if doing a training run of twenty-five miles instead of forty constituted being careful. He laughed, and I decided to just let him think it was a joke.

In December, I took Brett and Kevin up to Virginia to visit my mom. It was nice to see the boys with their grandmother, even though she was confused about who they were. Mom's friend Kimberly had been to visit her the week before and told me that she thought it was time to think about moving Mom somewhere. She was spending too much time alone and it wasn't safe for her anymore. I reluctantly agreed that something had to be done. Kimberly said we should do it in January. I was embarrassed to tell her that I would be in Brazil running a race. She kindly said she understood and so would my mom. We would move her in February.

The Brazil 135 Ultramarathon was set to start on January 17, 2013. Chris, Tony, and I started running toward the start on the morning of the fifteenth. I was still recovering from hernia surgery, so my training hadn't been great. Regardless, I wanted to test myself after almost three years away from the sport. Most pilgrims on the Caminho da Fé came with the goal of deepening their spiritual connections. I was there to purge some demons.

We covered about sixty-seven miles on day one and sixty-six on day two. I was hanging in there, but just barely. Day three brought us to the starting line of the official Brazil 135, where a couple hundred other solo runners and members of relay teams were waiting to begin. We didn't have any of the normal pre-race jitters because we already felt like crap. We had sore feet, stomach problems, and were sleep deprived and sunburned. The race began and we shuffled off with the pack. A few of the veteran Brazilian runners were off the front and out of sight in minutes. In most races, I would at least be trying to chase them. But I was here for the experience, to remind myself who I was.

As we neared the finish line, I felt as grateful as any human being could feel. We had run 268 miles in four days along the Path of Faith. For me, this was much more than just another adventure. It was the start of the next part of my life.

- - - -

In February, I made the long drive back up to Cape Charles to help Kimberly move my mom out of her house. But when it was time to drive her to Heritage Hall, an Alzheimer's care facility, I couldn't get in the car. I felt that I was betraying her. In her brief moments of clarity, she had said this was just what she didn't want—to be surrounded by sick people and cared for by strangers. I watched Kimberly drive away with Momma in the car, knowing that she would never live in this house again.

Later that day, a man from Emory University arrived at the house and put labels on a dozen boxes filled with her plays, journals, letters, and photographs. I stayed in Cape Charles for three more days, packing up Momma's belongings. While I was there, I received an e-mail from Chris Kostman, the owner and race director for the Badwater Ultramarathon, congratulating me on being accepted into the 2013 Badwater. I had already been crying off and on as I packed my mom's stuff. Chris's kind note opened the floodgates again.

On my way out of town, I stopped to say good-bye to Momma. I found her in a TV room at the care facility. I stood for a moment in the doorway watching her talk to an elderly man slouched in a wheelchair. She was only sixty-nine—so much younger looking than everyone else in the room. It broke my heart.

"What are *you* doing here?" she said with a look of wonder when I approached.

I hugged her. We talked about what a pretty day it was outside and how it wouldn't be long before the dogwoods bloomed. I told her about Badwater and how happy I was to be going back to the race.

She took my hand. "That's good. I love you." Her eyes told me there was more, but the words would not come out.

I left Heritage Hall grateful that the staff there would care for her and keep her safe. I hoped she liked having people around. I hoped she wasn't scared. I hoped she wasn't in pain. And a part of me hoped she wouldn't last long.

- - - -

By mid-March, I was getting worried about money. My job at the magazine wasn't long-term. I was grateful that Steve had helped me get back on my feet, or at least out of the halfway house, but now I needed a real job. I had contemplated getting back into the hail-repair business, but it had been a long time since I had fixed any dents. I wasn't sure I still knew how. I started calling around to some of the guys who used to work for me. I had no problem humbling myself and letting any of them be the boss. The problem was that it was March and a little early for hail. Then I called Scott Blind, an old friend and one of the best dent technicians in the world. He was happy to hear from me, and as luck would have it, one of his accounts in Atlanta had just sustained a lot of hail damage. He asked if I could get there by the next morning. I told him that I had to get permission to travel but I wanted the job, so please hold my spot.

I called my probation officer and explained the situation. She reminded me that a travel request normally takes a week to process. I practically begged her to let me go. She called me back thirty minutes later to approve my travel with some conditions. First, she wanted to call Scott to confirm that I had the job. And second, she wanted me to text her a photo of me working with the car dealership sign in the background. No problem, I told her.

I loaded my outdated tools in the Dodge Durango that a friend had helped me buy for $1,500. I hit the road at midnight, wanting to get there before the workday started. I drove all night, and despite the poor condition of my vehicle, I made it to Atlanta at 5:30 a.m. I slept for an hour in the truck, and when I woke up, one of my old employees was staring at me through the driver's-side glass. He laughed when I jumped. He took me over to meet the job-site manager and to get me set up.

Fixing hail damage on cars is tedious work under the best circumstances. It had been years since I had picked up my tools. I used to be one of the best techs in the business, and now I was the worst guy on the job. I even had to ask a couple of the guys to help me out with some dents I just couldn't fix. For the first few days, I was sore from head to toe, but eventually I started feeling better and doing better work. I followed all of my probation rules and stayed on the job until it ended two weeks later. Even though I was rusty, I made $15,000, enough to let me breathe for a while. I thanked Scott and the guys who helped me and drove back to North Carolina.

- - - -

She sat on the bike next to me in the gym. She had her earbuds in and her music on, the universal sign of "Don't talk to me, I'm here to work out." I struck up a conversation anyway. I hadn't seen her in the gym before. She said she'd recently moved back from Ecuador to be closer to her family. That was my cue.

"Ecuador! I've been to Ecuador."

She didn't take her earbuds out, but she looked me fully in the eyes for the first time with intrigue and skepticism. "Really? Most people around here don't even know where Ecuador is. They think it's in Africa."

I smiled and nodded that I understood. She continued to crank out intervals on the bike. She was clearly a cyclist, and I was impressed by her power and speed. After what seemed like a safe pause, I asked her about her cycling, did she run, what sports did she play. She lit up when she told me of all the rock climbing she'd done in the High Andes. She loved and missed it.

"Have you ever done any mountaineering? Ice climbing?" I asked.

"Well, I hate to be cold, so I mostly stick to rock, but I did summit Cotopaxi."

I laughed with delight. "I summited Cotopaxi, too!"

This time her gaze lingered. She pulled out one earbud and then the other, and soon her iPod was turned off, sitting on the front rack of her stationary bike. We laughed and shared adventure stories for the next twenty minutes. She'd worked in the heart of the Amazon; I'd run there. I'd explored the outer islands of Belize; she'd snorkeled them all.

To her family, she was Stacey, but close friends called her Astacianna. I told her that family, friends, and enemies called me Charlie. She seemed to think I was interesting. I was in awe of her athleticism and excited by her energy and the kindness I saw in her eyes. I couldn't stop thinking, *My God, she's so beautiful! I'm glad I came to the gym today.*

She smiled and said it was nice chatting and headed over to the treadmills. I told her I would come over and say good-bye before I left. She seemed surprised, but said, "Okay."

I couldn't tell if the door was open, but I was going to walk through it any way that I could. I interrupted her treadmill workout to tell her good-bye. Then, sliding my cell phone out of my pocket, I asked her if she'd like to go running sometime.

Her answer was a quick "No" and it threw me off-balance. "I don't run with other people. That's my time alone."

I stood frozen, feeling like an idiot with my phone in my hand.

She let me just hang there before she smiled. "But I'll give you my number anyway!"

My heart pumped so loudly that I thought she might be able to hear it. As I drove away, her number in my phone, I told myself to play it cool and wait a day or two before I contacted her. I held out for nearly four hours.

It was two weeks before we had our first date at a downtown coffee shop. I brought my iPad and romanced her with maps on Google Earth. She was an ornithologist and showed me the remote places around the globe where she had worked. When it was my turn, I showed her where some of my favorite races had taken me.

On our second date, we sat outside and ate hummus and pita triangles and salads at a small café. I went back to the car and grabbed a fleece jacket for her because it was getting cold and we weren't ready to leave yet. My head was spinning. I liked her, but she didn't know the truth about me. She had been out of the country for the past couple of years. She didn't know me as a runner, and she most definitely had no idea I'd spent over a year in prison.

When I came back with the jacket, I took a deep breath and told her that I had something I needed to say. Sensing my reluctance, she reached across the table, touched my hand, and then held it. That simple act let me know that it was safe. I laid it all out for her, holding nothing back. Arrest, trial, conviction, prison. She heard me out, smiled, and said, "Is that it? You didn't murder anyone, right?" I even suggested that she Google my name later if she wanted to know more. She shook her head no and said she wanted to learn about me, from me, not from a computer.

Then it was her turn to take a deep breath. She began to tell me some of her "story," things that she said she kept private, even from lifelong friends. She told me that she had always been uncomfortable with sharing these intimate details for fear that they would define her, but that she felt compelled to tell me now. She had survived numerous rare diseases, including lymphomas; she'd had an onslaught of invasive procedures beginning at age seven and lengthy hospitalizations as a teenager. The chemo and radiation had wreaked havoc on her body, and she'd suffered with a destroyed bladder for nearly thirty years. From that young age, she would never have a pain-free day again in her life. She'd been through dozens of surgeries and there would be more. She didn't complain; she just trusted me enough to share. The remarkable thing was, no one would ever guess any of this based on her glowing presence and lean, athletic build. She'd played professional beach volleyball, but when injuries ended that career, she went back to college, became a competitive cyclist, got married, and was on track for a PhD when lymphoma hit again, the worst one yet. Her husband left her on her deathbed, having already found someone to replace her. But she didn't die. She was here, sitting in front of me. And she was perfect. We were still holding hands, and it was my turn to squeeze. I felt as if my heart might explode. I had never met anyone else like her, and I wanted this feeling to last.

I walked her to her car after dinner and I asked if I could kiss her. She shook her head no, but then she smiled and said, "Yes." After that first kiss, I was certain that this was going to be serious and wonderful, if I didn't screw it up.

The next day, I left for California, and Astacianna drove south to the Uwharries, a densely forested area near Asheboro, North Carolina. I was off to do an eighty-one-mile race, and she was banding birds and doing field surveys. Neither of us had a strong cell signal, so we weren't able to talk for several days. In my event, the inaugural Badwater Salton Sea race in Southern California, teams of three runners racing together ran against other teams, over rough terrain. I was on Team Neapolitan with Meredith Dolhare, a redheaded former collegiate tennis player, and Mosi Smith, a black retired US Marine. I was the white ex-con. We had T-shirts made with the image of an ice cream sandwich with strawberry, chocolate, and vanilla. Under the different colors were the words A GINGER, A JARHEAD, and A JAILBIRD. It felt great to run against tough competition on a challenging course. Unfortunately for my team, my mind was wandering back to North Carolina when I missed a turn and got us lost for several hours. We still managed to finish fourth.

Steve Hilts was on my support team, and before the race started, I asked him to let me know if Astacianna texted or called. I felt like a lovesick teenager. After only one kiss, I couldn't stop thinking about her.

I returned to Greensboro in time for Kevin's graduation from high school. Dad and Molly came to the ceremony, as did my step-dad, Coke, whom I was especially happy to see. We'd stayed in touch over the years, and he had always been supportive. Pam was there, of course, and so was Brett. He was working as a personal trainer at a big fitness club in town. He had put on some serious muscle, thanks to hard training and sober living. We had been through a lot as a family; it felt wonderful to be standing together outside the site of Kevin's graduation ceremony. And Kevin hadn't just graduated; he had earned nearly ninety credit hours toward college. He would be entering the University of North Carolina at Chapel Hill in the fall as a junior. After the ceremony, he came up and hugged me hard and said, "I wish Nana could have been here. I miss her."

It took a second for me to compose myself enough to say, "Me, too, buddy, she would have been proud of you."

– – – –

Astacianna and I started spending as much time together as we could. She was still going out into the field several days each week for her work. She could identify thousands of birds by sound alone. I started calling her the bird whisperer. I was in awe of her talents—and I was falling in love.

I was already in pretty good shape after the Salton Sea race, but now it was time to focus on Badwater. I ramped up my training as much as I dared, walking that fine line every runner knows between too much and too little. I had never been a high-mileage trainer. Instead I focused on duration. I hated going for a "thirty-mile run," but I could happily go out for six hours. I liked knowing exactly when I would finish.

One day, I asked Astacianna if she wanted to come with me. I told her that I would understand if she didn't want to, but it would mean a lot to me. In other words, I guilted her into it. I knew she liked running alone, but I hoped that I could convince her that she was helping me. She reluctantly agreed.

About an hour into our first run, we had been talking nonstop and enjoying the trails when she said, "This isn't so bad. Do you always run this slowly? Now I see how you run for six hours at a time."

I stopped dead in my tracks and pretended to be offended. "Well, if you really want to see how I run, why don't you come out to Badwater as part of my crew?"

"Are you serious? I'm afraid I would be a distraction."

"Honestly, at this point, it would be a much bigger distraction for me if you weren't there. I would love for you to be with me. It's a hard race for me, but it will be nearly as rough for you. It's the same temperature for both of us."

She said she would think about it.

It was strange how badly I wanted her in Death Valley with me. I wanted her to see the absolute core of who I was. I wanted her to know me better than anyone else ever had. I knew that there was no hiding or faking at Badwater. I think in some way I wanted to speed things along and know if her love for me was too good to be true. I knew that she would see the real me, the bad, the ugly, and hopefully some good, at Badwater. I thought she would know if I was the kind of man she wanted to be with by mile 135. I already knew that I wanted her, and that loving her was the most honest thing I had ever done. The next day she said yes.

- - - -

"Wow, you sure are pretty."

Those were the first words out of my mother's mouth when she met my new girlfriend. I don't think my mom even noticed me. She always had great taste in women. I had decided to visit her before Badwater, and Astacianna had agreed to come with me. I watched as she walked up to my mother and introduced herself. Mom used her finger to trace the outline of Astacianna's face. When she reached her hair, she tilted her head slightly and said, "Just look at those things. How do they do that?" Astacianna's hair was impossibly curly, and Mom no longer possessed a filter.

Astacianna and I pulled up chairs so that we could sit with Mom. She looked a little disheveled today, as if maybe she hadn't slept well.

I left the room to visit the nurses' station to discuss some things about Mom's care and her clothes. When I returned, Astacianna was brushing Mom's hair as she sat in a chair. Her eyes looked sleepy. Astacianna looked up at me and smiled. She wasn't performing a chore; she was loving my mother, touching her, connecting with her, with what was left of her.

My mom was living entirely in the moment, so whenever she found herself able to say something, she just said it. She didn't have all the words she wanted, but she made her point perfectly.

"You make me feel peaceful," she said to Astacianna. "I trust you."

- - - -

I couldn't contain my excitement as we drove from Vegas to Furnace Creek on July 14 for the racer check-in at Badwater. I shifted around in my seat in the van as I pointed out familiar sites: Dante's View, Zabriskie Point, the expansive salt flats. As we got closer to Death Valley, I longed to feel the relentless baking sun once again. For weeks the national news had reported stories of unprecedented heat in Death Valley National Park, with five consecutive days reaching at least 129 degrees. Nightly news and NPR were issuing heat advisories. That only excited me more. The record temperature was exactly one hundred years old, 134 degrees in July of 1913. I told everyone that I wanted 135 degrees; the hotter the better. Sitting beside me, Astacianna looked at me bemused as if she was thinking, *Who is this guy? He's nuts!* But I think she liked it. She had told me more than once, "Normal is boring."

"In that case," I had said, "you'll *never* be bored with me!"

I went to runner check-in, not exactly sure of the reception I would receive. Chris Kostman had been incredibly welcoming to me at the Badwater Salton Sea race, and I knew he was solidly in my corner. But dozens of runners that I had known and raced against for years were going to be here. I got my answer as soon as I got out of the car in the parking lot.

Pam Reed, who had won Badwater twice, ran over and hugged me. "Welcome back!"

That's how it went for the rest of the day. One reunion after another. And I was glad that my Badwater friends got to meet Astacianna and to see that I was more than just okay.

I had thought about this race every day for the past three years. At last I was here, on the starting line. To my left and my right were some of the best ultrarunners in the world: Pam, Dean Karnazes, Oswaldo Lopez, David Goggins. Most of them probably assumed that I had come here to simply take part. Just before the countdown began, I overheard one female runner asking why I had deserved the #2 starting bib. My plan was to show her.

I continue to believe that life is all about adaptation. It is not the circumstances that we are dealt that define us. Instead, the fabric of who we are is crafted by how we react, cope, adapt; and now I have a new mantra that I carry with me. It's simple, yet undeniably powerful. Astacianna shared it with me right before the start, for me to use if the race felt too hard for me to continue. She told me that each of us has his or her own pain, and no one else's pain is greater or less than ours. In her eyes, we are only equipped to measure our personal pain in the context of our own life experiences. When faced with what might seem to be an overwhelming hardship, she calms her breathing and with each exhale repeats these three words, one at a time: *No. Big. Deal.*

After Chris Kostman played the recording of the national anthem over his megaphone, we counted down from ten to zero and moved off the start line. I forced myself to do what I had learned to do over the years during this part of the race: go slow. I was amped up, but I knew I would need energy later.

ACKNOWLEDGMENTS

I remember the first big public talk I gave years ago at a university event. I was being honored as a "Balanced Man" and held up as an example of someone who used a sound-mind, sound-body approach to life. As I stood before two thousand attendees, I spoke nearly without taking a breath, filling sixty minutes with the story of my entire life up to that very moment. I felt that the audience had to know every detail about me in order to understand anything about me. I was wrong. It must have been excruciating for them. After my talk, a long line of polite young college students shook my hand and thanked me. However, I knew that I had done them a disservice. I had not given them credit for being smart enough to fill in the blanks that I should have left empty. I had not trusted them to seek more information about me if they wanted it. This brings me to my collaborator for *Running Man*, Meg Lukens Noonan. I have immeasurable gratitude to Meg for not letting me write this book in that same tedious, detail-flooding way. Meg took my stories, and helped to craft them, massage them, and sometimes toss them in the wastebin. I told Meg early on that I intended to be funny in this book, so she humored me (pun intended) and allowed a few of my jokes to stay. I have always used humor as a way of deflecting and defusing heavy situations. But in the course of writing *Running Man*, Meg helped me to stay serious when the subject was serious, to feel discomfort instead of making a joke. Meg has been much more than a collaborator, and I would have been lost without her.

Thanks to my agent, Deborah Grosvenor, for believing in *Run-*

ning Man. And further thanks to Clif Weins for connecting me with Deborah, and thanks to Carrie Regan for connecting me with Clif. That's how it works with friends, passing along contacts with best wishes. And sometimes, things actually work out!

I have huge gratitude for Shannon Welch, my editor at Scribner. In our first talks I told Shannon that I did not want to write a book about running, but rather I wanted to write about how running has shaped me and changed me. You wanted that same thing and together, I think we accomplished what we set out to do.

A thousand thanks to everyone at Scribner, including John Glynn, Kyle Radler, Ashley Gilliam, Kara Watson, Mia Crowley-Hald, Erich Hobbing, Bryden Spevak, Olga Leonardo, and Nan Graham.

Thanks to Bart Yasso, Dean Karnazes, Cheryl Strayed, Pam Reed, Chris McDougall, Scott Jurek, and Rich Roll for the early encouragement to write *Running Man.* Your books helped me understand how to find my own balance between running and story. Each of you chose a different approach, but you all found success by the not so simple act of writing entertaining and honest books.

Thanks to Mary Gadams for your friendship and support. I finished the first draft of *Running Man* in Ecuador, only days before running another one of your fabulous races. Back in 2000, we sat at adjoining tables for a race briefing before the Borneo *Eco-Challenge* and we have been friends ever since. Thanks also to the entire 4 Deserts organization for always welcoming me back so I can make some new memories. My life today would not be complete without the friendships I made in those deserts.

When I began writing this book, I knew that addiction and recovery would be a big part of my story. In the early drafts, I used the term "12-step meetings," instead of AA, to indicate what type of recovery process I used. I did this out of great respect for the Traditions of Alcoholics Anonymous. But something just didn't feel right to me. To gain perspective, I asked people who were not in recovery about the term "12-step meeting" or "recovery meeting" to see what they understood it to mean. Nearly all of them linked 12-step meetings directly with AA and often perceived them as one and the same. For more than eighty years, the AA program has helped millions of people achieve sobriety through the simple formula of one person helping another. In the early days, the founders were concerned about AA being represented in "press, radio, and films," fearing that a public failure by a member would damage the organization. I have thoughtfully considered what might happen if I shared my experiences in AA and then relapsed, all in the public eye. Would that harm AA? I don't think so. AA is far stronger than that. It is so much bigger than any individual. It will not work for everyone but it does work for me. For many years, I have been very open about my addiction and recovery. Because of this, thousands of people have reached out to ask me how they can change their own lives. I can't tell them how they should do it, but I can tell them how I did it. I hope I have helped some of them find their own path to sobriety. And I hope people never stop asking me how I turned things around.

- - - -

I am sincerely grateful to . . .

Captain Duncan Smith, for those early years at Presidio Adventure Racing Academy. Michael Lucero and his legacy live on, as do many friendships that were forged at the Presidio: Chris Haggerty, Rolf Dengler, Ian Adamson.

Josh Gelman, Susan Zirinsky, and Dan Rather at CBS *48 Hours* for allowing me to carry cameras around the jungle in Borneo. That experience changed the course of my life. Josh, thanks for continuing to be my friend. And a special note to Mr. Rather: I apologize for wrecking those video cameras. Though it may be of little consolation to you now, my adventure videography skills have greatly improved!

Tom Forman, for hiring me as a producer on *Extreme Makeover: Home Edition*, despite my complete lack of qualifications. That show, and the incredible people I met while working on it, remains a top-shelf memory for me.

ACKNOWLEDGMENTS

Mike P. and Jason Martin, for your creativity, your belief in my wacky ideas, and, most of all, your friendship.

Steve and Tamara Lackey, for your love and support. You gave me a chance to earn a dime but, more importantly, gain an ounce of hope when I had so little of both.

Mario Lacerda, I will always be grateful that you invited me to run the grueling Brazil 135 in 2013. It was like hitting a reset button for my life!

Greg Clark and Scott Blind, for your friendship and for putting me to work when I needed it most. You both have gone above and beyond by always taking me at my word and believing in my work ethic, no matter the obstacles faced.

Rubin Hanan, Terry Montgomery, and Pat Burns, for placing your confidence in me and setting me in motion. Your guidance and friendship have helped to create a future that I can believe in.

- - - -

To those who have taken my crazy adventure ideas seriously, kept me hydrated, and remembered to never talk to me while I was peeing . . .

Thanks to all the people who have given up their time and energy to crew for me during expeditions and races over the years. I could not have endured Badwater, Running the Sahara, Running America, or dozens of other events without your help. I was the one running, but each of you was hit with the same weather conditions, hunger, thirst, and sleep deprivation. I have always maintained that running is the easy job. I have just one thing to focus on, running, while my support team is charged with every small detail. Not only have my crews kept me safe and healthy, you have raised my spirits and kept me moving forward. Because of you, I will always remember that "the chair is the enemy." In particular, I thank Chuck Dale, Kista Cook, Jim Siverts, Lisa Trexler, Rebecca Byerly, Dean Hart, Chris Justice, Bobby Christiansen, Danny Moy, Louise Cooper, Justin Andrews, Meredith Dolhare, and Marcus Edvalson.

Tim Beggy, thanks for your friendship. You started the ball rolling on *Running the Sahara.* Thanks also to James Moll, Matt Damon, Larry Tanz, Marc Joubert, and Keith Quinn for believing in the Sahara project and helping to make it happen and to Mia Hamm and Jacky Gilardi for the roles that you played.

Jim Van Eerden, you are a great friend and I will always be grateful for your support of *Running the Sahara.* More importantly, it was an honor to be a cofounder, along with you and Matt Damon and LivePlanet, of H2O Africa. The good we did together will always be a highlight of my life. Thanks to the great work that Matt Damon and Gary White continue to do today at water.org, the legacy of *Running the Sahara* lives on.

Mohamed Ixa and the crew at Tidene, thank you for your invaluable assistance and companionship across the Sahara. Without you, I would very likely still be wandering around in the desert. I worry about you and the safety of your families in Niger. You are always in my heart.

Kevin Kerwin and Kate O'Neil, you have my sincerest thanks for making *Running America* an incredible film. It was the hardest physical experience of my life and you guys made it bearable. Chuck Dale, Jenny Dengler, Dave Pearson, Brian Weinberg, and Dr. Paul Langevin, thanks for not letting me die somewhere in Utah. Thanks also to Marshall Ulrich and his wife, Heather. Life doesn't go in a straight line and things don't always work out the way we think they will, but I still remember the good times.

And to my 2013 Badwater all-rookie crew, which included the love of my life, Stacey Astacianna Hatcher, my longtime friends and former teammates, Matt Battiston and Mike Prstojevich, new lifelong friends George Myers and Chris Benjamin, and the ever reliable Louis Pitts, you were all-stars and helped me pull off my most memorable Badwater yet. Gas in the tank or no gas in the tank, it all worked out!

- - - -

For when I looked into the abyss . . .

I offer the deepest thanks to the 120 friends, family, and complete strangers who wrote letters of support to the judge before my sentencing. I confess that I did not see the letters until I was in prison and, at that time, I was incapable of reading them. I tried, but the emotions just cut too deep. And despite your generous assessments of my character, I felt that I had to remain hardened to survive my new circumstances. As time passed, I was embarrassed that I hadn't read your letters and thanked each of you personally. So, I stored them away. Finally, while writing this book, I dug them out and read them, one by one. I could not have felt more humbled. Your letters showed the judge that I was loved and respected. But of much greater value to me, your words have helped me to heal and move past some of my pain and grudges. This acknowledgment is flanked by the sentiment that mere words cannot do justice. Please just be assured that you each have my gratitude and love far beyond anything I can express.

David Willey, John Atwood, and the staff at *Runner's World* magazine, thank you for publishing my article about the Barkley Marathons while I was incarcerated. You took a chance and I am grateful. I am also proud that "Notorious" was chosen as one of the top fifty articles in *Runner's World*'s first fifty years.

Joe Nocera of the *New York Times*, thank you for answering my father's letter. The spotlight you shined on my case helped to make this book possible. Your passion for finding the truth is inspiring.

My fellow inmates, who were part of the Native American sweat lodge at Beckley FCI. I learned many things from that experience. You helped me come to terms with my incarceration and to be grateful for what I still had rather than angry about all that I had lost.

– – – –

I give my most heartfelt thanks to . . .

Richard Engle, my father, for devoting your heart, time, and resources to defending me during some of my darkest times, and against unimaginable odds.

Molly Engle, for taking care of me and always treating me as your son, instead of a pesky stepson that you had to tolerate.

Dina Engle, for being a supportive stepsister through the years and

ACKNOWLEDGMENTS

for reminding me of childhood stories that I had long forgotten. Your memory is sharper than mine. Maybe I can be a better brother someday.

Coke Ariail, my stepfather and friend, for sharing your lifelong love of literature and passion for storytelling. The books you have given me through the years will always be my favorites.

Mud and Daddy Bill, Nanny, Grandmother and Granddad Engle, for loving me when I was a kid. One of my greatest regrets is that I did such a lousy job of being a grandson. Boys often don't get a clue until it is too late.

Pam Engle, for being a good mom and for putting up with my crazy ideas even when you might not have been thrilled by them. Together, we have raised two of the best young men I know.

Brett and Kevin, my sons, for reading parts of this book and giving me your honest feedback. You know my voice better than anyone. Not a day passes when I am not in awe of the kind, compassionate, and uniquely gifted men you have become. I love you both without limits.

- - - -

Rolf and Jenny Dengler, for being amazing friends. You have all of my love and then some. Just no more disposable cameras!

David Faber, for putting up with me as a roommate during a crazy period of my life. I am your friend and always will be.

Dianette Wells, for being an amazing friend and teammate. Most importantly, thanks for loving my boys whenever they would stay still long enough to let you.

Rob Coyne, for sticking with me in successful times and also when I fall flat on my face. You are family.

Kevin Lin, for making me laugh even in the heart of miserable conditions and for being my pacing rabbit in the Gobi. You gave me your trust and your friendship and, along with Ray Zahab, we accomplished something that gives us an unbreakable bond. Ray, you remain my brother, lifelong coach, and favorite Canadian!

Chip Pitts, for taking me in when I had no place to go. You did this after my arrest and after my release from prison. You are a friend in more ways than I can mention here. I love you like a brother.

ACKNOWLEDGMENTS

Kelly and Bryson Walker, Chip and Minda Hunter, Lester Pace, and Jim Johnson for helping my kids while I was away. You were the village that it took to raise children who were not your own and you will always be family.

Elaine Daniels and Gary Misenheimer, for looking after my boys and for being the best friends I could ask for.

Meredith Dolhare, for being an amazing confidante and ally, for loving my boys, and for always supporting my adventures. I look forward to taking on more challenges together down the road.

Emily Wilson Oliver, for your friendship and for getting my audio-tapes transcribed.

Todd Eichler, for being one of the nicest guys I know, even if you did go to Duke. Go Heels!

Greg Fenton, for giving me a chance to fall more deeply in love with Puerto Rico and with Astacianna. Meeting you at Badwater 2013 was an unexpected and now enduring gift.

Chris Roman, for always being kind and supportive. You embody the true meaning of compassion, and I never doubt that you will stand by those in whom you believe.

Steve Hilts, for being a witness to many events in my life, from races in Ecuador and Borneo, to chasing records across Death Valley. You were the only guest at my barefoot wedding deep in the redwoods of Big Sur. That was a stellar day, and you are a stellar man.

Chris Justice, for telling me truths I did not want to hear, while very clearly remaining in my corner. You always had my back. And I know you still get a little nervous when my name pops up on your caller ID. Thanks for always answering and thanks for remaining my friend.

David Johnstone, for your steadfast support for more than twenty years.

- - - -

When there simply are not enough words . . .

Momma, you gave me my voice but you never told me what to say. In a lifetime, what else could I hope to achieve but your unflinching

ACKNOWLEDGMENTS

confirmation that I am worthy, that I have value, that I am loved even when I am at my worst. When your mind is wandering without your permission, and you can't find the words you've misplaced, I know that you see in yourself only what is missing. Rest assured, I see all that is still there. Don't worry about me, Momma. You have given me all that I need to get through this life. I love you today and every day.

Kim McCowan, your love and care for my mother throughout these heartbreaking years has meant everything to me. The love and compassion you have for my momma leaves me speechless. Alzheimer's disease has taken so much from my mother but thanks to you, her work and her memory will live on. Thanks to Randy Gue at Emory University for protecting my mother's work. And thanks to all of you who love my mother and supported her work, especially Taylor Gibson, Warren Johnston, Kelly Hill, Pici, Sharon Sanders, Bob Sellers, and my aunt Laura Ranson.

I am blessed to call Steve Lucey a great friend of mine. Without you, Steve, I would most likely not be capable of running at all anymore. Your brilliance as a knee surgeon is undeniable and for that I am lucky. Even more important to me is the warmth and generosity that you and your amazing family have shown me and my boys through the years. I will always look forward to the next meal at the Lucey house.

I have the deepest respect and gratitude for my friend Howell Woltz, whom I consider to be one of the finest men I have ever known. You taught me which lines to cross and which ones to accept. You helped me use my incarceration as a tool to help others rather than a weapon to lash out at the world. Thanks to you, I understand that what happened to me, what was done to me, was not my fault. More importantly though, you taught me how to thrive in prison, instead of just survive. Justice isn't always just, but silver linings are most often created through hard work and perseverance. Thank you, my friend.

I will be forever grateful to the Hatchers for raising such an amazing daughter, although I'm not sure who to thank for her stubbornness. My gratitude to Russell, whom I finally cornered in the driveway, for agreeing to let me marry her, despite the fact that I had

ACKNOWLEDGMENTS

already proposed. I never have been good at organization. Special thanks to Paulette for not tossing me out of the house after reading portions of the book, some of which contained very colorful language. Your feedback was truly valuable. I am proud to be part of your family.

Finally, countless thanks to my wife, Stacey Astacianna Hatcher, for helping me throughout the very challenging process of writing *Running Man*. You made sure that my voice remained clear. There were many times that I wasn't sure I was capable of finishing this book, but you never wavered. You read every word over and over, usually telling me what I needed to hear rather than only what I wanted to hear. This book would still only be halfway finished if you had not been there to encourage me to just sit down and write. I was inspired by your dedication and patience at every stage of this endeavor. Above all, thank you for loving me and for letting me love you.

COMPETITION HIGHLIGHTS

1989 Big Sur Marathon

1991 Napa Valley Marathon, Boston Marathon, and Big Sur Marathon

1992–

1995 Ran dozens of marathons, triathlons and 10K races

1996 *Men's Winner*, Nanango Forest 52K, Australia; Boston Marathon

1998 Raid Gauloises, Ecuador

1999 *Winner* (Men's Division), Southern Traverse Adventure Race, New Zealand

2000 Hawaii Ironman; *Eco-Challenge*, Borneo; Raid Gauloises, Tibet/Nepal

2001 *Eco-Challenge*, New Zealand; Expedition BVI Adventure race, British Virgin Islands; Discovery Channel World Championships Adventure Race, Switzerland;

2002 *Eco-Challenge*, Fiji; Raid Gauloises, Vietnam

2003 *Winner*, 250K Gobi March, China; 5th *US National 24 Hour Championships*; *8th*, Badwater 135-Mile Ultramarathon

2004 *Winner*, RAAM (Race Across America) Co-ed team division; Grand Canyon Rim to Rim to Rim run; *2nd*, 250K Atacama Crossing, Chile

2005 *Winner*, 220K Jungle Marathon, Brazil; *3rd*, Badwater Ultramarathon; *3rd*, Coastal Challenge 250K, Costa Rica; *3rd*, Mauritania Challenge 250K

COMPETITION HIGHLIGHTS

2006   *Winner*, 250K Gobi March, China, team division; *3rd*, Badwater Ultramarathon

2006–

2007   Record run across the Sahara

2007   *5th*, Badwater Ultramarathon; *13th*, Furnace Creek 508 cycling race; *2nd overall*, Death Valley Cup

2008   Running America—record attempt for crossing the United States

2009   *4th*, Badwater Ultramarathon; *4th*, Furnace Creek 508; *1st, new record*, Death Valley Cup

2013   Brazil 135 Ultramarathon; *5th, fifty-plus-age-group record*, Badwater Ultramarathon

2014   January 11—Married Astacianna Hatcher in a redwood forest, Big Sur, CA—*1st place*